Critical Reviews for *Donald's Story*

"THE BOOK IS WONDERFUL. Sandra Merrill has achieved the remarkable task of telling three stories at once...Donald and his family then, her experience of rediscovery now, and the overall history of the 4th Fighter Group in WWII. I was moved many times and salute her for it."
— Jeffrey L. Ethell, Aviation Writer

"FANTASTIC WORK. VERY MOVING. FASCINATING AND UNUSUAL. There are scores of WWII stories but the hook for this one is the way [the author] fell into uncovering it. This book transcends typical WWII accounts and exploration of family histories...I really believe she has created something unique and universally appealing. Very impressive."
— Gary Brueggemann, WWII Historian and Educator

"The idea intrigued me from the outset: Fifty years after the death of a fighter pilot during WWII, tragically on Christmas Day of 1944, his niece resolves to write a book memorializing his life and death. I could hardly wait for a look at her finished draft. I had been an instructor pilot and a fighter pilot myself, and had read many books written by other military pilots in this very unique profession. But how would a niece view this fraternity? ...The book was worth the wait. As I read it I saw my own innocence, hope, pride, patriotism and supreme effort as the author's uncle progressed from farm to heroic action in the greatest of all wars. I will admit tears were in my eyes as she visited his gravesite in Holland after fifty years. Could it possibly have been that long?"
— James L. Brewer, author of *MULES, MISSILES & MEN*

Donald's Story

Sandra D. Merrill

Tebidine

Berlin, Maryland

Published by Tebidine Publishing, 11431 Assateague Road, Berlin, Maryland 21811-2413.

Grateful acknowledgment is made for permission to reprint previously published material:

ONE MORE ARROW, by Elton John and Bernie Taupin
© 1983 Happenstance Limited (PRS) & Rouge Booze, Inc. (ASCAP)
All Rights o/b/o Happenstance Limited & Rouge Booze, Inc., for the USA, its territories & Possessions administered by WB Music Corp. (ASCAP)
All Rights Reserved   Used by Permission
WARNER BROS. PUBLICATIONS U.S. INC., Miami, FL. 33014

All photographs, unless otherwise noted, are from Emerson family collections.

Single copies may be ordered directly from the publisher for $14.95 (U.S. currency) per copy. Please include $2.50 per copy for postage and handling; Maryland residents add 5% state sales tax.

Library of Congress Catalog Card Number: 96-90046

ISBN: 0-9649541-4-1

Front cover: "Donald's Stuff" (Martin Photography, Minneapolis)

Back cover: Donald Emerson landing in England after Russia
                  Shuttle Mission. (CWO Edward B. Richie)

                  Bob Tullius flying his P-51 Mustang with
                  Captain Emerson's markings. (R.C. Tullius)

                  "Donald Duck" patch from Emerson's jacket

Cover: Lori Jenkins, HBP — Hagerstown, Maryland

Printed in the United States of America
by
HBP, Hagerstown, Maryland

For my mother, Uncle John, and Elinor.
And for anyone who ever lost someone to war.

Contents

It is with a grateful heart I sincerely thank the many who assisted or encouraged me in any way, just a few of them here by name: Fellow writers in *The Twisted Lits,* for helping me find my voice and pry this project off the ground—especially Bobbie Easterling, who took only candy bars in payment for her patient and ceaseless editing; writers and historians Jim Brewer, Gary Brueggemann and Jeff Ethell, for their expert criticism and advice—Jeff Ethell's *Escort to Berlin*, written with Garry Fry, was invaluable to me in my research of the 4th Fighter Group, and greatly simplified the monumental task of listing all its casualties; veterans and others associated with the 4th FG, the Eighth and Ninth Air Forces and the Veterans of the Battle of the Bulge, for welcoming my efforts to remember one of their own—deserving special mention, in approximate order of appearance, are Frank Frison, Ed Kueppers, Chuck Konsler, Jim Goodson, Robert "Buffalo Grass" Nelson, Otey Glass, Bob Planck, Don Patchen (my surrogate uncle), Joe Sills, Ed Nelson, Bob Tullius, C.J. Hein, Gil Kesler, Francis "Lefty" Grove, Don Groomer, Joe Higgins, Bob Beeson, Bill Gier, and Ed and Mark Richie.

Finally, I thank all of Donald's friends, my friends, and my Emerson, Torkelson, Troska and Merrill families for their love and support—from John Troska who got me started with a word processor in St. Paul, to Ted Merrill who dragged me across the finish line in Berlin. And to my dad (who never told me what to do) and Esther Troska (who loved me anyway), thank you EVER so much! Most of all, I thank Uncle Donald for his letters, and my mother for her memories.

Sandra D. Merrill

FOREWORD

BY DONALD J. PATCHEN
WWII Fighter Pilot and POW

To the author, Uncle Donald was only a name at the time of his death. Over the years that followed, remembering became somewhat easier for most of those who are part of this story, and as stories and pictures were shared at family gatherings, the seed of desire began to take root to know this boy who became a man in a few short months prior to his death. And as is so often the case, where there is death there is also new life, and so was born "The Donald Story."

It was not possible at the outset to visualize what would take place in the days, weeks, months, and years that followed as the process began to find answers to the myriad of questions that were beginning to come to the forefront. Where to start? At the beginning? And where was that? But believe in something strongly enough and help will arrive, and so, with hardly any recognition of its happening, "The Donald Story" began to unfold.

It is doubtful that a finger could be placed on any one point as the beginning, nor would there be a final question that would constitute the end, and it is of no real importance to try to justify a particular point as the start or finish. Rather, as with any good book, it's what lies between the covers that determines its validity and therefore its appeal.

Within the pages of "The Donald Story" one will easily find the validity that brings appeal to the story of this young man's life: through his own writings in letters to his family; through interviews and letters from his friends, both civilian and military, who were part of his short but eventful life; from the records acquired from his civilian life and military service; from his life on the farm, his dreams of things to come, and finally to one of those dreams come true: a pilot! And a fighter pilot no less! Certainly there was no wish that there be a war, but if it was to be then he wanted to be a part of it. Once committed, it was all or nothing, and as the reader will see, no one could ever have given more. His country, his family, his friends — that was his life in a too short lifetime.

The author has captured this and given life to what was only a face in a picture on the mantel for some, and memories, both happy and sad (more happy than sad it is hoped), for others. She has done this with the help of an untold number of strangers who now are like friends of old, found records by means known only to her, through places visited, and by hours spent in reflecting on what was and what might have been.

When others might have given up she found continued encouragement from many but especially from her family which gives credence to her total commitment to bring life, as near as it is possible, to this face on the mantel. Dreams are the spice of life. Without them life can be very dull. With them, fantasies can be fulfilled, if only in one's mind, but still enjoyed.

From the beginning, when a desire to know this person that others talked about with so much deep feeling and love began to surface, to the dedication of an exact duplicate, by another new friend, of the plane that was so important in the young man's life, a pattern developed that was even eerie at times. If a stalemate should arise there was an almost immediate response, completely out of the blue, from an otherwise unknown (to the author at that point) with information that would fill the void of thought that had occurred and allow for continuation of "The Story." That this happened many times leads one to believe that the writing of this account was predestined. For those who were involved, new friends, new places and shared memories were the legacy that this young man left. In return, the memorial airplane and this book — and the many who were a part of its creation — pay final tribute to a young man remembered and who is no longer unknown.

Don Patchen
March 1995

"One More Arrow"

He must have been romantic
He must have sensed adventure
And I feel the steel of his strong will
In the frame around his picture

And he's one more arrow,
Flying through the air
One more arrow landing in
A shady spot somewhere
Where the days and night
Blend into one
And he can always feel the sun
Through the soft brown earth
That holds him forever young

Elton John and Bernie Taupin

...I admit I'm sticking my neck out but I'd rather take my chances in the air than in the infantry, armored divisions, tank corps or the navy! Of course it's dangerous but name me a war job that isn't. Anyway I'm one of those that believe that if a guy is supposed to lose his life in this war it will happen no matter what or where and vice versa.

Donald R. Emerson
October 31, 1942

*F*or most of my life I have been aware of the abiding presence of a family legend: Donald. My uncle, my mother's youngest brother. World War II hero, ace fighter pilot of a P-51 Mustang, captain in the 4th Fighter Group of the Eighth Air Force at age 21. Killed in the Battle of the Bulge, at age 21. On Christmas Day.

I was only 15 months old when he went away for the last time, so of course I can't remember him, but I always felt as if I should. Pictures of him were on walls and in photo albums, and Grandma and my mother would often talk about him. They talked about him a lot.

In my grandparents' farmhouse hung a metal-framed 8 x 10 photographer's portrait of Uncle Donald — all in tones of brown except for three spots tinted blue: his eyes and a winged patch on the left sleeve of his military dress uniform. Though his facial expression was serious he had posed rather casually and stood with both thumbs hooked into the belt around his boyish waist. He was a total stranger to me, but I memorized his features early on: smooth, pleasant face; heavy brows shading clear, youthful eyes that were permanently fixed on something just beyond my right shoulder; medium-sized, slightly up-turned nose; a rather wide mouth with thick, full lips.

On another wall under a black-edged glass was an oil-colored portrait of a beautiful, brown-haired, brown-eyed lady. No matter how many times I would ask who she was, Grandma

*was always happy to tell me. It was Elinor — Elinor Lindemann
from New York — the girl that Donald had planned to marry
when he came home from the war — almost her daughter-in-law,
like Betty, my uncle John's wife. Elinor was married to someone
else now, Grandma said, but she still kept in touch.*

*Along with the pictures, there were other tangible reminders
to prompt reminiscences of Donald, especially Grandma's good
silverware. He had been born with an eye for the finer things,
and enjoyed buying beautiful, extravagant gifts for others as well
as himself. The shiny mahogany chest full of sterling silver was
the last Christmas present he bought for his mother. He had
chosen the exquisite pattern personally — a sculptured lily of the
valley curled elegantly around the handle tip of each piece. The
fancy table Grandma set for special occasions always reminded
us of Donald, especially at Christmas. And in the summertime
there was that amazing clothesline strung between the pine trees
behind the house — it didn't even require any clothespins — a
clothespinless clothesline! He had ordered it from some faraway
place — I don't remember where — with the intention of selling
them door-to-door as a money-making venture, but he soon
discovered he had no more affinity for selling than he had for
farming. When Grandma hung out the wash she'd show me how
it worked by sliding a little wheel-type thing along the double
wire that twisted and caught the corners of the wet clothes in its
grip. She may well have had the only such novelty in the entire
Red River Valley.*

*I loved to listen to Grandma's stories about Donald. She
never cried or looked sad when she talked about him; she mostly
seemed proud. She probably thought about Donald every day, I
figured, but I knew he monopolized her thoughts on holidays and
washdays.*

*She talked about Donald until the day she died in 1968.
Donald, the baby who had surprised everyone by his birth;
Donald, the boy who didn't like either school or farming very
much; Donald, the young man who loved to fly.*

*After Grandma died, my mother inherited a hodgepodge of
letters, pictures and other things Donald had left behind,
collectively known as "Donald's stuff." She had also spoken
often to us kids — and anybody else who would listen — about*

Donald. With Grandma gone it would be up to her to keep his memory alive, because even though Grandpa and Uncle John certainly missed and remembered Donald as much as she did, they were never able to talk as easily about him, so they rarely did.

On visits home since growing up, I loved to drag out the photo albums and the boxes full of unorganized snapshots which serve as visual aids in recalling our family history, and often I'd look through Donald's stuff, too; not only was it an activity that was encouraged, but it seldom went unnoticed by my mother.

"I see you're looking at Donald's stuff again," she had said when she caught me at it one recent time. I confessed, again, that it had always fascinated me, especially my two favorite pieces of memorabilia: the little V-Mail letter he wrote to her about falling in love with Elinor, and his little zippered Bible.

As I opened it I saw my name childishly scribbled in pencil on the first page. "Why'd you let me write in here?" I asked her.

"I didn't know you had!" she replied. "I think I let you take it to Sunday School once in a while. Turn to John 20:31...see? Donald underlined part of that verse, '...but these are written that you might believe that Jesus is the Christ, the Son of God, and that believing, you might have life through His name .' When his stuff was sent home, Mama unzipped it and it fell open to that page."

And with that we were off on yet another recounting of Donald's story.

My mother was going on nine years of age and her brother Johnny was almost seven and a half when their baby brother was born.

His impending birth had been a big surprise to them, since their mother was supposedly unable to have any more children. She had suffered a tubal pregnancy a few years before, and after Dr. Waldron had performed the surgery necessary to save her life, he said there was no possibility of that happening again, and that her child-bearing days were over. When she turned up at his office and told him she was sure that she was pregnant again, he bellowed, "IMPOSSIBLE!" He had done the surgery, himself, he said, and refused to examine her. Unconvinced, despite her doctor's adamant pronouncement, she made an appointment with one of his colleagues who concurred with her diagnosis. There would be one more child.

This was one of my grandmother's favorite stories: the time she had outsmarted that doctor. I could still see Grandma's sly half-smile as my mother's voice began reciting the story for her, mixing it with some of her own.

"So a few months later, after she had gotten really big, she went back to Dr. Waldron and said, 'Well, what do you think now?' "

My mother always stopped to laugh at that line before moving on. "I remember talking with Johnny about the new baby that was coming — we were getting so excited — it was soon time for it to be born. We were in the little bedroom where the baby was going to sleep — on our backs, crosswise on the narrow bed with our legs straight up against the wall. 'I'm wishing for a girl,' I told him.

" 'I'll wish for a girl, too,'Johnny said; 'then it will be a boy.'

"When we came walking home from school that warm spring day — the 17th of May, 1923 — and saw the doctor's open-top car in the yard we went running into the house as fast as we could. Donald had just been born. He was a cute baby — so round and fat, but I was mad it was a boy and told Mama, 'You have to have another baby right away! I want a girl! And I'm not going to help you take care of him, either!' She was not exactly in the mood to hear that right then, so she just looked at me and said, 'You can have the girls, yourself.' She never let me forget that," my mother said, laughing again.

Yes. Grandma's hex. It had become a family joke — the curse she had put on her disgruntled daughter to have only girls. My mother gave birth to five babies, not a boy in the bunch; I was number four. Uncle John had apparently been affected by her spell, too; his pessimistic practice of wishing for the opposite of what he wanted had long-term effects — all of his children were boys.

My mother's narrative began speeding up, and she went on effortlessly, and even though I knew most of the story by heart, I never tired of hearing her tell it.

"I remember Donald holding you when you were a couple months old — he really liked you — I named you after him, you know — your middle name, Dawn, is for Donald. He thought you were a nice little baby; he said, 'I must be getting paternal.' "

"Yeah, I remember — I mean I remember you told me that before," I said almost absently, settling in to hear the rest.

But instead of picking up the story where she left off, she surprised me by abruptly asking, "Do you think you might write about him someday? It looked like you were copying something down from my scrapbook."

"OH, MA! Why do you always expect me to start writing?"

"You wrote me the best letter one time," she said proudly.

"When was that? I hardly remember writing any!"

"Right after you moved into that house on Lincoln."

"THAT WAS 25 YEARS AGO!" I sputtered, after mentally subtracting 1964 from 1989.

"It was long, too," she said. "At least six or seven pages!" She admitted she still had it and sometimes dug it out to reread it. I could imagine her doing that. She loved getting letters and saved most of them.

" I wrote only once in all those years?" I asked.

"Oh, you may have written more than that — but it was such a good one, I keep it handy. Do you want me to get it so you can read it?" she offered eagerly.

"Nah, maybe some other time. I'd rather read Donald's letters — I just love the way he wrote. Are there others around somewhere?"

She told me there should be quite a few more — she was sure that Grandma had saved all of her letters from Donald, and despite the wear and tear from the frequent handling of her own precious letters, many of them were still readable.

"Johnny has a big bunch, too," she added, "but I bet he's never looked at them again. I wonder if he's ever talked to his boys much about Donald — probably not; it's always been so hard for him; he'd rather try to forget — block it all out. It would be nice if someone would write up his story. Johnny's boys should know something about him — what he did in the war — what he was like. He should be remembered."

"I know, Ma. But there are MILLIONS of war stories."

That was what I had said, my automatic answer, because that was what I had thought for such a long time. I was conscious of listening to Donald's story for nearly 40 years, but I had listened as if it were some homespun fairy tale. It wasn't until I had sons nearing draft age that Donald suddenly became more than a deified, storybook figure — a real human being, my own flesh and blood. And then the dormant obligation I had felt to tell Donald's story began to stir, and I knew that even though he was just one among countless thousands of unknown heroes, he still might speak for many of them — reason enough for his story to be told. I was about to set out on an odyssey of discovery, and by reading Donald's letters, finding his friends and recording old memories, I was going to do my best to remember an uncle that I never really knew.

Chapter One

HOTEL MEDFORD
Milwaukee, Wisconsin

Nov. 15, 1941

Hello Mom, Pop & Bro. John,

I didn't get around to sending you a card today so I'll use some of this free stationery and do a little scribbling.

Phil Kiner and I got a room in this joint together - we have been staying in cabins along the way so far but when we pulled into Milwaukee Bill B. said he was sick of cold cabins so we drove to the heart of the city and stopped at the first hotel we saw that didn't look too dam high class. Boy Milwaukee is a bigger place than I thought it was - it seems to be a city of big bugs too, every other car you see is a Cadalac or a big Packard etc.

Phil and I just came back from a show house. What a show house. I bet the darn place would hold 3 or 4 thousand people. We had a heck of a time to even find where the seats were - we went through 3 lobbies and up and around and all over before we got there. Oh well we live and learn and boy I sure have learned a lot on this trip! I wouldn't have missed it for anything. I'll explain more in detail later on what we've done but it would take about 10 of these pages to do it so whenever time hangs heavy on my hands when I'm in Chicago I'll tell everything. We've been picking up the Chicago papers and the want ads are just crammed full of men and boys my age wanted for work - all kinds of it. Bill says he's certain we'll have no trouble getting work. Phil is going to get a job for the winter too. I guess we'll pull into Chicago tomorrow about noon. We intend to get an early start in the morning and it's 1:00 o'clock now so I'd better hit the hay. Phil is getting ready for bed now.

Love, Don

D onald Emerson was eighteen when he first left his sheltered, provincial life near the Canadian border. He had graduated from high school in Karlstad, Minnesota, earlier that spring, but without any passion or goal to pursue, he was still operating more or less on whim. He knew only one thing for certain: his future would never be on the farm. He not only had no love for farming, but lacked the easy working relationship with his father that brother John commanded. After the harvest season he decided to check out Chicago where several of his school friends were already employed, and with some North Dakota neighbors — Phil Kiner, and Bill and Ella Barron — drove there in search of work for the winter.

Donald was really going to miss the close communion of his family, but an ambitious exchange of letters would be a substitute. His rapidly expanding world view immediately provided fodder for ceaseless correspondence, and soon he'd be nudging his family to consider adding some modern amenities to improve their rustic lifestyle. With so much information to report, Donald had begun writing home in his left-handed scrawl before they made it to their final stop.

Donald's parents, C.F. (Frank) and Mabel, had moved several times, but they always lived in the upper Red River Valley, and always on a hard-scrabble farm. When they lost their Joliette, North Dakota, homestead in the Great Depression, they moved from Pembina County in North Dakota to rented farms in Minnesota's adjoining Kittson County. In 1938, they moved back permanently to Pembina County to manage another Joliette farm inherited by a favorite Emerson cousin, the brilliant and musically talented Max Short. Since surviving the luckless fate of having his legs shot off in WWI, Max had been working as a mineralogist at the University of New Mexico. Having no desire to farm the land himself, he offered the job to his cousin Frank; thus Frank, wife Mabel and sons were settled in time for Donald to attend high school in Pembina during his sophomore year.

But Donald, who had received all but his first year of schooling in Karlstad, missed his friends so much that he finagled a return for his junior and senior years by staying with his sister Eleanor while school was in session.

Eleanor had, in 1935, married a shy Norwegian man of many talents, the brother of her best friend, Alice: Harold Oliver Torkelson, "Hot" for short. When Donald joined them in their rural home, they already had a good start on their family of girls. Deeply saddened by the stillbirth of their first daughter in 1936, they were consoled a year later by the birth of healthy Beverly; baby Bonnie was born in the spring of '39.

Eleanor was a soft touch as far as Donald was concerned, and taking him in as a boarder was not an imposition to her. She had been won over by her chubby-cheeked baby brother soon after his birth. Her spiteful oath not to help with his care was soon recanted, and she became a second mother to Donald.

Their own mother was a tiny, frail woman weakened by too many pregnancies in too few years. Her first baby, James, died just hours after birth; Eleanor was born the next year, and John 16 months later. In a short time an ectopic pregnancy prompted emergency surgery to save her life. By the time Donald arrived, Mabel's fragile health made her prone to a variety of chronic illnesses, and her young daughter Eleanor had already assumed responsibility for many of the household chores. Taking on the additional chore of caring for an infant was instinctive, and Eleanor had lovingly watched Donald as he developed into a much shorter version of their handsome father. Helping him finish high school was merely an extension of her nurturing.

Donald was called simply that at home and school — never Don or Donnie. Later on he'd also be known as Don, Emmy, and just plain Emerson. A friendly, popular boy, he was much more interested in having a good time than in either his studies or sports; he much preferred activities such as joy riding around with friends who had access to automobiles. One of his good friends, Dale Turnwall, had a clunker of his own called "The Blue Lizzie," so named because of its thrifty do-it-yourself paint job; the old car stalled so often that most riders would have to get out and push, smudging themselves and their clothes on its water-based calcimine paint. Another long-time friend, and infamous driver, was Nordie Swenson. Nordie and Donald at one time secretly schemed of joining the Royal Canadian Air Force after high school. (Canada accepted American volunteers without any college education.) Tragedy put a quick end to their pipe dream, however. On a cold night in late November, 1940, while driving his father's week-old, two-door Chevrolet, Nordie missed a sharp curve on a country road; the warning sign had just been knocked down by a snowplow. The car rolled completely, landing in the ditch. Donald and the other six passengers were not hurt, but Nordie was thrown out of the vehicle and broke his back.

Donald did not distinguish himself in any way during his school years, but once, after being goaded into it by his friends, he joined the band when another clarinet player was needed; hating everything about it, he quit after a year. Of his own free will, though, he tried out for the senior class play: "Jiminy Crickets." He was typecast as the "chum" of the main character played by Dale, an easy part to play. On the autograph page of his School Day Memories book reserved for special friends, Marcella Carlson, Lawrence Hageland, Avis Hennissen, and Jennie — a girl in the junior class, were the first to sign their names. It was said that Donald and Jennie were sweet on each other.

In May of 1941, when the senior class graduated, they chose as their class flower the American Beauty Rose. Their class colors were red, white, and blue, and their class motto was: "Thank God I am an American." They had felt safe and secure, and thankful to be oceans away from the warring world. When Donald walked across the stage in the Karlstad High School Auditorium to receive his diploma, he was innocently unaware of the role he was destined to play in global events; his real education was about to begin.

Nov. 19, 1941

Hello everybody,

I suppose you have been looking for a letter from me. I've been so darn much on the go since we got here I just haven't had time to write. We got here Sun. about noon. I'm not staying with any of the others yet. Phil K. and I are still here where Bill and his wife are staying. Elmer Hanegan is the name and boy are they ever swell to Phil and me. I'm sure glad I came with Bill. He dragged Phil and I all around Chicago Monday looking for work but we didn't have any luck. Monday night Bill went to the hospital so we lost our guide. This Elmer H. helped us get a job yesterday. He's a pretty influential man and he called up one of the big boys in Montgomery Ward and Co. He got us an appointment and we didn't even have to go thru the employment office etc. Gosh is that outfit ever big here. It's in the loop and I bet the two buildings that make up the M.W. mail order branch cover about 3 square blocks and they're 15 stories high. Phil and I will be in the shipping dept. (filling orders etc.) 60 cents per hr. It won't start for a week tho but anyway we know we got a job if we can't get something better in the meantime. This Elmer H. told me this morning that he was pretty sure he could get me a government civil service job being I'm not of draft age and that I have high school education. Don't underestimate this Hanegan fellow, he's really got pull in this burg. He's manager of all the Auto Parts Co. stores in this city. He owns two racing cars that he races at the Indianapolis Speedway. One of the cars holds a speed record at that track. He sure gave us the thrill of our lives Sunday night. He's an official at the Midget races here in Chicago. They're held indoors at the International Amphitheater - it's an enormous place.

The track where these midget cars race is about 1/4 mile around and then the seating is all around it like in a football stadium only this has a roof over the whole thing. I guess it's very much like Madison Sq. Garden in New York. Anyway

Elmer gets us all press tickets so we got in free so we saved the cost of the tickets ($1.70 ea.) There were about 40 midgets entered but they had short elimination races so only about 15 midgets got in the final race. It was 100 laps long. I only wish I could explain the hair-raising thrill of seeing those little cars skidding around that track. Every once in a while a car would lose control and then there was thrills plenty. What those little cars can stand is something awful. I saw one car go right over the back end of another one and they kept on going. A friend of Elmer's got killed a short time ago. He got his head cut right in half. (Driving one of those midgets.)

I haven't even seen any of the gang yet but I've talked to them all over the phone. This Elmer lives about 30 miles from the Loop and yet this part of the city looks about like the main street of Grafton [N.D.] or Thief River Falls [Minn.]. That should give you a slight idea of what Chicago is like. Phil and I went down to the loop for the first time alone yesterday and did we ever have a time getting back. We're learning fast tho. The round trip to the loop and back here takes about 3 hrs. by street car. Elmer Hanegan said I'd have to have my birth certificate if he was to get me in any Gov. job so if you get it you can send it to this address. I don't know how long we'll be here but this will be my address anyway. They sure are swell people - they've practically forced Phil and I to stay here until we feel we can find our way around the city better and know definitely what we'll be doing. She is Polish but pretty as a picture! And just as nice. Here's my address: 6332 So. Fairfield Ave. - Chicago, Ill.

Love, Don

While most of the so-called civilized world was engaged in war with Hitler and the Axis powers, the United States remained officially neutral. The country was still recovering from the effects of the First World War — "the war to end all wars" — and was extremely wary of being dragged into another; and although by this time America was patrolling the seas, giving aid to the Allies, and had initiated its first peacetime military draft in history, President Roosevelt was clinging to his vow never to send another mother's son to fight on foreign soil.

The Allies had tried to avoid war with Germany, and in a futile attempt at appeasement had allowed the takeover of Austria and Czechoslovakia without opposition. Still not satisfied, Hitler went on to invade Poland on September 1, 1939, forcing England, France, Australia, New Zealand and British India to declare war two days later.

Aggressive acts in Europe snowballed. After Communist Russia marched into Poland and divided the country with Germany, it attacked and overpowered Finland. Fascist Italy, Germany's ally, seized Albania, and Germany went on to overrun Norway, Denmark, Holland, Belgium, Luxembourg, and France. With the collapse of France in the summer of 1940, England was left to fight virtually alone.

Hitler then concentrated his energies on conquering Great Britain and ordered Germany's powerful Luftwaffe air force to bomb the British homeland and wipe out its Royal Air Force. The "Battle of Britain" was the first major aerial conflict of the war, and the first Allied victory. The outstanding courage and stubborn resistance of the English people during the Blitz inspired Prime Minister Churchill to label these months Britain's "finest hour" and to praise the RAF by saying, "Never in the field of human conflict was so much owed by so many to so few."

Discouraged by England's surprising strength Hitler turned elsewhere, and by the spring of 1941, the Axis powers had taken Yugoslavia, Greece, and the Island of Crete. Next Germany invaded neutral Russia, which before long would become allied with England. It took an act of war to make allies of Communist Stalin and anti-communist Churchill, but as Churchill put it to the British House of Commons, "If Hitler were to invade Hell, I should find occasion to make a favorable reference to the Devil."

Dec. 1, 1941

Dear Mom, Dad & Johnny,

Well it's 7:00 at night and I've just got up. You see I've started working nights at Montgomery's. Working at night is sort of hard to get used to, but the work is easier and you get 10% more pay. I and Phil get 55 cents an hr. It sure is a nice place to work at. A person has a good chance to work himself up too. You get advanced as you learn. They claim this store is the largest in the world. That may be a lot of baloney but I wouldn't be surprised if it were true. They have 50 million dollars worth of stock in the mail order dept. where I work, and they employ 65,000 people and that doesn't include the extras like me that are taken on for the Xmas rush.

Last week when I was waiting to get on at Monkey's, I helped Elmer H. take inventory at his store. Taking inventory at a store like that is no joke. They have hundreds of different articles like gaskets, bearings, bolts, etc. I worked three whole days and did nothing but count gaskets! It really put me in shape for starting my job at Montgomery's tho. You know everything there goes by numbers too. Incidently all Montgomery Ward employees get a 10% discount on everything they buy at the store. Also there's a bargain dept. where only M.W. employees can buy. This is where the goods go when there is an overstock yet there isn't enough to put on sale in any catalog. Everything there is slashed 35 to 50%. You can buy everything from peanuts to stoves there. Too bad it's so far from home. I saw some very nice living room sets with 50% price cuts. First thing I'm going to get is a wrist watch. I really need one on my job and I can get good $15 & $16 ones at the bargain dept. for $7 & $8.

I spent Sat. night and all day Sun. over at Belle Plaine Ave. with my old gang. By the way, Ember Turnwall works in the same Dept. at M.W.'s as I do. Belle Plaine Ave. is near the Lake so Sun. morning Lawrence [Hageland] and I walked along the beach and out on a breakwater about half a mile. There was hardly a wind yet the waves were about 10 to 15 ft. high. There's a hotel along the lake called the Edgewater Hotel. Boy is it ever a beautiful structure!! I've seen so many things here in Chicago that have bulged my eyes out, it would take a book to tell about them all. I intend to get some pictures tho and send you. Phil and I are going to take an airplane ride one of these days and get a decent look at Chicago. The Chicago Municipal Airport is only a half mile from here. It's the largest among Chicago's 10 or 12 airports. It covers 640 acres, one mile on each side. It's got all paved runways too.

Sun. afternoon Lawrence, Dale, Morlan [Turnwall] and I went down town and took in a show at the Chicago Theater - one of the best. It cost 75 cents for admission but you really get your money's worth. The show was "Yank in the R.A.F." and then of course there was the floor show. That really was good. Chorus girls, dancing teams from Hollywood, Benny Goodman's band, etc. The usual price you pay for shows here is 55 cents. For that you always get a double feature - good ones! It's worth 55 cents to even get a look at the inside of some of these places they call show halls. There's one on 63rd street 10 blocks from here that has a big water fountain and live swans and other water fowl swimming around in the lagoon around it.

I hope this finds you all well - I'm fine.

Love, Don

P.S. Have you heard anything about that electric line?

On the other side of the world the tiny, overcrowded country of Japan had been systematically gobbling up Pacific territories with the intended goal of controlling all of Asia. By December of 1941, it held Indochina, Manchuria and parts of China. While eyeing American holdings Japan tried unsuccessfully to persuade the United States to stop aiding China and Russia, and the diplomatic and trade relationships existing between the two countries rapidly deteriorated.

Early on Sunday morning, December 7, 1941, the Japanese attacked the U.S. Pacific Fleet at Pearl Harbor, and the still officially neutral America was dragged into the war. On December 8th, the United States declared war on Japan, and three days later, in accordance with a previous treaty held with Japan, Germany declared war on the United States.

The European Allies finally had reason for optimism. Now Churchill, upon hearing of the attack on Pearl Harbor, knew that the U.S. had no choice but to join in the fight, and that with their help, the war would be won. The American people, once sharply divided on the issue of getting involved in other countries' battles, quickly joined together to solidly back the war effort.

As the first reports of Pearl Harbor were broadcast, Donald's family was gathering for Sunday dinner at the Halma, Minnesota, farm where his mother had grown up. Mabel's parents had since died, but her sister Nannie and three brothers, Tom, Arvid and Lester Roswell were still living there. As Eleanor, Harold and the girls drove into the yard, the men came out of the house and met them with the news. Conversation that day was of little else; they knew that before this war ended few families would escape having at least one son called to serve in the armed forces. Being married and the father of two, Harold would be exempt from the draft, but one of his own younger brothers, Glenn, had been called up in August, and now it was expected that Uncle Sam would soon be greeting John.

When the commercial rush of Christmas was over, the temporary jobs at Montgomery Ward ended for Donald and Phil. A return trip home to North Dakota too impractical, the Joliette foursome spent the holidays with their gracious hosts, the Hanegans. Any pangs of homesickness Donald may have felt during his first Christmas away from home were thoroughly obliterated by the thrill of his first airplane ride. Thanks to Bill and Ella, whose friend ran a small airport, Donald's wish to have an aerial view of Chicago was granted. Phil remembered that during the week between Christmas and the New Year he and Donald circled high above the metropolis for about a half-hour in a small plane, but at that time Donald gave no indication the event was in any way a turning point for him.

In January Phil got a new job in a transistor factory, and Donald found work at Wilson's Meat Packing Plant.

January 11, 1942

Dear Mom, Pop, & Brother John,

I seem to be in a letter writing mood today, so I guess I'll scribble a letter to you all too. This will be my third letter this afternoon. One to Eleanor and another to a <u>certain</u> somebody.

It's been slightly cold here the past week. I say slightly but the Chicago people say it's terribly cold. It hasn't gone below 6 below tho. The papers describe it as the worst cold spell in years. It held on for a whole week and I guess that's very unusual. I'm still wearing summer underwear tho. I haven't had a cold since I came here either.

Thanks for your letter John - I sure enjoyed it.

I saw that picture "Sun Valley Serenade" a month before I saw the Ice Review. In fact Sonja Henie went through that same dance that she did in the picture in one of her five appearances at the Ice Review. Another thing Johnny - those two negro dancers that were in that picture (they danced the "Chattanooga Choo Choo") appeared in the floor show at the Chicago Theater when I was there.

I bummed around all day yesterday in the Loop District. I paid 25 cents and went up to the observatory in the Chicago Board of Trade Building - the tallest in Chicago (45 stories). Boy you really get a wonderful view of the city from the obs. The sun was shining but there seemed to be a haze in the air so I couldn't see more than about 5 miles out. If a real clear Sat. or Sun. comes along, I'm going to take my camera and go up there and take some pictures. They have a telescope up there too, that you have to put a dime in to make it work. Weather permitting you can see buildings in three different states. When you're on the elevator going up to the obs., your ears hurt due to the change in air pressure. They have a lot of free literature in the obs., and I picked up some that describes some of the buildings and other things about Chicago and I'm going to send it to you.

Well it's Sunday night again so it's "off to the races."

Due to the government restrictions on rubber etc., this may
be the last of the midget races too. Boy it sure is lucky we
got that car when we did! Better take it easy and remember,
Johnny, the faster you go the quicker the tires wear out.

   Ann just said we were leaving for the races in a few
minutes so I better quit and get ready.

                    Love, Donald

At his new job, Donald ran a machine that manufactured
medical sutures from the intestines of sheep. This operation was
not very mentally taxing work and, apparently, nothing to write
home about. While he toiled away the hours stringing catgut, he
began working out his personal war strategy.

   During America's early days at war only men between the
ages of 21 and 36 were required by law to register for the draft,
but any and all men and women between the ages of 18 and 45
were invited to enlist. Those who volunteered for military
service before their numbers were called by a national lottery
were given a little more choice in assignment, plus the additional
incentive of the chance to qualify for officers' commissions.

   Donald reasoned, correctly, that the draft board would give
at least a temporary deferment to one of the Emerson sons for
necessary farm work, and he knew there was an excellent chance
that if he did nothing — just let the events already set in motion
run their natural course — the oldest son, his 26-year-old
brother John, would very likely be drafted. The next unsavory
probability was that when Donald was of draft age, a hardship
deferment would mean he'd be stuck on the farm, maybe for
life. Although he didn't feel completely at ease about joining
the military, either — with its intrinsic possibility of mortal
combat — Donald was determined that if one of the Emerson
boys were to be spared, it should be his brother John; he, at
least, loved being on the farm. When Donald got a letter from
home the next day telling him that John had received his first
draft notice, he knew what had to be done, and he was ready to
act.

Mabel Roswell Emerson & son Donald, 3 months old.

Mr. & Mrs. C. F. Emerson on their wedding day

Frank, Mabel, son John & daughter Eleanor

Eleanor & John

Donald

*John & Eleanor,
holding brother
Donald*

*Emerson picnic: Ray
& Hilda Emerson with
daughters, Frank &
Mabel's family, Jim &
Elsie Ferguson*

*Visiting Grandma Roswell: Mabel,
Nannie, Donald, Tom, Eleanor, Lester
(on motorcycle), Grandma & Arvid*

Baby Donald

Donald, Eleanor & John

Donald, Eleanor, John & pets

7-year-old Donald

Grandpa John Hay Emerson & Donald

Emersons in 1934

Rev. E. B. Kluver's confirmation class, Donald upper right

Donald, Lawrence Hageland & Lloyd Johnson across from school in 1940
[Art Folland]

Karlstad High School
Class of 1941

PRINCIPAL
RAYMOND DORDAL

SUPERINTENDENT
L. E. WERMAGER

LAWRENCE F. HAGELAND
THELMA G. SPILDE
DALE G. TURNWALL
SHIRLEE E. MELBYE
PRISCILLA E. ERICSSON
WALLACE B. OLSON
INYOE G. BENSON
GRACE I. HAUGELAND
CURTISS L. LINDBERG
FLORENCE M. LE DOUX
MARCELLA C. CARLSON
LLOYD H. JOHNSON
BERNICE J. RYDBERG
CAROL G. DANIELSON
VALBORG H. TORKELSON
MORLAN G. TURNWALL
BERNICE G. ANDERSON
RUTH C. NETTERLUND
ARTHUR I. FOLLAND
MARJORIE G. THON
SHIRLEY M. VAN DELSEN
DONALD R. EMERSON
HARRIET V. HULTGREN
RAYMOND J. NORDINE
ELNA JANE JOHNSON

Monday nite
January 12, 1942

Dear Folks,

I don't suppose this will make sense to you at first. I sent off one letter to you last night but I got your letter this morning and that's why I'm writing this second letter. To tell you the truth I've been waiting all along to hear if the army wanted Johnny or not. I imagine you can smell what's coming now - well anyway as soon as I had read the letter I hiked down to the Cook County Court House here in Chicago to see what division of Uncle Sam's service I could get into. Now I didn't even consider the Aviation Corps, the Navy, or the Army. I don't think I'm enough of a "man" (physically) to get in the Marines so I went to see what the Coast Guard offered. I didn't sign up or anything but I asked a lot of questions. The Coast Guard is just what the name says. It's better than the Navy or Marines in that a person is stationed along the coast somewhere instead of way out in the ocean or on an island for months at a time. A person can enlist in any branch of the Coast Guard he wishes. If I was going to enlist, I'd take up the radio end of it. The pay is about the same as the Army, Navy, etc., starting at $21.00 per month and you can work yourself up so you would get about $150.00 per month at the end of 3 years. Of course you get your room, board and clothes free. They give you $118.00 worth of clothing when you enlist. If a person stays in the service, he retires after 30 years with 75% of the salary he happens to be making at that time. I expect this war to last a long time and I'd be drafted anyway so I think it would be better to enlist now in something good like this. The fellow at the desk said he couldn't see why I wouldn't pass the physical if I had my teeth fixed a little. If I was to get my teeth taken care of in the next two weeks and signed up then I would leave for New Orleans Feb. 15th.

Of course they have to have your written consent to all this so I'm putting it up to you. What do you think? I myself think it's a pretty good thing.

As soon as you can decide which way on this, write and let me know. Soon.

Your Son, Donald

P.S. The Coast Guard gives one month vacation with pay each year - most business concerns only give two weeks at the most.

Donald's family did not object to his idea of enlisting — many of his friends were doing the same; Dale Turnwall had recently enlisted in the Navy as an airplane mechanic.

This war was for everyone, and soon, whether by invitation or out of patriotic fervor, the sons and daughters of diplomats, politicos, blue bloods and plutocrats were joining the armed forces too — along with all four of President Roosevelt's own sons.

January 26, 1942

Dear Mom, Dad & Bro. John,

It's 4:30 in the afternoon and I don't go to work until 8:00. I don't believe I told you in my last letter, but my new job is night work. I start at 8:30 and quit at 5:00 in the morning. I get home at 5:30 and instead of going right to bed I read the morning paper, or lay down on the sofa until the others get up. I eat breakfast with them and then I "hit the hay" and sleep until about 4:00. Sort of a cock-eyed routine, eh? Usually if I haven't anything else to do after I get up, I go down to the public library just 3 blocks from here. I have been spending quite a lot of my spare time there. They have a wonderful collection of every type of book or magazine.

I got your last letter Sat., so I looked up Charles Short [nephew of Max] yesterday. I couldn't imagine at first what he could be doing here and especially at that address. Lake Shore Drive is at the northeast part of the city right on the lake shore. What I'm leading up to is this - that section is where all the "highbrows" live. I mean the kind whose evening attire consists of high silk hat, white gloves and a cane, etc.

I soon found out what was what when I got there tho - 710 LSD turned out to be Abbott Hall - dormitory for the medical students of Northwestern University. Charles didn't recognize me at all. You know it's two years since he did see me and then I was in work clothes. We had a swell visit. For some reason they have condensed the four year course into just 3 yrs. They have to do a lot of hard studying - he and his roommate stay up until 1:00 most every night. He's from Santa Anita. They have classes six days a week and they usually have studying to do at night or on Sundays, so Charles has seen very little of Chicago. We plan to arrange a date for some Sunday afternoon and go out and do something.

After I left Abbott Hall I went over to see how my old gang was getting along. I hadn't seen any of them since before Xmas. We went downtown and saw the show "Babes on Broadway" with Micky R. and Judy Garland - Oh boy! This show has been running at one of the biggest loop theaters for a whole month now and it's still going strong.

Love to all, Don

P.S. I wonder what's eating Eleanor. She hasn't answered the last two letters that I've sent her.

Once I started working on Donald's story, communication between my mother and me picked up considerably — usually through the modern counterpart of letter writing: the telephone. I wanted to know what Donald had meant when he wrote, "I wonder what's eating Eleanor?" Had she been worried or depressed, or upset by his plans to enlist?

She said it was nothing like that, that she probably was just busy. "I had my hands pretty full, you know," she reminded me. "Two little kids and all. I NEVER was depressed."

"I SURE WOULD HAVE BEEN," I snapped in disbelief. "How about after Pearl Harbor? And during that first Christmas? What were your thoughts then?"

She just remembered everybody was talking about the war, and she remembered wondering if the war would ever get to Donald.

The attack on Pearl Harbor had sparked a vehement suspicion in America of all Japanese people. Charts purporting to differentiate them from the Chinese by their physical characteristics were circulated to aid in separating the guilty from the innocent, and by early 1942, American citizens of Japanese descent who lived on the defense-critical West Coast were being rounded up and relocated in internment camps throughout the United States. But while they were held captive and closely observed for any signs of treachery, their sons joined the U.S. military, and along with segregated units of Black American soldiers went off to fight for the oppressed and dispossessed in other lands.

Almost overnight the United States had to shift its industrial gears to aid in what had become its own battles. Factories and automobile plants were adapted to produce tanks, planes and other necessary military goods, and the production of civilian cars was stopped in February of 1942. With the rubber supply from the East Indies blocked, the sale of new tires was banned, and shortages of other staple goods — especially sugar — made · rationing a way of life. Citizens were urged to cut back, do without, gather scrap metals and old tires for recycling, and to invest in War Bonds to help win the war. The military draft quickly accelerated, and by the war's end 15 million Americans would serve in some branch of the armed forces. For the first time in history large numbers of women were going to work to supply the necessary labor, and to replace the missing men. And Lela Pederson, the teenaged girl hired to help Mabel in the Emerson household, would soon be pitching in with the outside work to make up for Donald's absence.

Restrictions caused by the war couldn't halt all normal social life or conventions, and folks still enjoyed such simple pleasures as playing whist and going to the movies. The movie theaters offered a new feature film or two each week, and escapist comedies and westerns alternated with flicks more apropos to current events such as *Dive Bomber, Navy Blues,* and *You're in the Army Now.* Love and marriage still found a way, and the first of Donald's pals took the matrimonial plunge when Donald's first girlfriend, Marcella Carlson, married Bruce

Turnbull. The Red Cross and the USO were collecting used "Books for Boys in Service," and the American Legion furnished service flags for their families to display in the windows of their homes. To aid pilots training in aircraft recognition, Pembina High School students carved model airplanes for shipment to Wold Chamberlain Field in Minneapolis.

In Karlstad, students began selling defense stamps, and Henry Peterson, a local entrepreneur, was buying used tires and scrap metal for 40 cents/100#. And within a month's time of the U.S. entering the war, the village mourned and memorialized its first war fatality. Elwood Monroe Swenson, who had enlisted in the Army the year before, was killed during Japanese bombing of a Manila hospital where he was working as a medic. Karlstad's American Legion Post would later be named in his honor.

The decision regarding military service would ultimately be left to Donald. Brother John was not slated to appear before the draft board until sometime in the spring; this gave Donald ample time to agonize over all the alternatives. He said nothing about any of this to his friends, but they remembered that he seemed to have trouble deciding whether he should stay in Chicago or quit his job and go back to North Dakota with them, and almost until the last minute they weren't sure if he would get in the car.

But by winter's end Donald was back home in Pembina County. He had stated his case for voluntary service and his brother John had grudgingly acquiesced to Donald's plan — primarily because he mistakenly assumed he would always exert enough influence over Donald to chart the course he'd take. An introvert by nature, John had never made friends easily; because of this, his closest personal relationships would always be those within his own family. Consequently, when John gave his mindful advice to his young brother, he was also counseling his very best friend.

John had prudently calculated the safest jobs in the armed forces, and taking heed, Donald abandoned his original idea of joining the Coast Guard and enlisted in the army, specifying air corps mechanics — ground work — as his preference. Then,

after helping put in the crops one last spring, Donald took the
train to the Army Induction Station at Fargo, North Dakota;
from there he would be sent to the military reception center at
Fort Snelling in Minneapolis to receive his assignment.

*When I asked my mother if it bothered her that Donald had
talked Uncle John into what had amounted to letting him go in
his place, she said it hadn't, because it was a sensible idea.
Donald would have had to stay home to work on the farm if John
had gone, and then neither of them would have been happy.*

*But even with the unanimous approval of the family, it had
been a time of unmitigated anguish for Uncle John. She told me
about the party Donald's friends and neighbors gave him at the
Harold Tisdale farm near Joliette; she remembered at the end of
the evening they all sang, "God Be With You 'Til We Meet
Again."*

*"It was awfully hard on Johnny to see him go," she added.
"When we got back to our folks' house after Donald's farewell
party, Johnny went upstairs and broke down and cried — he just
sobbed. He told Donald that when he came back home he was
going to buy him a new car."*

Chapter Two

Private Donald R. Emerson

June 25, 1942
Fort Snelling

Dear Mom, Dad & Bro.,

Well nothing much has happened since I left home but I imagine you'd like to hear from me. I didn't get into Fargo until 6:15 Tues. night and so had to lay over until Wed. at my own expense. I left Fargo at 11:40 Wed. night for Minneapolis along with four other fellows. We got to Minneapolis at 7:10 this morning and got out here at the Fort around 9:30. It so happens we got here at a poor time cause the medical building is being enlarged and fixed up so we won't even get our physicals until Mon. morning. I'm already sick of laying around doing nothing but eat, sleep, and walking around looking dumb. I've had two meals on Uncle Sam here at the Fort and they've been O.K.! We had dinner at 9:50 and supper at 3:50. This sounds sort of funny but you see the day starts at 4:30 in the morning. I'm going to hit the hay rather early tonight cause we couldn't sleep at all on the train last night.

I'll write again as soon as something breaks around here. Don't try to write to me tho cause it's hard telling where I'll be after next week.

So long, Don

America had been unprepared and underequipped to wage war at the time Pearl Harbor was attacked and spent the next several months stepping up production of the urgently needed equipment and materials. The military branches began rapidly coordinating their offensive strategies with the Allies, with top priority given to defeating Hitler and Mussolini in Europe. It would be the middle of 1942 before U.S. participation began to show positive results.

During this time Japan continued its program of conquest almost unopposed, taking American and British island territories in the Phillippines, the Dutch East Indies, Malaya, Guam and Wake. In April came the surrender at Bataan and the infamous "death march" of the Allied soldiers taken prisoner.

In another two weeks, however, the U.S. Army B-25 bombers of "Doolittle's Raiders" had made it all the way to Tokyo; and in June, Marine and Navy bombers staged a tide-turning three-day attack on a Japanese invasion fleet on its way to Midway Island, and at last, as Admiral Nimitz, commander in chief of the Pacific Fleet, stated, "Pearl Harbor was partially avenged."

July 1, 1942

Dear Folks,

At last, after a wait of five days, I'm in this "Man's Army." I was sworn in last night along with 30 other enlisted men. One of the reasons for all the delay is that they wanted at least 30 enlisted men to work on at one time. The percentage of enlisted men as compared to draftees is very small. Just to give you an idea of how efficient this reception center is - they are pushing through about 900 a day. They really put us guys through the mill today! First we had our classification or aptitude test. This test was designed so that no one could possibly get a perfect score. It was made up of vocabulary, mechanical (gears, pulleys, etc.), and mathematical problems. Some of the problems were too hard to monkey with and nobody finished in the 80 minutes allowed us. I got 230 out of the possible 300 points. This score falls in the above average group. Several of the older fellows with no high school education got scores as low as 125. After this test we were classified as to what branch of service we were to be put into. There were five of us who applied for Air Corps ground work and three of us made it. Everyone over 20 years old could not state any preference whatsoever as to what he wanted to get into. The sergeant classifying us was going to put me in the Tank Corps because of my tractor operating experience, but I objected and said I had been very definitely told that I could choose my branch of service. He then went to one of the "higher-ups" and found that I was right. I am classified for the Air Corps unassigned. If I get to be a mechanic or not I don't know, but at least I'll be doing something in the Air Corps.

We got our uniforms today too. It's rather hard to put in writing but getting the uniform on does give one a proud feeling. Altogether, the clothing issued to us weighs over 80 pounds and is valued at $125.00. I got a perfect fit in my uniform and they fit you over again if a person gains too much.

We also got three vaccination shots at one time which just about knocked us cold. About an hour afterwards I got a stiff headache and the chills - just like when a person is coming down with the flu. At this moment the chills have gone and I've got a fever instead. Our misery doesn't end yet though cause we got five more shots to take after this.

We signed up for our insurance today too. I signed for the limit of $10,000 which will cost me $6.50 a month. This insurance can be turned into a 20 year pay policy after one year. At the end of 20 years it will be paid up and will then have a cash value of $6,000 and will pay $10,000 if left as a straight 20 year life policy. Of course it also pays the full amount if death comes in the service or afterwards. I think I got this straight - anyway it's a good thing. The payments will amount to $78.00 a year but that's still cheap compared to other corresponding policies.

There is free entertainment here every night at the U.S.O. or recreation hall at the Fort Snelling Post. Last Sunday night Carmen Miranda was here, and Phil Harris and his band were here one night before I came.

　　We will be leaving here in three to five days from now for a permanent camp (Maybe). Anyway they told us not to have letters sent to us unless it's important. If letters are sent to us and we have already left they have to forward it and I gather they aren't keen on doing that. If you do have to write this is the address.

　　　　Private Donald R. Emerson
　　　　Company 3 Reception Center
　　　　Fort Snelling, Minneapolis, Minn.

　　　　　　　　　　Love, Don

As America began the massive build-up of its armed forces, a European theater of operations (ETO) was formally established, with Maj. Gen. Dwight D. Eisenhower in command, and the creation of one of the greatest air striking forces ever to participate in combat was under way. The Eighth Air Force, first under the direction of Col. Asa M. Duncan, was to be one of 15 separate army air forces during the war, and in the next 2 1/2 years "The Mighty Eighth" would grow to number more than 200,000 men and 4,000 aircraft.

　　Early in 1942, Eighth Air Force personnel began streaming into England as the leaders of the American and British Bomber Commands, Ira Eaker and Arthur "Bomber" Harris respectively, worked to correlate bombing tactics. Initial British skepticism to Eaker's proposal of daytime bombing dissolved and plans were laid for Britain's RAF to continue its bombing raids on German cities at night and for the U.S. to begin hitting their industrial targets during the day. Using this strategy the Allies would soon be bombing "around the clock," in Eaker's words, which Churchill gleefully quoted, "and keeping the devils from getting any rest."

　　On May 5, 1942, Maj. Gen. Carl Spaatz took over as head of the Eighth Air Force, and by July 4, 1942, U.S. crews flying British planes bombed German targets for the first time.

July 5, 1942

Dear Mom, Dad & Bro. John,

Well here it is Sunday and I haven't moved out yet. Of the original 30 men that were sworn in together, only 3 of us are still here. I haven't the least idea when I will be called for shipment either. It's like Warren Hart said - The Army don't tell the men anything until the last moment. A person hears a deuce of a lot of rumors about this and that but you can't believe anything unless it comes from headquarters.

Yesterday was the quietest 4th of July I ever spent! Holidays and Sundays are just like any other day here at the reception center. What they don't find up for us guys to do around here isn't funny. I've swept and scrubbed barracks, mowed the grass and been parking lot director. Yesterday morning they couldn't find any work for us to do, so they sent us out to pick up all the cigarette butts that were lying around (Ha). The only thing I've missed is K.P. duty and am thankful for that. The guys on K.P. have to start work at 4:30 A.M. and don't get off till 6:30 P.M. Each mess hall serves 1200 individual meals a day, so you can understand why K.P. is dreaded. There are nine mess halls here at the reception center and each one serves two breakfasts, two dinners and two suppers.

The Army sure does give us wonderful food though. To give you an idea, we had a T-bone steak that completely covered our plate for dinner yesterday. Here is the menu for today's dinner; Pork chops (I had three), mashed potatoes and gravy, dark bread, string beans, celery, lemonade, cookies and ice cream. Since I've been here we've had fried chicken twice and turkey once. They give us ice cream for dessert about every other day. Considering the mass cooking they do, those cooks sure turn out tasty dishes.

We have a very interesting character in our barracks that I have talked to a lot. He is a native prince of India. He is the color of a light Negro, is 6 ' 6" tall and has a splendid figure. He's 26 years old and has been in the U.S. for eight years getting an education. You never seen a smarter guy nor one that can talk better English.

I hope everything is going O.K. back home. I might be here for another week yet. Some guys have been here for three weeks before they were shipped. I talked to the Post Master and he said it's O.K. for you to write. If your letter gets here after I've left it will be sent back to you.
Say Hello to Lela

Love, Donald

Donald's detachment left St. Paul July 7, 1942, for Jefferson, Missouri, on the Silver Castle — the Rock Island Line's fastest train, until engine trouble slowed it down. They missed their connection in St. Louis and killed the day by doing the town. At the YMCA they had a free swim and a free lunch, and at the USO center, a free show. One more stop along the road. One more chance to write home — but just this brief bit of news on a postcard that day.

Regardless of the purpose of his travels, Donald was an avid adventurer, and each place visited yet another exotic land for a wide-eyed boy to explore. He eagerly gobbled up each new location like a hungry pup, quickly adapting to its people and adopting the jargon. But he always took the time to share it all with his family, sending a card or letter to somebody nearly every day — a rate that wouldn't slow until he was in active combat.

It was completely natural, this propensity Donald had for letter writing. His parents were both prolific letter writers, and along with that talent, he had also been gifted with the best qualities possessed by each. Their cross-bred intelligence, together with Frank's calmness of spirit and Mabel's spunky assertiveness, was strung together by a double strand of common sense. In Donald their genetic combination had produced the jauntiest, most colorful hybrid possible.

His father was a man of regal bearing, with the views of a philosopher and the heart of a poet; family circumstances and the poverty of the times had made him a farmer. While still a young boy, an epidemic of scarlet fever had killed two of his brothers and had left him with severely diminished hearing. Later that same year the two-week-old baby, one of his two sisters, died of an unknown illness. Although he hadn't been able to finish high school, he had, when he was in his twenties, studied for a couple of semesters at the agricultural college in Fargo before being called home because of his father's declining health. With unflinching "Emerson pride" he stifled his keen disappointment and obediently accepted his inherited role as the responsible eldest son. He withdrew from the pleasurable cocoon of academia, and never left farming again.

With his head in the clouds, Frank might never have noticed the charms and domestic abilities of Mabel Roswell, the family's diminutive hired girl — if not for his mother. After she first shot down his idle fantasies of higher-flying city girls, she brought him down to earth and steered him toward a more sensible choice. Her matchmaking was successful, and Frank and Mabel were soon married. Mabel was 21; Frank was 32.

Nine years later, in 1921, with a good wife and two healthy children, he decided he was a lucky man. He had convinced himself that he was indeed fortunate to have been given the farm free and clear. His younger brother Ray was not yet married and was not skilled in farm management, Frank said, and had "a very highly developed taste with corresponding ability to make returns deficient."

Frank still had hope of someday moving his family to Ontario, Canada, where the Emersons had originally settled when they emigrated from Durham County, England, in 1817. This was for his children's sake more than his own, and he wanted to live near the train station so they would have easy access to Toronto. "I want my children to go to college," he said. "I certainly do believe in college — it helps a man or woman to round out a life."

But this dream he had for his children met the same fate as the dreams he'd had for himself — as it turned out, not one of his children was interested in higher education. And although he did not dwell on disappointment, it was sometimes apparent that he more often respected the opinions and generally sought out the company of intellectuals.

Eleanor, though very creative and industrious, had never exerted herself in school. Donald not only wasted most of his time at school, but was also quite lazy in general — and his lack of enthusiasm and speed when doing mundane chores was often downright exasperating to the rest of them. Of the three, only John had excelled in high school; when he graduated he was the salutatorian of his class. But John wanted just to farm.

It wasn't long before John proved to be a consummate farmer, and Frank was then able to leave all the practical decisions to him, thereby allowing himself the mental freedom to consider more ethereal interests. He was frequently inspired by his lofty and noble thoughts to scratch out semi-legible poems, essays and editorials which he'd submit to area newspapers for publication, and for mental stimulation he corresponded with a variety of interesting personalities. Because he delighted in watching nature unfold, Frank did find some satisfaction in farm life. But perhaps even more he loved musing upon the words to best describe it all, and at harvest time he surveyed the ripened fields of grain and proclaimed them to be "great golden oceans." The recipients of his numerous compositions were undoubtedly relieved when he traded his pen for a typewriter.

Donald had his father's poetic powers of observation, but bolstered by the sometimes brash candor of his mother, he ably put his to far more interesting and effective use. He was known for always speaking his mind and "calling a spade a spade," his sister said.

When the new enlistees arrived at the air corps replacement training center in Jefferson Barracks, Missouri, on July 9th, Donald wrote that the campsite and surrounding country were very nice — just like a big park. "Sorry to say," he added, "that's as far as the good part of J.B. goes. Everybody — even officers — told us this place has the worst dam climate in the world and I already agree with them. It's hot in the daytime and it rains every night. The humidity is so high a person's shirt gets wringing wet in the morning and stays that way until you take it off. The first night I was here it rained 6 1/2 inches in 12 hrs. The paper called the main storm a cloudburst. The Mississippi is at flood stage and the Missouri R. has been over its banks for a week. On the train Wed. morning I saw fields of wheat in the swath that were completely covered with water. On top of the heat and rain we sleep in tents. Imagine a tent during a good thunder storm."

Located ten miles from St. Louis, the camp was a tent city over two miles long, set up to handle 50,000 men. Here the recruits would undergo four weeks of intensive drill training, eight hours every day, before being sent on to other schooling. There would be no time or need to go elsewhere for anything. Each squadron had its own church, with a chaplain for every faith, and the camp had five motion picture theaters plus an open air theater — larger than any county fair grandstand — where touring USO shows performed. Jeanette MacDonald was set to be featured late in July. (A "beautiful singer," Donald said.)

They got there just in time to take part in a parade the next day, marching and standing at attention for three hours without a break. "By official count 157 individuals had to be given first aid for fainting, sunstroke, etc.," Donald wrote. "Of course that's not a bad percentage considering the fact that 25,000 took part in the parade."

July 15, 1942

Dear Folks & Bro. John,

I've just come from the last "chow" and as usual it's too darn hot and close to do anything but sit. It don't seem to cool down at night here at all until about 12:00 midnight. The mercury hit 95 degrees today but that wasn't as bad as yesterday when it hit a high of 98 degrees with a humidity reading of 57%. There's so much moisture in the air here that envelopes seal themselves if not kept away from the open air. Right at this moment, the soldier that is sitting across from me at this writing table is trying to find a usable envelope out of a new bunch of them. So far he hasn't succeeded.

Yesterday we fellows that came from Fort Snelling, went thru the final process of our classification. We were given a series of five tests to find out if we were smart enough to go to school and also if we had aptitude for whatever schooling we wished to take up. We were given another I.Q. test and a mathematical test first. If we flunked either one of these tests we were put out of things right then. Fellows who didn't pass cannot go to school and will be put on general duty. Both tests were quite easy for me, in fact I got a perfect score on the math test which included some algebra. In the mechanical aptitude test that I took, 84 was the passing grade. Anything above 120 in that test gave one a rating of excellent. My mark was 129 - not bad, eh? I'm going to take up aircraft mechanics. This course gives me 4 1/2 months of schooling and will cover everything on a plane from tail to engine inclusive. By the way, you may be surprised to know that the total number of men required to fly and service each B-17 bomber is 31. I'll be a happy soldier when they ship me off to school - this basic training is plenty tough.

I haven't got any news from you at home as yet but I hope everything is hunky-dory.

Love, Donald

President Roosevelt proposed lowering the speed limit to 40 MPH, the nation went on "War Time" (one hour ahead), and farmers were urged to plan for seasons in advance by readying their equipment and stocking up on machinery repair parts and supplies. It was expected when war production reached its peak, the demand for raw materials would cause even more shortages and further hardships.

The list of area men leaving for military service grew to include a couple of Donald's former teachers, Hans Koland and Ken Kunny, who ended up at Jefferson Barracks too. Donald was hoping to find them there — he thought it would be nice to see a familiar face, even if it did belong to an old school teacher. Also swept up in the draft — despite being well past draft age — was his 42-year-old uncle, Lester Roswell; as the result of a snafu at the draft board, he would submissively march several months in the infantry before the error was corrected and he was discharged.

July 17, 1942

Dear Folks and Big Brother,

I got your very welcome letter yesterday. Believe me, nothing helps a soldier's morale more than a letter from home!

You mentioned having sent me a letter in care of Fort Snelling, but I haven't seen anything of that as yet. I'm not at all surprised, tho. They say it takes about two weeks for letters to be forwarded from one camp to another. Glad to hear that you're managing as well as you are with the work and that the crops still look good. I wasn't very much surprised to hear that Lela was helping outside. In fact, I expected that would happen. Nothing she would tackle would surprise me very much.

We had another one of those dam parades today. Some Brigadier General decided to visit J.B., so we had to get out on the parade grounds in our summer dress uniform (tie and all) with the temperature crowding the 100 degree mark. Tonight at supper time the temp. inside the mess hall stood at 98 degrees with the ventilation system going full blast. The only time it cools off here is when it rains and that's just as bad as the heat. Getting back to the subject, these parades are something to see. We march to the time of the 170 piece J.B. band. I got a date with the dentist on the day of the next parade, but from what I hear about the army dentists I don't know which would be worse, parade or getting my teeth filled. Whenever it's possible they drill us in the shade under the trees. When we get our daily 30 minutes of exercise we strip down to our shorts. I guess I've been painting a rather tough picture of the life here at J.B. If it wasn't for the heat it wouldn't be too bad. We work hard but we get good eats and entertainment.

I'm afraid I'm going to run short of money before Uncle Sam gets around to paying us. To start with I bought myself a good pen and the initial expenses at Fort Snelling and here took quite a bit. Even tho I do most of my own washing it costs us $1.00 per week to get our khaki uniforms dry cleaned. No matter how long we're here we won't get any money until we leave and then it will only be $19.00. If you could manage it $5.00 should tide me over. Incidently it must be sent in cash or postal money order. We can't get personal checks cashed here.

I think I'll leave my camera at home until I get sent to school but you can use those films if you want to. Johnny should be able to figure out how it works.

I don't care to have the Karlstad paper sent to me. I'll depend on "Sis" to supply me with the news from there.

Love, Don

Donald's mother was also a great correspondent, but unlike her husband, she wrote letters that were very direct and to the point, seldom leaving any room for misinterpretation. So very plain spoken herself, she liked to brag that her husband was "a writer," even though many of his fancy words and metaphorical phrases were lost on her, for she never implied anything.

Quite the opposite of Frank in nature, she was a feisty little scrapper and made no pretense of hiding any dissatisfaction. Though perfectly happy when she could keep busy with her garden, as the days grew shorter and colder her mood could mirror the bleak northern landscape. To break the monotony of winter and lift her spirits, she liked to go away somewhere — anywhere she could have the company of other people, if only to spend time with her daughter and family at Karlstad, or her sister and brothers at Halma. When confined to the house she spent her days working at various needlecraft and tatting, or poring over her well-worn medical encyclopedia, eagerly diagnosing the ailments of others when she had none of her own. By the time spring came to the farm, the melting snow and the April rains had turned the rich black earth to a sticky gumbo, and she would complain there was nothing to look at but mud.

July 26, 1942

Dearest Sis, Harold & Kids,

It's Sunday afternoon and I'm going to try and catch up on my letter writing. I got your letter Thursday along with three others. The other letters were from Mrs. William Barron, Jennie and E.B. Kluver. You can believe this or not but I read your letter first. Kluver sent me a very nice note and also the

Army Bible Kit given by the Karlstad Luther League. Kluver got my address off of a postcard I had sent Nannie and the Boys. He ended the letter "With kind greetings from the parsonage at Halma and from your Pastor and friend E.B. Kluver." Pretty darn nice, eh? I'm going to answer his letter this afternoon too.

I didn't dream Lester would have to go so quick. I don't imagine he is very keen on letter writing. It would be kind of fun to correspond with him if he would care for that sort of thing.

You asked if it was as nice here as in the good old "northwest." Well I must admit it's very pretty here. The campsite is a regular park with the Mississippi River alongside. If they had Minnesota weather here it would be O.K. I know this much, I'd never want to live here. I don't have to worry about spending the winter here tho as I won't be here very long. Just where I'll be shipped next I don't know but I'll be sent someplace to go to school for five months to study aircraft mechanics. I hear that those that do real well in school get a chance to go to advance schools, etc. If there's any such thing I know one soldier that's going to take advantage of it!

So Beverly is singing in the Karlstad church today. If she can make a good impression in town it will be a lot to her credit. I've got my fingers crossed for her.

No I better quit this and get started at the other letters. We don't have much time on week days and we're almost too tired after drill to write anyway.

Love to all,

Don

P.S. I noticed that your letter sent by airmail didn't get here any faster than the other ones so save that extra 3 cents for postage on other letters.

The Emersons had bought a new black Chevrolet sedan in 1941, and now they purchased a new swather — a machine that cut grain into rows for harvesting. With the promise of a bumper crop, Cousin Max had an additional granary built on the farm.

These were days of frenetic activity for sister Eleanor, as well. Along with the usual housework to be done without benefit of electricity or indoor plumbing, there were berries to pick, a garden to plant and weed, followed by the job of canning and preserving the produce. And every morning and night there were cows to be milked while battling thick swarms of biting flies and mosquitoes. The impromptu sloppy slaps in the face by fetid, stringy bovine tails made the barn a favored backdrop for Eleanor's wry and frequent refrain to Harold: "Ain't love grand?"

Her social life was centered nearby in the Hegland Lutheran Church, where she sometimes played the piano while her five-year-old daughter Beverly sang. Later, when little Bonnie turned four, this became a sister act, and together they would sing their songs of innocent faith: "Jesus Loves Me" and "Trust and Obey." Any spare time Eleanor had was spent in sewing nearly all of the clothing worn by her daughters and herself, and in writing voluminous letters to young brother Donald.

July 29, 1942

Dear Folks and Bro. John,

I got the sweetest news tonight that a soldier at J.B. can get. I'm going to get shipped out of this ____ place within the next two or three days. Four other fellows and I got put on a special shipping order. We don't know where we're going except that it will be some aircraft mechanic training center. Why they're shipping us out before our basic training is over, I don't know, but it makes me very sad indeed. I have only one regret and that is I'll miss rifle, pistol and submachine gun practice which would have come in the last days of drill. Spencer Shamp qualified for a mechanic too and we're getting shipped together. We have stuck together ever since we enlisted at Fargo.

A rather amusing incident happened here tonight after "chow." Two weeks ago a shipment of men came here that included some genuine "hillbillies." One fellow hadn't taken a bath since he was born - at least he hadn't taken one since he came here. Anybody who doesn't take a shower every night in this place gets in bad shape in a hurry! The other fellows in this guy's tent couldn't stand to be around him any longer so they took him over to the shower house by force and actually scrubbed him with G.I. brushes. He screamed and fought like a wild man all the time, and I'm telling you it was more fun than a circus to watch.

If you haven't sent any letters to me by the time this reaches you, do not send any as I'll most likely be shipped by the time they get here. I hope I get a letter with some "dough" in it before I leave. Of course if you haven't sent it by the time this reaches you, just forget about it. I think we will get a partial payment of some kind when we leave here.

I hope this finds you all well and everything is going "on the beam," as we say in the Air Corps.

Love, Donald

In the middle of North America, volunteers organized as "plane spotters" to work in four-hour shifts and watch for enemy planes 24 hours a day. The blare of air-raid sirens alerted the community to shut off lights for trial black-outs, and weekly radio forums were held featuring a panel of experts addressing such topics as, "What are we fighting for?"

Turnwall Mercantile in Karlstad and Heneman's and Hartz Stores in Pembina displayed photographs of the uniformed local boys in their storefront windows, along with the advertised specials: "Cheerioats" — a new oatmeal cereal — 15¢ for a 7 oz. package. Ring Bologna — 17¢ a pound. Radiant Roast Coffee — 59¢ for a two pound tin. And shoes "for every occasion" were priced from 98¢ to $3.49. V-mail letter sheets, which were reduced to microfilm for shipping and enlarged and printed for delivery, were available at all Post Offices. Anyone writing to the boys overseas could receive up to three free sheets per day; the cost of mailing was 3¢ regular, or 6¢ by air. The Pembina Civic League was writing letters to those in the military service, collecting names, addresses and coins for postage in jars put in each place of business, and the Busy Bees women's club of Karlstad's First Lutheran Church was sending them cookies. Private Donald R. Emerson's name was on both of their lists.

AIR CORPS TECHNICAL SCHOOL
LOWRY FIELD, COLORADO

August 2, 1942

Dear Folks and Bro. John,

I left Jefferson Barracks Friday night and arrived here at Lowry Field last night. Lowry Field is just three miles outside of Denver, altitude 5300' above sea level. I know after only 18 hours that this place is heaven in comparison to J.B.

The air here seems so pure and fresh - one good breath of it makes one feel like "superman." It gets warm here too but there is very little moisture in the air and that makes a lot of difference. The nights are rather cool. Anybody coming from J.B. can really appreciate this climate! The mountains are about 50 miles from here and are plainly visible. They seem to rise very abruptly and the tops are snow covered.

I know now why we were pulled out of J.B. and sent here. I was very disappointed and angry when I found out but it's army orders and there is nothing we can do about it. It seems there is a surplus of mechanics and a shortage of armorers in the air force so we were sent here to go to armour school. An armorer in the Air Corps takes care of everything connected with the firing and destructive power of a bomber. This includes machine guns, bomb racks, and power turrets on which the small cannons are mounted, etc. I'm sure it will prove very interesting work but I can't see that it will be of any great value to one after the war. I talked to a major on the train about it and he gave me some encouragement. The Armour course is a lot harder than the mechanics. Only 40% actually graduate and those who do make good get a higher rating. The major asked me what mark I made in my mechanics test and when I told him he said there's the reason you were pulled to be an armorer. Everybody here got a mark of 115 or better in the mechanical aptitude test. We won't start school until August 10th. Classes will be held 8 hours a day, six days a week.

We crossed the state of Kansas en route here. The southern part reminded me so much of the Red River Valley that I actually got homesick. The land is slightly rolling with not a tree in sight. We traveled 600 miles across Kansas and Colorado without seeing a tree except those along rivers and creeks. The crops in Kansas have already been harvested and the stubble showed evidence of a very heavy crop. I could see that the harvesting is done almost 100% with combines. There was one thing that struck me as rather queer. I didn't see one set of farm buildings that had a grove around it.

Please send my camera. Pack it good and mark it <u>Glass</u> so it won't be damaged by rough handling. Say, I wonder if you would send for a case for my camera and call it an advance Xmas present. You'll find it in Sears and Roebuck under the picture and description of my camera. I wouldn't have a chance to get one myself cause we never get a pass in the daytime except on Sunday and they don't carry them in the post exchange.

I haven't told you before but I signed up to buy a $18.75 bond each month so that amount plus the $6.50 for my insurance will be taken out of my pay each month. The bond will be sent direct from Washington, D.C., to you at home. I think the first one will reach you sometime after August 30th.

I'm writing this in the USO Club building and there is a dance going on so it's pretty hard to concentrate.

Love, Don

P.S. Say hello to Lela and tell her that if she ever finds herself with nothing to do she can drop me a line or two. (If she wants to.) Don't be afraid to write more often. If I remember right I've received two letters and a card from home since I left.

Although it must have seemed to Donald that he had been away a long time, in reality it had been less than a month since he left Fort Snelling, and the mail he kept looking for still hadn't caught up with him. He was eager to get a good look at Denver, but its numerous parks and attractions would have to wait; no passes would be issued until he'd been at Lowry Field for a week. As soon as he could he went down to the Post Library and consulted a Railroad Atlas to calculate just how far he was from home — about 1200 miles now.

Everything here was superior, in Donald's opinion, to anything at his previous camps — and the food, of course, always rated special mention. "I'll tell you what we had for dinner today," he wrote in one letter. "The menu contained vegetable soup, mashed potatoes and gravy, pork chops, corn on the cob, head lettuce salad, cake, cream pie and ice cream, bread and coffee or milk. Yesterday we had fried chicken for dinner. For breakfast we get toast, eggs in one form or another, our choice of cereals from oatmeal to shredded wheat, some kind of fruit and coffee, milk or tomato juice to drink..."

August 14, 1942

Dear Folks and Bro. John,

I got your last letter today and also the one containing the $5. I realize now why I haven't seen anything of your letters and I'm sorry I rebuked you for not writing. I didn't expect the money. I could tell by the nature of that letter that you had already sent it before you got mine telling you that I was shipping and wouldn't need the "fin" as I was going to get a partial payment when I left Jefferson barracks. (The above is known as a "Shakespearian" sentence. Ha.) If I had known that the $5 had been sent, I wouldn't have asked for that camera case. What you can do tho is tear out that catalog page with my camera on it and send that to me. I'll try to send for it myself.

After leaving the Red Rocks Theater Sunday night we drove to the top of Lookout Mountain. This mountain rises very abruptly from the floor of the plain. It's impossible to give a true word picture of the view from lookout point. Denver seems to be directly below but it is actually about 15 miles away. Buffalo Bill's grave is on the top of this mountain and there is also a Buffalo Bill Memorial Museum there. I am enclosing some post cards that show some of the views that we saw. You will notice on the card that shows Clear Creek Canyon that there is a road on the left side of the stream. We traveled on that road for about 20 miles and it's the most beautiful drive one could imagine. The road itself is an engineering feat. In many places it's blasted out of the side of rock cliffs.

We started school Monday and I'm telling you it's tough! The instruction in this phase of the course is given by the lecture method. The amount of stuff fired at us in one day is terrific. We don't have any textbooks and the only reference we have to study by is the notes we take during the lectures. We have a test every day on what was covered the day before. We will have this type of work for the first two months and then we'll move into the practical application phase of the course, that is, working on the actual plane and guns, etc. For the past week I have been studying small arms and electrical machine gun and bomb rack controls in school. We took apart and learned the nomenclature (name of each part and its function) of the automatic pistol (54 individual parts) the Springfield cal. 30 rifle, the new Garand rifle, the Thompson sub-machine gun and the Browning automatic rifle. The Garand rifle is by far the best shoulder arm, yet it is the simplest in construction of all. In about a week's time we will go into the cal. 30 and 50 machine gun and the 20 & 37 mm. cannon course. We spend three full weeks on those guns so I imagine there will be a lot to learn.

Yes, I have been thinking ever since I started this school that it would be duck soup for Johnny. During these first two months we will study:

1. Small arms -- Cal. 30-50 machine guns and 20 & 37 cannon

2. Low explosives -- Used in small arms

3. High explosives -- Used in bombs

4. Bombs -- Demolition, fragmentation, armor piercing, and six kinds of chemical bombs

5. Ten types of bomb fuses (nose & tail)
6. Synchronization of aircraft guns
7. Electrical gun controls
8. Bomb racks (light and heavy)
9. Pistol flares

This isn't all of them but it's all I can think of at the present. It's all very interesting but I can see now that mechanical ability is going to help a lot cause most of the guns, bomb fuses and power turrets, etc., are a complicated mess. I've only gone to school for four days but I've written three perfect test papers out of the four I've taken. I don't want to appear to be bragging but so far I've got the highest average in our class of 40.

That reminds me - I don't exactly care to have my letters read to everybody. I quite often tell you of my accomplishments and tho they are absolutely true, others may have slightly different ideas. Anyway, what they don't know don't hurt them!

I'm going to have a harder time keeping up with my correspondence from now on. To give you an idea why, I'm going to give you my daily schedule: Get up at 6:05, make our beds and scrub barracks, etc., go to breakfast at 7:20, study or do what we want from 8:30 to 11:00, fall out for one hour of exercising at 11:00, go to school at 1:30 and don't get out 'til 10:00 at night. We can't get to sleep until 11:00 so that gives us seven hours sleep (enough, but not too much). This goes on six days a week and on Sunday it's Denver or bust! I'll write whenever I get caught up with my studies but it probably won't be so often.

I got the usual fat letter from Eleanor yesterday. She gave me a lot of news.

No, it's soon time for calisthenics (exercises) so I have to close. I hope the harvest is going along O.K.

In haste,
Don

Pvt. Donald R. Emerson

*Harold's brother,
Glenn Torkelson*

*"Hot" & Eleanor with daughters Beverly &
Bonnie*

Wartime weddings were becoming quite common, and while home on furlough in August, Hot's brother Glenn married his sweetheart, Margaret Bakke. Donald had been hoping he'd "get a break" like Glenn and be given a furlough before shipping out, but notices were soon posted that all furloughs were canceled; all heavy bombardment armorers would be on their way to bomber bases as soon as they finished school. "I suppose this all sounds pretty bad to you," he wrote his sister, "but I still consider I'm getting a 'break!' I'm in the Air Corps."

Also in August, the U.S. Army Air Forces announced their first fighter groups would soon be operational in England. One of these was being formed around the three "Eagle Squadrons" of the British Royal Air Force — squadrons comprised of American fighter pilots who had voluntarily fought with the RAF before the United States entered into the war. These men were veterans of the full range of combat operations and had already been credited with destroying 73 1/2 enemy aircraft for the RAF. This prior experience gave them the distinction of being the oldest American fighter unit in combat. Now under the new American command of Col. Edward W. Anderson, these volunteers were transferred to the U.S. Eighth Army Air Force and the "Eagle Squadrons" were officially formed as the 4th Fighter Group.

August 15, 1942

Dear Sis, Harold and Beverly & Bonnie,

I got your letter Thursday. I imagine our letters passed en route. Your letters are very welcome sister! Somehow they make me feel good all over.

I got two letters yesterday that both turned out to be jokes. The one letter was addressed to a Sgt. Donald A. Emerson. Of course I knew it wasn't for me because it was from an address I had never heard of - and then, I'm a private not a sergeant! The right addressee turned out to be a colored Sgt. in the quartermaster corps over at Lowry No. 1. That's the first time I've ever heard of another person with my name. The other letter was one from home that had been sent July 8th. It was one Mom had sent to me in care of Fort

Snelling and it took this long to catch up with me. The front
of the letter was completely covered with forwarding
addresses.

I was sorry to hear that Lester hit the infantry. Field
artillery or something like that would have been better than
the infantry. I got plenty sick of drilling with only three weeks
of it. About all the training that an infantry man gets
consists of drilling and long hikes with a pack on your back etc.
I gather that you would like to know just what drilling is. The
purpose of drill is to teach a group of soldiers how to move in
an orderly manner and in perfect unison. This is accomplished
by marching in step and everybody doing the following
movements at exactly the same time.

Love, Donald

*My mother was so comfortable remembering Donald, and she
tended her memories like a cozy, warming fire, vigilantly stirring
and stoking them with faithful recollections. She still could see
baby Donald taking his first proud, stumbling steps into the open
arms of their father. And she remembered the little boy she led
by the hand on his first day of school in Karlstad — he was
wearing a brown tweed jacket and short brown pants. A sweet
young woman with a soft voice had come to meet him at the
classroom door.*

*"Bertha Turnwall was his second grade teacher," my mother
reminded me. "She was 'Miss Strand' back then."*

*Taking another haphazard leap in the chronology, she took
me to the day she found the enraptured ten-year-old Donald
sprawled out on the grass by the gasoline tank; he had sniffed the
tantalizing fumes until he passed out. Then, standing near the
sink, she pantomimed the distinctive way he had of washing his
face. With cupped hands he had scooped water from the white
enameled wash basin and moved his face around in his hands,
instead of rubbing his hands over his face. Remembered, too,
was the high school Donald who got a kick out of sitting in the
big rocking chair, impishly savoring a bagful of candy while his
two small nieces — her daughters — patiently watched him,
anticipating the unpromised, but sure-to-be-shared treat.*

And she'd never forget that when the phone call came from her brother John, five-year-old Bonnie had cried out — sensing the bad news before hearing it, and for many months after, Bonnie would awaken in the night crying for Uncle Donald.

September 3, 1942

Dear Mom, Dad & Bro. John,

It seems we have been so darn busy this last week that I haven't had time to do any letter writing at all. Last Friday the commanding officers got the bright idea that all students on "B" shift should live in the barracks at the north end of the Field. We had to get settled in new barracks all over again. I made sure I was the first one in tho so I got myself a room again.

I gathered from your letter, John, that you're having a pretty tough time with the harvesting. I wish I could be back there helping you. As things turned out, I guess I got the best end of the deal even tho I am in the army. There is one thing that has to be taken into consideration tho and that is the fact that you wouldn't of had any choice whatsoever as to what branch of the army you wanted. When I went in anybody who had been registered was given no more consideration than the drafted man even if he did enlist. I have heard that in some places they won't let a man enlist now if he is registered. Back in civilian life you hear a lot about soldiers getting jobs that they're best qualified for. Well I can tell you that's a lot of B.S.! The air corps is supposed to be the highest and best branch of the army, yet there are fellows going to armorer school here that have been mechanics and radio technicians, etc., for as many as ten years in civilian life. I was plenty "burned up" about being sent to armorer school myself but it's proving such interesting work that I've forgot about it. True, it won't do me much good after the war but I've come to the conclusion that there will be so dam many aircraft mechanics it would be hard to make use of that experience also.

We finished up with the four basic courses last week. Here I am boasting again but I got a final grade of over 90 in all of them. A grade of 90 or better here is considered as good as 100 if given in a college course because of the great amount of material we have to digest in the limited amount of time given. We are in what are called the advance courses now. They cover aircraft machine guns, cannons, synchronization and bomb racks. Right now we're studying the Browning automatic Cal. 50 aircraft machine guns. Boy this is a real gun and how. It fires 14 rounds per second and has a maximum range of 21,375 feet. The cost of this gun is $850.00. The B-17 carries 13 of these guns so it would have approximately $11,000 worth of guns.

We got paid Monday and I got $40.00 after two months expenses and bonds were taken out. You should see the gambling that goes on here after payday. I saw some suckers lose their whole pay in one night and I also seen some guys clean up as high as $250!

Love to all, Donald

P.S. I'm sending you two days notes on explosives & ammunition - we had our final test on that part of the course so I won't need the notes anymore. They should prove interesting to you Johnny.

P.P.S. I'm sending this by air mail and I want you to tell me how long it took to reach you and if it's any faster.

Donald got to Denver a few days later. It was a nice, clean city, he said, about the size of Minneapolis, with perfect weather and close to the most beautiful scenery he'd ever seen; he mastered it by streetcar, roller coaster and speedboat before getting rained on once. He thoroughly enjoyed his leisure time there, and when he wasn't posing for a camera, he was toting one. He told his folks and brother John that the female population wasn't much to look at and he guessed northern Minnesota couldn't be beat for good looking girls. He revised his opinion two weeks later when he found his next girlfriend, but he didn't mention it to them — just to his sister.

Her name was Esther Rome, age 19, with a personality and figure much like Jennie's, Donald's Karlstad girlfriend. He had been strolling around the Lakeside Amusement Park one day — just looking at the flowers, when he saw a very pretty blonde sitting on the grass leaning against a tree. He adjusted his camera and took a candid shot of her. She noticed him before he snapped the picture, but instead of covering her face, gave him a nice smile. Ice broken, they started talking. One thing led to another and before he knew it he had made a "show date" with her for that night. This boy who wrote his parents the particulars of his activities — including how to fuse live bombs — reserved this category of news for his romance-minded sister, always with the understanding that she not tell their mother.

September 13, 1942

Dear Dad, Mom & Bro. John,

This is Sunday afternoon - the first Sunday that I haven't spent in Denver since I came to Lowry Field. I had such a swell time last Sunday and Monday that I don't mind staying in today. It's easier on the pocket book anyway and it gives me a chance to catch up on my letter writing.

Thanks for your letter Daddy, even tho I did have quite a time reading it. I spent so much time on it that one of the fellows asked me if I was learning that letter by heart. I told him, no - I was only deciphering my dad's writing. I believe it's your birthday today, so here's wishing you many happy returns of the day!

It burned me up when I heard about Johnny getting another draft notice. I personally gave Zimmerman that letter that I got from Fargo proving that I had enlisted. I also told him to make sure it was given the proper attention and he said he would.

Have you received my insurance policy from the War Dept. yet? It should have reached you by now but you haven't mentioned it. I'd like to know so I can check up on it here if you haven't got it yet. I'm not sure as to how soon but you should receive my first war bond in the near future too.

We had both Sunday and Monday off last week because of Labor Day. I went to a football game at the University of

Denver Stadium, Sunday. The game was played between the Chicago Bears and the Army All Star team. The Army beat the Chicago Bears 13-7. I enjoyed being in a big stadium for the first time more than the game itself. The money taken in was given to the Army-Navy Relief Fund, so at the half the army put on a little show. They ran some jeeps over ramps so the people could see them bounce and shot off some cannons, etc. Then a squadron of B-17 bombers and one of the P-38 pursuit ships from Lowry Field roared overhead. This is the latest thing in U.S. fighter planes and is the fastest plane in the world! It goes so fast it makes a whistling sound as it goes thru the air. I've gotten so I can recognize planes just by the sound.

We didn't have to be back in camp until 11:30 Monday night so Spencer S. and I blew ourselves to a hotel room <u>with bath</u> and stayed over night in Denver. Monday was Victory Day at the Lakeside Amusement Park with everything free to men in uniform. We went out there in the afternoon and took every ride in the place. We rode the roller coaster eight times straight.

No, I got three more letters to write so this will have to be all.

Love, Don

The course of instruction for armorers had been nine months long before the war started; now to meet the needs of the rapidly expanding air forces it was compressed into three. Donald had surprised himself by his previously untapped facility for learning, and for a while he had even thought of applying to become an instructor at Lowry, but then, he said, the Government started handing out civil service jobs to the "darn draft dodgers" and was training them for those positions instead.

The last part of their training was given in Lowry Field's hangars. Here they studied the P-38 Lightning, the P-40 Warhawk (made famous by the Flying Tigers) and the P-39 Airacobra fighter planes — as well as the four-motored heavy bombers they would be working on overseas: the B-24 Liberator and the B-17 Flying Fortress.

Of course Donald wished he could take pictures of all of this, too — those big bombers looked pretty small sitting in the corner of the enormous Lowry Field hangar No.1, he said, but this was strictly against the law. "The army don't want us to take pictures of anything, but they don't seem to care when 'Life' and 'Look' magazines publish all kinds of pictures showing military personnel and equipment."

September 21, 1942

Dear Folks & Bro. John,

We are starting a new phase this afternoon so we haven't anything to study. We finished three weeks on machine guns and cannons Saturday. We had a 3-hour essay type final test on it Saturday night. Boy was it rugged! We also had a malfunction test on the Cal. 30 machine gun. They handed each of us 29 guns that had something or another wrong with them. We had to attempt to fire each gun, then diagnose the trouble and put it in working order. The first gun I worked on turned out to be a runaway gun. As soon as I had chambered the first round and let go of the charging handle it started firing and I couldn't stop it. It scared heck out of me because I wasn't expecting the gun to work at all. The Cal. 30 fires 20 rounds per second so you can imagine the racket they make in automatic firing. The Cal. 50 gun fires 14 rounds per sec. These two guns were invented by Browning and are identical except for size. The aircraft cannons proved very interesting. The 20 mm cannon was originally a Spanish gun. The French took it over and we were manufacturing it when France fell so we just kept on making them - but for ourselves. It really is a wonderful gun! It has a comparatively high fire power (12 rounds per sec.) and is much more simple than the 37 mm. It fires high explosives and armor piercing projectiles. The 37 mm is another invention of Brownings. It only fires 2 rounds per second, but has a 1 lb. high explosive projectile that is capable of completely demolishing a plane. The 37 mm with a fully loaded magazine (60 rounds) weighs over 350 lbs. so you can see it's no play toy.

Here's something else that may be of interest. They were doing a little experimenting on a P-38 here at Lowry Field. They took out the regular engines and installed two 2,000 H.P. engines in their place. They red-lined it in level flight at 600 M.P.H. and climbed to 40,000 ft. at a 87 degree angle. What do you think of that? Of course that kind of speed wouldn't be practical because of poor maneuverability. As it is the P-38 takes 2 minutes to make a 360 degree turn.

I don't suppose the above is of much interest to you Mom - it's more or less directed at you Johnny. I imagine you're pretty busy, but how about a letter John?

I hate to do this Mom, but I'm afraid I'll have to disappoint you on the furlough business. I may as well tell you now that I don't expect one. After we graduate we go to another field for some actual line practice and from there -- ?

I'm sending some snaps of myself.

Love to all, Donald

The campaign to collect scrap metals heated up with slogans such as "Hit Hitler with Junk," "Scrap the Japs with Scrap," along with more graphic, guilt-provoking ads depicting the ghosts of soldiers haunting farm yards full of abandoned machinery with the accusing caption, "This could have saved our lives."

Henry Peterson's scrap metal recovery business was booming and it would hang on him the life-long nick-name of "Junk Henry." Before finding this niche in Karlstad's business sector, Junk Henry had, among other enterprises, run a restaurant — where customers ordering hamburgers paid in advance so he could run to the store and buy the meat. He had also sheared sheep for a time, but had tired of that and sold his gas-powered equipment to his friend and hunting buddy, Harold Torkelson, and Hot added still another trade to his already lengthy list of skills.

Tues. Eve. after school

Dear Sis, Harold, Beverly and Bonnie,

I got your newspaper length letter Sunday morning. As

usual I was glad to get it. Don't write any more letters like that or I'm afraid I'll get too puffed up (Ha). I will admit they make me feel good tho.

Hearing about Mom doing a little bragging didn't surprise me any. I remember once last spring, when we were driving home from Halma one night, I scolded her about that very thing. She had been spouting off at Chris Davises. That sort of thing just makes other people jealous. Oh well - we all have our faults.

I stayed inside the Field gates Saturday night and Sunday. All I did over the weekend was see a couple shows at the Post Theater. You see it's the end of the month and after paying for my pictures I was almost broke. Tomorrow is payday so everything will be hunky-dory again. I'll go through the usual routine of standing at attention while the Commanding Officer gives me my money. Then I'll give him a snappy salute, do an about face and walk away.

I got my finished pictures Saturday morning. I was very well satisfied with them and I'm sure you'll like it too when you see it. I'm wearing a garrison hat (the kind with the visor). The army doesn't issue these hats - in fact we aren't allowed to wear them in camp. I bought one in an army store in Denver. It cost $4.50 but it flatters me a lot more than the regular overseas cap the army issues. You're going to be flabbergasted when you hear what I paid for my pictures, but you know only the best is good enough for me. I had them made up in the 5 X 7 inch size and had them oil colored by a person who is supposed to be the best oil-color artist in Denver. I also got them mounted in a gold metal frame with a glass front. As a result I paid a total of $12.25 for three pictures! I'm sending one home, one to you, and Jennie has been asking for a picture of me in every other letter so I sent one off to her today. Don't tell anybody I sent one to her. Above all don't tell Mom - she talks too much! Roswells might feel slighted if they knew I sent a picture to Jennie and not to them. I picked a smiling pose this time cause my graduation picture is on the sober side. I'll try to get yours in the mail tomorrow so it will reach you a day or so after this letter. Incidently the emblems on my coat lapels are part of the Air Corps uniform.

Tomorrow is our last day in the classroom and boy I'm glad! The work has become increasingly hard during these last phases but I've still kept my marks up. I don't know if that will ever do me any material good tho. We will spend 2 1/2 weeks out at the hangers before we graduate where we will familiarize ourselves with all the different types of planes and their machine gun and bomb rack installations, etc. Graduation will be the 17th of October as far as we know - they never tell us anything for sure in the army.

By the way My Dear Sister, I wish you wouldn't show my letters to everybody. I'm usually a little more intimate in my letters to you than anybody else, so naturally it's intended for you only. If there are parts of my letters that you think are worth repeating and don't give away any secrets, you can read those portions to whoever you wish. You can consider this a mild scolding (Ha).

As to your birthday sister, I honestly did think of it the day after it was past and it was too late to do anything about it. It's a good thing you reminded me about Dad's or I'm afraid I would have forgotten his too. When the time comes, be sure you remind me of Mom's birthday. She's pretty sensitive about us not remembering her on her birthday.

You asked if I get lonesome here. To tell you the truth I really don't. We are kept so busy all the time with studies, etc., that I don't even think about it. The main reason is that I like it here so well. If I was back at J.B. I think the situation would be different.

Thanks for asking me but you don't need to send me anything in the line of "eats" or candy. The Post Exchange restaurant and soda fountain is only half a block away from our barracks and we get candy there a lot cheaper than civilians can buy it. If you ever do get the urge to send me something just slip one of those green folding things in a letter.

Your letter reminded me of the fact that I received a package of cookies from the Karlstad "Busy Bees" about three weeks ago. It had been sent to me in care of Jefferson Barracks, so it was almost three weeks in reaching me. The cookies were so broken up and dried out that they weren't eatable, but if you see any member of the Busy Bees I want you to thank them for me.

I guess I've scribbled enough for now so I'll sign off.

Your loving Bro.

Donald

I don't suppose H.O.T. looks forward to driving the bus six times a week - not much time to haul hay, etc.

H.O.T. Hot. My dad. He was an Emerson in-law for the last half of Donald's life, years when he'd been busy knocking himself out to support his growing family. Although he preferred country living, the farm income was never quite adequate, and to supplement it he took whatever extra jobs he could get, along with hunting and trapping innumerable wild animals for the food, fur or bounty they provided. In varying seasons he drove a school bus, sheared sheep, and hired out as a carpenter or as a farmhand. In later years he drove a truck for the creamery and worked as a county tax assessor. When he retired, he was working for the Wikstrom Telephone Company as a utility man.

Though he may be, as he describes himself, "a bashful Norwegian," there were a few stories he liked to tell. Of how he nearly drowned when he fell in the river while checking beaver traps with Oscar Hageland — the ice had just broken up and he had been swept downstream by the swift spring current, and how he saved himself, finally, by grabbing hold of a fallen tree limb.

"April 9th," he said. "Still ice on the river. Got out just in time to drive the school bus in my soaking wet clothes — didn't have time to change! Big boots full of cold water and all. FOUR-BUCKLE OVERSHOES! Never got sick, either!"

And he could talk about his sheep-shearing days — of how he sometimes even had to catch the sheep before he could shear them, and how at times their wool was caked with manure. And those awful karakul sheep, "THEY WERE THE WORST!" he said. Shaving away their coats of tightly kinked fleece took extra time, and was so hard on the steel blades that they needed constant resharpening. Shearing was back-breaking work, but at 15 cents per sheep, big money, and on a good day he could clip as many as a hundred. But he paid for this windfall in his dreams. Tormented in his sleep by nightmares of wrestling with these woolly adversaries, he once awakened to find he had kicked out a window next to the bed.

He must have kept other memories, too.

Although my dad was often in the room during visits, or on an extension when my mother and I talked on the phone, he usually listened quietly, interjecting comments only when he had something funny to say. Once, when they were at my house, I realized that I'd never asked him about Donald.

"Pop — what do you remember about Donald?"

He hesitated briefly, carefully choosing his words for comic effect. This gave my mother another chance to answer for him.

"Oh, Donald was just crazy about your dad," she said to me. "Wasn't he, Harold?"

"HE WAS A PEST!" Pop chuckled.

"OH, HE WAS NOT!" protested my mother. "He was a wonderful boy and he was absolutely wild about you."

"He's joking, Ma," I said, attempting to head off a dispute.

"Oh, I know that," she admitted. "Why do you always have to talk so foolish?" she asked, flinging Pop a critical glance.

Ignoring her, my dad continued, "He used to hang on me all the time and sit on my lap — right here," he said, patting his knee. "He was too old for that."

"How old was he?" I asked.

"Musta' been about fifteen," Pop estimated.

"OH, HAROLD! Don't be so silly — he couldn't have been more than nine or ten when you first came over to our house."

"Prob'ly why my knee's so bad now," he added with a wily smirk.

"Oh, the way you talk!" my mother mumbled in his direction.

"Did Pop start coming to see you right after you first met — when you went home from school with Alice?" I asked.

"It wasn't much later," she answered.

"I thought you were so shy, Pop."

"I am!" he insisted. "I didn't start anything."

"That's right — Ma noticed how kindly you treated your dogs, and she decided on the spot that you would be a good father. You didn't stand a chance, you know."

Holding up a short letter I tried to proceed. "I found a note that Donald..."

"It wasn't just because of the dogs! He was real good with his little sisters, too," my mother explained.

"...wrote especially to you from training camp."

" I REMEMBER THAT LETTER!" Pop cut in.

"Says, 'Dear H.O.T., I wish I were back there so I could take your new gun...' "

"HE THOUGHT HE WAS GONNA TAKE MY NEW GUN APART!"

"Well, Harold! He could have done it — he knew how to do it by that time," she said in Donald's defense.

Pop was clearly unmoved. "NOBODY touches my guns," he warned unyieldingly.

"Maybe he just said that to tease you," I said, reading on. " 'Someday if I have a lot of spare time I'll write you a letter...' "

"Oh, he wasn't teasing — he meant it!" Pop decided.

" '...and describe in detail the ten different types of machine guns, cannons and rifles that I know by heart.' "

"No, he wouldn't tease," my mother agreed. "He wasn't like that — he was a wonderful boy. He never drank or smoked, either."

"Nicest gun I ever had," Pop said, almost misty with nostalgia.

But my mother was sticking with Donald.

"I remember one time when he was a little boy he was in the toilet for such a long time that I went out and asked him what the trouble was. He said he'd been praying God would keep him on the narrow path."

"That path to your outhouse WAS real narrow," Pop allowed.

My mother guffawed in spite of herself. I did, too, and then tried to plow through their habitual banter by forging ahead.

" 'Those machine guns that fire 20 shots per second have as many as 200 separate parts in them!' " I read. " 'The only thing I hated was learning the exact names of every part. <u>Oil buffer tube assembly plunger rod spring</u> is the name of one little spring in the 50 caliber machine gun.' "

But Pop kept going back to his gun.

"It was a 30-30 Winchester. Paid twenty-eight dollars for it. A gun like that would cost two or three hundred dollars today."

Muttering to myself to give it up, I surrendered, completely overrun, and joined the sideshow.

"So what happened to that gun, Pop?" I asked.

"Traded it a couple years later for a horse — to Severt Setten."

"That's another thing I never could understand about you," my mother grumbled. "You always thought you should have horses! Whatever for? You had no use for them — you had a tractor!"

"No," he said, ignoring her, "it wasn't Severt Setten. I traded it to Herbert Pearson. Sold the HORSE to Severt Setten for fifty dollars, so I guess I did all right."

"Donald never did try to touch your gun, so it doesn't even matter," said my mother, at last returning to the subject.

"Oh, I know," he said. "But it made me kinda' mad, anyway."

"Did Donald like to hunt?" I then thought to ask.

"No," she answered. "He never cared for anything like that."

"That's what I always say," Pop said. " 'I don't care, but it makes me mad anyway.' Sure was a nice gun, though. Nicest gun I ever had. Another thing I like to say is, 'I've got lots of time, but I'm in a hurry anyway.' "

"That's a good one, Pop — I should write this down so I'll remember it," I said.

"Oh, stop with that," my mother ordered. "She's not writing about you — she's writing about Donald. He was a Christian, too. Be sure you put that in there."

My mother may not have said that last line aloud, but I heard it, anyway.

U ntil its pact with Italy, Germany held no territory and had no interests in the Mediterranean; but once aligned with Mussolini, Hitler sent Germany's Gen. Rommel to North Africa to help the Italians maintain their holdings and launch an offensive against the British. Rommel's Afrika Korps rolled into North Africa intending to capture Egypt; they were able to push through British troops and advance 250 miles, taking Tobruk and Libya before being stopped at El Alamein. On November 2, 1942, Gen. Montgomery, the new leader of the British 8th Army forced Rommel to retreat, bringing about the first major British victory over Germany in the war. Plans were made for an Allied invasion, and on November 8, 1942, American troops launched a surprise attack, called Operation Torch, by landing in French North Africa where they quickly took Algeria and Morocco. Even though his forces were caught in the squeeze put on by the Americans from the west and the British from the east, Rommel did not give up. It would be another six months before the Afrika Korps was crushed, forcing Rommel's surrender.

By autumn of 1942, a week seldom passed without news of several local boys going to war — or a report of one who was wounded, missing, taken prisoner, or killed in action. And in England, on September 21st, just nine days after the 4th Fighter Group was officially activated, its first casualty was recorded when Lt. John T. Slater was killed in action.

The American military academies could turn out only a

fraction of the aviation cadets needed for combat flight training, and in order to recruit enough mentally and physically qualified candidates, the U.S. Army lowered the minimum age from 21 to 19, and replaced the once requisite college education with a high school diploma. To further attract potential airmen, the army promoted the Air Corps by putting on impressive air shows featuring stunt pilots, and by advertising: "UNCLE SAM NEEDS PILOTS — BE A U.S. ARMY FLYING CADET — LET'S GO! U.S.A. — KEEP 'EM FLYING." What they did not publicize was the exorbitant rate of attrition of the glamorous flyboys during war.

These opportunities for excitement, as well as military career advancement, were not wasted on Donald, but his unsuspecting family had no idea he was already immersed in the paperwork necessary for applying to become an aviation cadet.

October 22, 1942

Dear Folks & Bro. John,

I imagine you have been wondering why I haven't written. Ever since we graduated I've been expecting to be shipped any day. I sent my diploma home - did you get it? I just got off of a 16 hour K.P. detail and I feel like a physical wreck. If it wasn't important I wouldn't be writing this now. Yesterday the thing that I have been working on for a full month finally went thru. I never told you but ever since I've been in this army I intended to try for Aviation Cadet. I had my doubts about passing the mental and physical examinations so I didn't say anything about it. Yesterday I went before a board of high ranking officers for a personal interview. They decided I was a fit prospect for becoming a commissioned officer after training as pilot, bombardier or navigator. I've already been taken off the regular shipping list and put on the cadet list. I will stay here until my turn comes and that may take as long as two or three months as there is quite a large waiting list and cadet shipping orders only come out once a month. In the small self-addressed envelope you will find a statement consenting for me to take cadet training, which you must sign and have notarized. Being there was a danger of my being shipped out of here they consented to accept me if I felt sure you would give your consent, which I'm to turn in as soon as possible. I don't think you're going to say "no" but just to make sure - if I don't get that consent I'll be accused of fraudulent application! The reason I didn't dare wait for your consent was because of a rumor that was floating around. It turned out to be true and today all the rest of our class signed overseas books and received extra equipment such as gas masks and helmets. That means only one thing - foreign service after leaving here! We were expecting this as the Air Corps needs 13,000 armorers for overseas duty at this time. The school here is going on a 24-hour day, 7 days a week basis starting next week. As far as overseas duty is concerned I wouldn't have cared but the bad part about it is that ratings are almost impossible to get once you're out of this country and be darned if I want to remain a buck private forever.

If I do O.K. in cadet training I'll become an officer and that's nothing to sneer at. I have investigated every other way of getting a commission and this is the only thing that doesn't require at least two years college. I could have signed up for Armorer Cadet because of my good grades going thru this school. One of my classmates got into this and he had a lower average grade than I. He will take a two months advance course and then be commissioned. I think the college requirement is just a method of elimination because I can't see what good it does an armorer!

Before I could apply for Aviation Cadet I had to secure three letters of recommendation and pass a difficult mental test. As you seem to already know, Harts & Bill Barrons supplied two letters and I got the other one from L.E. Wermager [Karlstad High School Supt.]. Wermager's recommendation carried the most weight. It was a full typewritten page long and even mentioned my fine home background (Ha). The test was plenty hard and I just finished in the 3 hours allowed time. I can justly feel proud of the mark I got which you can see for yourself on the qualification card I'm sending you. The test consisted of current events, mechanical ability, mathematics and some questions on a few of the more common bombers and pursuit planes. The minimum passing mark on that test is 75.

You don't know how hard I've worked on this application! Once the army gets a guy trained for something they don't want to let you apply for anything else.

I've gone into detail about this to let you know what's what and also that it's not a sudden infatuation of mine. It's been on my mind for quite a while and in the meantime, I've been working harder than I ever did in high school so I would stand a better chance for advancement as an armorer too.

Excuse writing - I'm too tired to think straight.

As ever, Donald

P.S. That qualification card must be returned to me also!!

After reading my mother's letters from Donald I became hooked on exhuming his story, and I wanted to read the rest of them. It seemed time to go after Uncle John. I made the six-hour drive up north from the Twin Cities in order to interview him, only to discover I was too late; he had just left on a trip to Alaska to visit David, his youngest and most adventurous son.

A letter would have to suffice. I had blithely — and ignorantly — assumed that any old sorrows about Donald had surely been put to rest by that time, and when I returned home I wrote to Uncle John asking a barrage of intimate questions, all of the things I needed to know.

He efficiently answered my request for his help. A small box containing letters from Donald and the Stateside log book tabulating his flight time had arrived almost by return mail. In a handwritten letter to me he said he would have to rack his brain to recall Donald's activities. He remembered that before Donald enlisted he had helped him on the farm, and together they had worked picking potatoes for other farmers. Then, when the military draft was threatening, Donald had decided he should be the one to go.

"He thought there were better ways to make a living than farming," Uncle John wrote. "I had him enlist in airplane

mechanics, but he decided once he got in he wanted to fly... He seemed to have a fatalistic attitude he would be shot down but felt he would survive... If he had stayed in mechanics he would probably be alive today..."

October 31, 1942

Dear Bro. John & Folks,

Received your letter and the consent Monday.

Last Saturday every one of my classmates shipped out and I was left all alone in the barracks. I spent Saturday night there but it was so quiet it gave me the creeps. Sunday morning I got permission from the guy in charge of quarters to move into Barracks 877. There are only six of us here - just enough to have fun. These other fellows graduated the same time as I did but are being held here for a reason unknown to themselves. We go to bed when we please and get up when we please. In general we don't do anything but clean our rooms and fire the furnace, etc. We spend most of our time at the Service Club or Post Theater. We don't dare hang around the barracks much during the day cause they're always looking for guys to grab for some detail. Some life, eh? In this squadron I believe there are only eight of us who are future Cadets. This is not a very large percentage considering the fact that there's about 1600 men in the 10th Squadron.

When I get sent to the cadet replacement center I'll be given further physical examinations and aptitude tests to determine just what I'm best suited for. What they decide on is what I'll be and we have no choice in the matter. All I know now is that I'll be one of the three - pilot, navigator or bombardier. When we are getting our training the pay will be $75.00 per month which is equal to a buck sergeant's pay. The cadet training lasts from five to seven months depending upon what we become.

Speaking of money reminds me that I'm forced to ask for a little handout. As I write this letter my billfold contains $1.56. I have clothes at the cleaners that will require $1.00 to get out and I have my watch at the jeweler's getting it cleaned, the bill for which will be $2.00. I have to get a good pair of gym shoes too so you can see I'll be needing money - soon. It will be a month before my next pay day so you can send me as much as you wish (at least $10 - $15). The best way to send it is by money order and keep the stub so if the letter gets lost you won't be out anything.

In reply to what you wrote in your letter John, I admit I am sticking my neck out but I'd rather take my chances in the air than in the infantry, armored divisions, tank corps or the navy! Of course it's dangerous but name me a war job that isn't. Anyway I'm one of those that believe that if a guy is supposed to lose his life in this war it will happen no matter what or where and vice versa. The biggest factor that made me apply for cadet was the officer's commission, not the fascination of the air. After I was finally approved by the Cadet Board almost all of my classmates congratulated me and wished they were in my place. I got a card from S. Shamp today and he's in South Carolina. They will be shipped overseas as soon as a complete squadron is formed.

Have no more news -

Love to all, Donald

P.S. When you write remember I'm in barracks 877 instead of 878.

My collection of Donald's letters had grown to at least 100, counting the additional ones I got from Uncle John, but he had left many of my probing, personal questions unanswered. I wasn't sure if it was a simple oversight on his part, or if it was too much of an ordeal for him to dredge up the past. My mother believed he probably just didn't remember.

"Go ahead and write to him again," she said when I called. "He's got nothing else to do, except drive Betty crazy."

I suggested that maybe he'd rather be left alone, but paying no attention to me she went on to say, "He never should have moved off the farm when he retired — he hasn't been happy since."

"I hate to bother him if it's painful for him," I said, trying to explain. But she was unswayed.

"He gets depressed when he has nothing to do — he's like Mama that way," she firmly decided. "Thank God I'm not like that — I never get depressed!"

"Never?"

"NEVER!"

"Don't you ever feel bad? Or sad? Or get the blues sometimes?" I asked incredulously.

"Oh, sure, maybe a little bad or sad sometimes," she admitted, "but I NEVER get depressed!"

"Fancy that. So you think it's okay if I ask him again?"

"Why not? It can't hurt."

My mother was such a compelling optimist, an incurable Pollyanna to the core. I'd try again. I could never stand to be a reporter.

Nov. 12, 1942

Dear Mom, Dad & Bro. John,

I got your last letter the first of this week. I was plenty glad to get the money order as I was down to my last nickel.

You will remember I told you that I expected to stay here at Lowry Field for 2 or 3 months before getting called for Cadet Training. Well I got notice yesterday that I was on shipping orders and was not to leave the Field. About 2 hours ago they told me to pack as I'm leaving at 5:00 tomorrow morning. I sneaked a look at the shipping order and I'm going to Nashville, Tennessee. I'm due to arrive there Sunday the 15th so will probably be there when you get this letter. I can tell you I'm plenty glad about it too. I was getting fed up with doing nothing but K.P. detail all the time. There are five of us leaving together. The funny part of it is I'm getting shipped before some guys in the 10th Squadron who have been waiting as long as 4 months.

I'll write as soon as possible. I'll soon be "Cadet" D.R. Emerson instead of Pvt.

Love, Donald

After L.E. Wermager's letter of recommendation on Donald's behalf, a correspondence developed between the two of them, but to Donald's chagrin, the high school superintendent was so impressed by it that Donald found himself being quoted in an article written for the *Karlstad Advocate,* entitled "Donald's Advice":

A letter carrying advice for all students was received by our school last week. One of our graduates is now entering his work as an aviation cadet and reports back to his high school. An excerpt from his letter may be interesting to every high school student.

"I am beginning to realize now that a high school education comes in handy. I only wish I had applied myself more when I was in school."

This seems to be the sentiment of so many who are now being taxed to their best abilities in the armed forces. Why not take this man's advice? Start applying yourself now. We congratulate Donald Emerson, Class of 1941, on his progress toward his commission in the U.S. Air Forces.

In Nashville the cadet candidates would go through the classification process, a meticulous screening that would eliminate many brilliant and seemingly physically fit young prospects. Just being bright and healthy was no guarantee of acceptance; to be classified as potential aviators in combat demanded much more. Besides the often quoted "eyes of eagles and reflexes of cats," they needed internal organs and gastrointestinal tracts that would not seize up or explode from extreme gravitational forces, and it was imperative that they possess the mental and emotional stability necessary to keep their heads and do their jobs, even when under attack. Equally important — though it was not always noticeable in the shy and soft-spoken, or self-mocking among them, every flyer had to possess a very healthy ego, because there was no way they could succeed at what they would be called on to do if they didn't first believe in themselves.

November 22, 1942

Dear Folks & Bro. John,

Not a great deal has happened to us as yet. I haven't seen anything of Nashville as we are restricted to the camp for the first two weeks. I'm sort of anxious to get into town and see some of these southern belles. They say the gals really go for cadets. The civilians down here have that genuine southern drawl. It's actually fun to listen to them talk.

All we have done is have an interview and another physical. The interview was given by a psychology expert who tried to determine if we had enough on the ball to take cadet training. He asked a lot of silly questions - not for information but just to see how we answered. For instance he asked me if I had ever had intercourse with a girl and other embarrassing questions concerning sex. Then he asked some current event questions and why did I want to fly, etc. I know of two fellows who got washed out on this. The one was given the high sign because he just stammered on a couple words. I thought I got a tough physical at Lowry Field, but they really went over us with a fine-tooth comb here. It took two days to go through. The first day they gave us x-rays, urine test, two blood tests and the eye test. I was a little afraid of the eye test but I guess I have perfect vision. They test the eyes for strength, angle of conversion, depth perception and did a lot of other tests with optical instruments that I didn't understand.

Yesterday we got the general physical on hearing, teeth, height, weight, limbs, etc. The most important part of this is the part on the heart and blood pressure. They use what they call the "Snider test." They take your pulse and blood pressure laying down, standing up and after exercising. I was glad to get this physical over with. About 10% of the bunch were so unfortunate as to be washed out on the physical.

Next week we get two days of mental and psychology tests and the results will decide what we will become. The way it used to be everyone wanted to be pilots and those who washed out as pilots later became navigators and bombardiers. That system was O.K. in peacetime but now they want to be sure the first time. I haven't set my heart on becoming a pilot like most of the guys have. Personal preference shouldn't come first if we expect to win this war!

Things are pretty strict around here. Some of the rules are almost silly. The idea is to prepare us for the Cadet training where rules and orders have to be obeyed to the line! They keep telling us that we are future officers and to start acting like one now.

It's a good thing I got that $10 before I left Lowry Field. They tell us not to expect to be paid until just before we get shipped out of here. I'll try to stretch that $10 as far as I can. I should get quite a substantial sum when I do get paid tho. Cadet pay is $75 per month with the insurance paid by the government. A Sgt. in the regular army gets $78 per month but has to pay about $7.00 for his $10,000 insurance.

Have you done anything about getting a phone put in yet? I wish you would so I could at least talk to my family even if I can't get to see you personally. Night and Sunday rates are quite reasonable. I'm writing this in the recreation room and you'd be surprised to see the guys calling home. One fellow just placed a call to California and it came thru in less than 10 minutes. I think I'm about 1400 miles from home.

Love, Donald

A/S Donald R. Emerson
Sqd. E Group 5
Nashville Air Center
Nashville, Tennessee (P.S. A/S stands for Aviation student.)

I could tell from reading Donald's letters that his mother must have done most of the writing to him, so I brought up Grandma's letter-writing proclivities to my mother.

"She was good at writing letters," she said.

"I got quite a letter from her myself, once," I reminded her. "A real scathing one — shortly after I broke up with some guy. Did she ever chew me out!"

"What did she say?"

"I don't remember all of it — I just remember the best line: 'Good men are scarce and hard to come by.' Priceless! I think she also took a couple of pokes at you while she was at it."

"Oh, that wouldn't surprise me any," my mother conceded. "I was her favorite pincushion. Whenever she was feeling low, she'd fire off a letter to someone, usually me."

"What did she pick on you about, Ma?"

"Nothing. Everything." She answered rather wistfully.

"I wish now I had saved the letter I got," I said. "Did you save any of yours?"

After a brief pause she answered. "I only kept the good ones. I threw the rest away."

Thanksgiving Day

Dear Folks & Bro. John,

I received your air mail reply today. I was at the recreation hall playing pool when it was delivered to me. Words cannot express how much a soldier enjoys a letter from home. Until I got the letter I was in sort of a mood being it was Thanksgiving Day away from home and all. It wasn't too bad here in camp today tho. They put on a swell turkey dinner in our mess hall. Also they deviated from the regular style of serving ourselves the cafeteria way by being seated and getting served individually by the cooks here.

Some generous people visited our squadron today and left a box of oranges and a basket of apples for us. They looked as though they could afford it as they were driving a '42 Oldsmobile. Maybe that's a sample of southern hospitality (Ha). The southern people will have to go some to beat the Denver people in that respect tho.

I have taken all the physical and classification examinations but don't know anything for sure yet. They take the results from all the tests and scramble them together, then decide from that. Of course this all takes time.

Don't worry about getting me anything for Xmas. I have received a total of $15 from you so will consider that as my present. Of course I won't be able to send anything home to you either. If I have to stay here too long I may have to call on your help again. I believe I explained the financial situation to you in my last letter.

I haven't much to say to you, Mom, on that matter of your and Eleanor disagreeing so. I have heard from both sides on it and I personally think it's darn silly! In answer to one of Eleanor's letters I said the same thing. I am positively neutral!!

No it's soon time for evening chow and I have to be there to call roll at the formation. I was appointed Cadet Corporal of our squad and have to call roll at all formations such as reveille, drill, chow, etc. A squad consists of 15 men. When we have drill I have to be the drill instructor. Drill is duck soup to us but it's not so easy for the guys that just came out of civilian life.

Lots of love to all,
Donald

December 11, 1942

Dearest Sis, Harold & Kids,

As I write this I am in a hospital bed, but don't get alarmed - it's nothing serious. I went on "sick call" Tuesday with an extremely sore throat. The "Doc" took one look at it, then took my temperature - which read 102 degrees - and said, "Son, you're going to the hospital." My temperature is back to normal this morning and my throat is better so I should be out of here pretty soon. They give a guy good medical care here anyway. Incidently the nurse is just too cute for words!

I almost felt like tearing my hair out when I read about Wermager putting that "Donald's advice" in the paper. I wrote to Wermager some time ago thanking him for his recommend-ation and I said something to the effect that I now realized the value of high school and wished I had applied myself more when I was in school. I sure didn't think he would put anything in the paper about it. I can just see the grins on my old class-mates' faces when they read it. I am not ashamed of it but you know what I mean. I would appreciate the Advocate but I'm going to make sure it don't contain any more "Donald's advices"!!

Mom said she was taking my picture to the store in Pembina. They have the same thing as Turnwalls. When I took that picture I never dreamed it would get such publicity (Ha). Mom also had a few things to say about you. She said it was your turn to write. Personally I think your differences are rather silly and no good will ever come of it. Mom has a funny constitution and things like this affect her so why don't you swallow your pride and write.

I got a long letter from Dad in which he complimented me for the first time since I've been in the army. You know he never did think I could ever do anything. I guess I gave Dad every reason for thinking that way tho. The folks had seen that piece in the Advocate but they didn't send it to me either.

Well it came thru last week. After two weeks of waiting with my fingers crossed, I finally got officially appointed as an "Aviation Cadet." I was classified as a Pilot. I guess that means I'm disgustingly healthy (or at least I was) and I have the necessary aptitudes and coordination. My rank now is A/C (Aviation Cadet) instead of A/S. We turned in all of our government issue clothing and got $200 worth of cadet clothing. They gave us seven complete uniforms - four summer and three winter. Contrary to your dream, cadets do wear uniforms! It's the same color as my old uniform but it's of better material and cadets wear officers' insignia except for the bars of course. They gave us a $7.00 officer's garrison hat with the wings and propeller design on it instead of the officer's "eagle."

Being classified as a pilot I have a long tough road ahead. According to facts and figures there is a 50/50 chance that I will wash out somewhere along the line. The army gives the cadet just so much time to learn each phase and no more. They will also wash a guy on carelessness, insubordination of superior officers or even wearing a dirty uniform. You see we are potential officers and are watched very close because of that.

I think we will stay here until Jan. 1st. Meanwhile I hope your dreams come true. It is highly improbable tho and I'm not counting on it. Our commanding officer has a dry sort of humor. He gave us a little speech the other day in which he told us that we would get all the privileges that are given cadets - for instance "no furloughs." I think it's a practice to give all newly commissioned officers a furlough tho. That would be something to look forward to in case my appointment goes thru.

I quit writing to Lester cause he never answered my last one. Anyway I know he don't care much about writing letters. I have lots of time on my hands here in the hospital so maybe I'll write a letter to Tom. I wrote a long letter home yesterday and I should answer Jennie's last letter. Marjorie S. must have "talked" cause Jennie asked me what that girl back in Denver was like.

I'm glad to hear Nordie is making the best of it. Before I left he told me he intended to go to business school. I wish I knew his address as I'd like to hear from him.

Excuse hen scratching. I'm using somebody's pen and writing in bed you know.

Lots of love,
A/C D.R. Emerson

His sister's dream did come true, and Donald came home for Christmas. The mildly euphoric state he was in from his recent cadet appointment fueled his stride as he made his rounds. He had obviously taken his superiors' admonitions to heart because he had already arranged every bit of his five-foot, six-inch frame into a very good likeness of an officer, and the official bearing affected by this cocky little rooster came dangerously close to rubbing his loved ones the wrong way.

Donald wasn't the only one with news, however. Eleanor and Hot announced that they were expecting another child come midsummer, and this time even non-gamblers were betting that Harold would get his boy. They planned to name him Virgil.

The newly formed 4th Fighter Group — still taking orders from the RAF and flying British Spitfires — had now experienced its first few months in combat. Although much of their early activity consisted of rather routine, unexciting convoy patrols, they had begun making fighter sweep and bomber escort missions to German-occupied France and Holland. In spite of the fact that operations were in low gear until the end of 1942, they destroyed 8 1/2 enemy planes — the fraction indicating a "kill" had been shared with another group. R.N. Beaty survived a crash coming home, but 13 more pilots were lost. Captured by the Germans were Robert Smith — who escaped and made it back to England, Edward Brettell, Charles Cook, Marion Jackson, George Middleton, George Sperry and Gil Wright. Robert Sprague was killed in a flying accident; William Baker, Gene Neville, Leonard Ryerson, Dennis Smith, and Anthony Seaman were all killed in combat action.

The Russians had been doggedly battling the Germans since the 1941 invasion. In the early months of their offensive the more highly trained German armies had been successfully gaining ground, but eventually they were done in by a combination of impediments: Hitler's blundering leadership, the overpowering Russian troop strength, and the harsh, debilitating winter weather. The savage fight for Russian territory was finally coming to a head in the city of Stalingrad, and by early February, 1943, the Germans would be defeated.

The British had assumed command of all operations in the Indian Ocean with the Americans directing everything east of that, including China and Australia. And once organized, the Allies began showing the Japanese that they were not too busy fighting Hitler to ignore the war with them in the Pacific. America's superior technology for cranking out war supplies would weight the scales, and after the victory at Midway Island its military advantage over Japan grew. Although the fighting began bringing more positive results, the Japanese were formidable opponents, and their tenacity of spirit contributed greatly to the length and intensity of each conflict. The Allied offensive in the Solomon Islands and the vicious battle for Guadalcanal would take an excruciating six months to drive off the Japanese.

Rationing continued in the States, with sugar, coffee, processed foods, leather and rubber shoes in short supply. Housewives were asked to conserve and save fat, used cooking oil and tin — with instructions given to clean tin cans, remove both ends, and flatten for salvaging.

The American Legion Auxiliary was conducting its second statewide house-to-house drive to collect old phonograph records. These records would be sold back to the recording companies as scrap at ceiling prices. With the funds obtained, newly released recordings at lowest prices would then be purchased for free distribution to U.S. fighting men.

Another of what would be a series of big War Bond sales had started; Uncle Sam said at least $13 billion more was needed and no amount of money was too small to invest. Defense stamps could be bought for just pennies; three 3¢ stamps could buy two sandbags — which could stop "any kind of rifle or machine gun bullet." One 25¢ stamp bought film for an aerial photograph, eleven would pay for a steel helmet, thirty-seven paid for one gas mask, and twenty-five were enough for a first aid kit.

Soon after Christmas Donald was on his way back to camp. A 12-hour layover between train connections in Chicago gave him a chance to surprise his old friend and benefactor, Elmer Hanegan, by walking in on him at his store. When Elmer's eyes had adjusted to the metamorphic sight of last year's artless country boy turned up-and-coming aviation cadet, he insisted Donald hang around until quitting time and go home with him for supper. The Hanegans lived 18 miles away in Oak Lawn now, Donald noted, but Elmer could still drive to work "...cause his tires are good and he has a 'C' ration card." Visit over, he was back on the train bound for Nashville, in a car full of soldiers returning from furloughs and a bunch of WAACs being transferred to a camp in Alabama. "There was an officer with them but he was a good fellow so we enjoyed ourselves!" Donald wrote.

January 19, 1943

Dear Mom, Dad & Bro. John,

I got your letter today Mom and I'm
going to answer it right now. I'm sorry
to hear that you were worried about me
cause I didn't write sooner -- I guess I
should have sent you a card or something.
I meant to but just didn't get around to
it.

I suppose you're already wondering why
the typewritten letter so I'll explain
right away. I have a permanent job here in
the office in the capacity of "Charge of
Quarters" so I have access to one of the
typewriters. It's really a "gold-brick"
job-- all I have to do is keep the records
straight on what men are in what barracks.
You see, if a phone call or a telegram
comes in for a man it's imperative that he
be located in a hurry. That sums up my
duties. I'm not eligible for any other
details and wouldn't have to take calisthenics if I didn't want to but I take
them anyway cause I figure it's for my own
good.

I shook off that cold I had when I left
home and I feel a lot better now. My
appetite returned as soon as I came back
so I should gain back some of that lost
weight.

I didn't get on that shipment I spoke
of in my letter but the tactical officer
was just saying today that there was
another pilot shipment being made up. I'm
leading a pretty easy life around here but
the sooner I get shipped the better. I
want to get started with my training.

Here's a little something that might
interest you. A bunch of cadets from
Puerto Rico have just arrived at this camp
and some of them are in my barracks. They
are all of the dark skin type and talk

Spanish. Of course they can speak English
but they prefer to speak their native
language among themselves. They all seem
like a pretty good bunch of fellows but I
think they should speak the English
language while they are here because
they're not so good at it. They sound like
a bunch of monkeys when they get going in
Spanish.

A long distance phone call from Denver,
Colorado, just came in for a fellow in our
squadron. That reminds me, when I was over
at Harts we got on the subject of getting
a phone in at home. Hart said there was
some idle line somewhere that you could
use. He suggested that you get the phone
in now and string the line on the fence
for this winter. There is some logic to
that because as soon as spring comes
around you will be as busy as a cat
shitting on a marble floor and won't have
time to fool with it. Gosh only knows how
much the big Emerson farming concern needs
a phone and I'm going to chew your a__
out until you get it in. Don't mind me --
I feel important today or something.

I've caught up on all my letter writing
since I got this job because I have lots
of spare time and I love to type. Learning
to type is like learning to swim or ride a
bicycle -- you never forget it. I hadn't
typed for two years but I timed myself
yesterday and I can bang out about 50
words per minute.

I was glad to hear my bonds have
finally started arriving. You can expect
one every month now regular. Of course
they will always be dated five months
behind. If you should ever need money for
medical attention, you are welcome to use
them, Mom. Look at the bonds and let me
know if I had them made out with you as
co-owner or beneficiary. I can't remember

which. If you are just the beneficiary
they would have to go through my hands
first.
    I was also glad to hear you got the
wheat out, John. That $380 over sounds
pretty good. You're "on the beam" when it
comes to selling out at the right time. I
can't think of any more news so will
close.

                    Lots of love,
                    Aviation Cadet Don Emerson

U.S. ARMY AIR CORPS
MAXWELL FIELD, ALABAMA

                                February 14, 1943

Dear Folks & Bro. John,

    Well peaceful Sunday has rolled around again so I'd better
write "you all" while I have the time. Boy you would be
surprised how fast the days go by around here. I guess it's
because we are rushed so. Sunday is the only day we get any
spare time and I spend that writing home and studying.

    They sure do keep us on the jump - we have to get up at
4:45 in the morning and we're on the go all day long. This
preflight school is really officers' training school and boy it's
tough! This field is the southeastern headquarters for the air
forces. It also has primary, basic and advance schools and is
a sub depot (center of supply and repair). It has seven large
hangars and is seven miles around. Incidently we run around
the field on our cross-country runs. It will be another five
weeks or so before I actually start to fly. I think I'll get my
primary flying in Florida. If everything goes according to
schedule, we will graduate the 1st of December 1943. That
means a lot of hard work ahead.

    We just finished a course in aircraft recognition. This
included the planes of our army and navy, England's,
Germany's and Japan's. Not as easy as you'd think. They

flash silhouettes on a screen in the tests. My final average was 99.16. On one of the daily tests I identified a British naval plane wrong.

The upper class is going to graduate ahead of schedule so we have only about ten more days to go as underclassmen. Incidently one of the underclassmen talked back to an upperclassman last week and got 100 tours as punishment for it. That goes to show how much they mean business around here. A punishment tour represents one hour of walking and they are walked off on Saturday nights and on Sundays so here's one little boy that's strictly on the beam!

Friday we paraded for the benefit of some visiting high-ranking Brazilian officers. Saturday, 200 local Boy Scouts watched us. Some contrast, eh?

They put on an air show for our benefit this morning. When you see the planes flying in formation, doing loops, snap rolls, slow rolls, recovering from stalls and spins, it just makes you feel like you'd go thru anything to be able to fly.

We went to the cadet valentine dance last night. I didn't actually do any dancing but I did enjoy myself. I love to hear these southern gals talk. Boy the females really go for Aviation Cadets in a big way!

I have a stiff neck today but it wasn't caused by necking. At athletics yesterday we spent most of the time on tumbling mats. We were doing forward and backward "summersalts." Athletics here isn't the same routine every day. Each day they specialize on and stress the exercising of certain muscles. Some days we use dumbbells, other days the "wand" (four foot broomsticks shown in that folder I sent home) then once a week comes the much dreaded cross-country run. With getting up so early in the morning, the heavy schedule and the parades and athletics, we sure don't have to worry about sleeping nights! We have a saying around here that goes like this -   "Late to bed, early to rise,
                  Makes a Cadet saggy, draggy and baggy
                  Under the eyes."

I'm going to list my academic courses so you can see what we study.

1. Radio code and visual code (blinker)
2. Mathematics (algebra and graphs, etc.)
3. Maps, charts and aerial photos
4. Air craft recognition
5. Ground Forces (organization and how the regular army operates)
6. Military customs and courtesies
7. War department publications
8. Signal communications
9. Physics (dealing mostly with aeronautics)
10. Air Forces (organizations and operations)
11. Naval Forces (this is hard because we have to identify warships by their silhouette, etc.)
12. Cryptography (deciphering codes and secret messages)
13. Chemical warfare defense

All this is for the training of potential pilot officers. We will get academic work like this all through the cadet training. If anybody tells you that being a cadet is a snap you can tell him for me that he is plumb loco. I'm sure glad I am one tho!

No - it's "chow time."

Love, Don

Valentine's Day was almost a high holiday for my mother, that hopeless romantic. For the occasion she would make heart-shaped sugar cookies with pink icing, and for her daughters, when we were very young, there were homemade cotton dresses appliqued with lace-trimmed hearts. In addition to that, the day also called up yet another endearing memory of Donald, when he was only seven.

Donald always had a girlfriend. In high school, before Jennie, there was Marjorie Dagen, and she had been preceded by a string of since forgotten others — going all the way back to the second grade, and the memorable first was Marcella Carlson, a lively tomboy, and a farm kid like himself.

A February never passed without the retelling of the Valentine's Day Donald asked his mother to cook up a batch of divinity candy. He wrapped up a few pieces to give to Marcella, and wrote a little poem to go with it: "This candy is sweet, you can bet. But you are sweeter, yet!"

March 10, 1943

Dear Folks & Bro. John,

This is going to be late in reaching you but I spent all day Sunday in Montgomery so didn't get my usual letter off. Our studies are getting rougher as we go along so letter writing is secondary.

We get "open post" from 5:00 Saturday night to 8:00 Sunday night. We don't have to come back to the field Saturday night so three of us got an $8.00 room with bath at the Graystone Hotel and stayed in town over night. We stayed in bed 'til the unnaturally late hour of 9:30, then ordered room service and had breakfast in bed. All three of us are Methodists so we went to 11:00 services. Incidently the minister took a check of the Service Men attending and there was over 100 cadets representing 28 states. I really had an enjoyable weekend. I could tell you about a U.S.O. dance Sat. night and the show Sunday afternoon but that would be dry reading. Oh yeah!

I got your letter Dad and appreciated the fact that you took the trouble to send me your latest composition. I usually don't tell "little white lies" so I can't say that I enjoyed it too much, but then I haven't a very receptive mind for that type of material. I also got your letter, Mom. I hope things get better by the time this reaches you. I'm in perfect health and never felt better in my life despite the strenuous schedule. Maybe it's the vitamin pills they give us for breakfast every morning.

We have been getting instructions lately in high altitude flying and the use of oxygen, etc. Yesterday we took a simulated flight to 28,000 feet in a low pressure chamber. The important thing to watch is keeping the pressure equalized on both sides of the ear drums. There is three ways of doing this, namely, swallowing, yawning, and holding your nose and blowing hard. You have to equalize the pressure every 1,000 ft. Oxygen is necessary in order to stay normal. They had one cadet leave his oxygen mask off and he passed out at 25,000 ft. When a person lacks oxygen, he feels like everything is O.K. and will pass out feeling good. There is no ill effect from passing out from lack of oxygen.

I'm going to enclose some solution sheets to daily tests that we had in Naval Forces and Physics. We cover a college course in physics in 30 days. Take a look at it John, and tell me if you remember having that type in high school -- I don't. You'd think we were in the navy the way we study about it. We have learned how to identify each class and type of warship of the navies of Germany, England, Japan and ours. We also learned how much vertical and horizontal armor plate each type of ship has and how the guns operated, how much range they have, and what battle dispositions and tactics our navy uses. It's very interesting, but at the rate we cover these courses, it becomes work. Incidently we have learned a few things about our submarines that are confidential and not to be disclosed. Speaking about subs, that baby sub captured from Japan is touring the country and was here last Thursday so we had a chance to see it. It is all intact except for being slightly caved in on one side. Its only means of propulsion is by electric motors. The batteries in it when captured were American made by "Exide" and the radio equipment was made by R.C.A. The sub has two torpedo tubes in the stern.

Sorry to hear about your stomach Johnny. I suppose it's a result of your trouble before or maybe it was ulcers all along. You will just have to be a good boy and drink your cream. I hope that kind of a diet won't leave you too weak for spring work. How about a line from you John old boy?

Love, Donald

Of the Roswell siblings, Mabel, the oldest, was the only one to marry. Sister Mildred had been engaged, but rather abruptly and without explanation called off the wedding. Before long it became obvious that she was seriously ill; her abnormal thyroid condition went untreated and soon caused mental derangement. She was cared for by the family until she became unmanageable and was then committed to a state hospital; she died there a few years later during an acute asthmatic attack.

Tom, the oldest brother, had served in France during World War One. Bright and gregarious, he had the best head for business and handled all the family bookkeeping and financial transactions.

Arvid also served in WWI, but had never left his army camp in the States. Rather taciturn and aloof in nature, he often kept to himself. His job on the farm was tending the cows, when they had them, and putzing around with the yard work and the garden.

Easy-going Lester, the youngest in the family, had worked in Milwaukee for the Nash Automobile company until he lost his job in the Depression. He then came back to Halma and started selling the gravel he shoveled by hand from the Roswell's gravel-rich homestead, beginning a moderately successful family business that would develop into deep, water-filled pits mined by dragline.

Nannie was the youngest of the girls. Amiable, but timid, she had never ventured forth at all. When she was old enough to leave home, her aging parents needed her help, and by the time they died, her job as cook and housekeeper for her brothers was firmly established and taken for granted. If she ever had dreams of independence, or had any objections to her lot in life, it is unknown. She never said.

Lester was the first of "the boys" to die. In 1957, at age 57, a head-on crash while driving his beautiful blue Buick killed him instantly. Tom and Arvid both lived to see their early 80s, and died of problems related to old age.

After Arvid died, Nannie had lived alone for just a few months when she fell and broke a hip. From the hospital she was sent to a convalescent home for the physical therapy needed to get her back on her feet, but either unwilling or unable to put forth the necessary effort, she soon passively gave in to a life spent between wheelchair and bed and never walked, or went home, again.

Donald, Louis Franklin, Charles Wilson & Edward Walden

**Donald with Charles Wilson, in a "stuck-
up pose" he didn't want shown around**

Tom & Arvid Roswell in World War One

NWA passenger plane enroute from Pembina to Canada for use as a training ship

March 15, 1943

Dear Tom, Arvid, Lester, Nannie & Mom,

That's sort of a long salutation but I want to include you all. I sure was glad to hear about you getting released from the Army, Lester. I don't imagine you have any great love for the infantry. I'm taking it for granted that you're at Halma, Mom. Time has wings around here and we have only two more weeks to go in Pre-flight. This field also has Primary, Basic and Advanced flight training and it's rumored that my squadron will stay right here for Primary. That would suit me fine cause Maxwell is a swell field and the city of Montgomery is tops. Of course one can never bank on these "latrine" rumors. I bet Lester will agree with me on that.

Love, Junior

P.S. My roommates started calling me "junior" cause I'm the youngest and I'm afraid it's going to stick.

Somehow it was always Great Aunt Nannie who came to mind whenever I considered Donald's short but purposeful life; there wasn't another person in the family more different from him. Nannie's safe and small existence had already stretched to hold more than four times the number of years Donald was given, but she hadn't experienced a minuscule fraction of the life he lived.

"She never did anything or went anywhere in her entire life!" I sputtered in near disgust to my mother.

I'd been trying really hard to locate any half-significant landmark in Nannie's long, dull life. She'd gone out on a double date once, along with my mother who had arranged it, but she'd never had a boyfriend, never learned to ride a bicycle or drive a car. Had she ever gone shopping? Except for her infrequent trips to Karlstad or Thief River to buy something important — like a pair of shoes or a coat, the boys brought home everything she needed. The only buying I ever saw her do was from the Syrian peddler who came to the door.

"She hardly left the house," I reiterated in frustration. "She never went anywhere!"

"She went to Pennsylvania once," my mother offered, as if refuting my entire tirade.

I stood corrected, and unable to keep from rolling my eyes at my mother as she expounded.

"With my folks. They took the train and visited some cousins there. She didn't want to go, but Mama made her — she thought Nannie should get out more."

Wow.

Chapter Four   *Fledgling*

H ome town boys were serving in every part of the world, sending back word from the Solomons, Aleutians, Africa and Europe. Three Pembina men in the 164th infantry — Vernon Johnson, Charles Walker and Llewellyn Renville — were part of the 1st army regiment to be sent to aid the marines in Guadalcanal, and a couple of Karlstad's soldiers reported having served in very prestigious company: Harry Shodin had been stationed at Biggs Field in Texas when the famous movie actor, Clark Gable, received part of his training, and Torjus Sylskar was cooking for Gen. MacArthur in Australia.

The former "Eagles" in Debden, England, were now in a period of transition as the 4th Fighter Group began the shift from British to American leadership. In addition to the change in operative lingo came some more than welcome American food, but a somewhat less than welcome fighter plane of their own: Republic Aviation's P-47 Thunderbolt. Quickly tagged the "jug" because of its close resemblance to an enormous, recumbent milk bottle, it received mixed reviews from the pilots.

The bulky, snub-nosed, seven-ton aircraft took some time to get used to, and before its baptism in combat four more pilots were casualties while still flying their borrowed British "Spits." Hazen Anderson was shot down and taken prisoner; Chester Grimm, William Kelly and Jap Powell were all killed in action.

March 28, 1943

Dear Folks & Bro. John,

Guess it's about time I was scribbling a few lines home.
This past week has been pretty busy with final exams and all.
We graduated yesterday and I'm telling you, it was quite a
relief. Our graduation ball was held last night. It was a pretty
big affair but a little too formal for my liking.

We are not staying here for Primary like I thought. My
squadron is going to Albany, Georgia. I think we will ship out
of here on Wednesday. Albany is about 180 miles southeast
of here. I get farther away from home every move I make.

I have managed pretty well the past two months but it's
the next two months that I'm afraid of. The army is clamping
down more than ever now and they say the wash-out rate at
Primary is about <u>60%.</u> If a guy can get thru Primary he has a
pretty good chance of going all the way. It's no disgrace to
wash out because one isn't adept at flying but little "Dono" is
going to be one sad little boy if that happens to him!

I had the pleasure of seeing a very good air show this
morning. I think they put on these shows for the benefit of our
morale. This pre-flight is a pretty stiff grind and one is apt to
get discouraged. After seeing a good air show, one gets that
"do or die" feeling. The show this morning was put on by a
young 23 year-old <u>Captain </u>who had just returned from combat
in the Pacific. He gave a spectacular demonstration in an
A-36 which is a dive bomber version of the P-51 Mustang
fighter. He made simulated dive bombing and ground strafing
attacks using us as a target. To give comparison there were
basic trainers, primary trainers and B-25s in the air at the
same time. The P-51 is a very maneuverable plane for being a
fast fighter. Its liquid-cooled in-line engine makes very little
noise in flight. The scream of the super charger makes more
noise than the engine. Enough of that.

Spring should be on the way up north. It's getting hot here
now. They say Georgia is a hot state, also it's the home of
lots of insects. Nuts - I'm getting spring fever. I wanna go

home and ride the "putt-putt." Nope - better stop thinking or I will get homesick.

So long, Donald

For their graduation parade the entire Pre-flight school of 10,000 cadets passed in review for the visiting VIPs: Anthony Eden, Britain's Foreign Minister; Sir John Dill, the British Army Field Marshall; and the United States' own General Marshall, U.S. Army Chief of Staff; and Gen. "Hap" Arnold and Gen. Royce of the Army Air Forces. The next night, well known radio commentator, Lowell Thomas, whose son was one of the cadets, gave his evening broadcast from Maxwell Field.

A week later Donald arrived at a smaller civilian flying school being operated under army supervision; that same day the cadets were given a lecture on the use and proper handling of parachutes. The next day they were issued flying clothes and started their academic work, and the day after that they got their first taste of the air.

DARR AERO TECH
Albany, Georgia

April 20, 1943

Dear Folks & Bro. John,

It's Tuesday morning and no flying cause of a high wind. I'm all burned up because my instructor told me yesterday that I was due to solo today. The first solo trip is a big obstacle to make and missing a day is like missing a step in your stride. I now have nine hours in the air and we have to solo before 12 hours. The only bad thing about it is that whenever a guy solos, the rest of the fellows throw him in the pool - clothes and all.

All we have done the past two days is shoot landings. I've had a little trouble with mine. It all boils down to the fact that I have poor judgement, that is, I have a hard time determining when to cut the throttle in order to hit the right spot and when to level off and stall in for the landing. My depth perception isn't too good. I guess I'm not the only one tho. I got sort of discouraged yesterday and Mr. Watts, my instructor, jumped all over me. He said the rest of my flying was good and with extra practice I would be able to train my eyes and overcome my difficulty.

There is a great deal more to this army flying than one would think. I believe anybody could learn to fly if he spent enough time at it. What the army wants is men who show and have that certain touch and not one who flies mechanically. One's personality plays a big part even. About 10% of the fellows are already on the way out. If the instructor doesn't think the cadet shows any promise he recommends him for a check ride which is given by the flight commander. This is just a formality cause the cadet is just as good as washed out at this point. The flight commander's plane is called the "washing machine" and rightly named! I'm not going to say if I think I'll make it or not. It's usually the guys who think they're "hot" who eventually wash. I don't think any less of a guy who can't make it and I have a hell of a lot of admiration for an army officer with silver wings on his blouse! With that I'll change the subject.

I sent $40 to Sister yesterday. I told her she didn't need to worry about paying it back but if she did, she could buy me two $18.75 bonds. Incidently I had intended to help Eleanor out before you suggested it, Mom. If I get paid as expected at the end of this month I may send some cash home to you "big operators" if you figure you need it - otherwise I'll help Uncle Sam out. I do intend to stick $50 cash away as a permanent reserve tho. I don't want to get caught with my pants down again like I did at Xmas and have to borrow money to get home on. I paid back that Red Cross loan the first month I was at Maxwell Field.

In case you'd be interested in knowing exactly where I am, Albany is located about 50 miles north of Florida. Georgia is known as the "Peach State" but I don't know if there are any right around here. The farmers in this section grow mostly peanuts. They are planted in hilled-up rows something like potatoes. In case of forced landings we are cautioned to land with the rows regardless of the wind directions. Every day our instructors will pull forced landings on us and we have to pick a suitable field, but quick! Here I am flying again.

Love, Donald

P.S. I wrote this in a hurry so excuse scribbling.

Easter Sunday

Dearest Sis,

Your Easter card arrived on exactly the right date. Thanks Sis! It was sort of a coincidence, you sending me $1.00. I couldn't help but feel amused but the situation doesn't alter the fact that you sent me a present - so thanks a heap. I got your card today.

I was out late Saturday night but managed to go to Easter services. I have been in town all day. Jake, Charles Wilson and I attended the First Methodist Church this morning. The pastor preached a very stirring sermon. He was the kind of preacher who wasn't afraid to say what he thought - for instance he wished everybody a Merry Xmas cause he was afraid he wouldn't see the majority of the people in the church again until next Easter.

We had a $1.60 T-bone steak for dinner and went to a show afterwards. When we were having dinner, a cadet from Turner Field (advanced twin engine school) sat at our table. He started talking and to my surprise found out he was from Thief River Falls, Minn. His name was Cummings and he lived on the same side of town as Gabrielsons. It does one good to meet someone close to home and talk over - well everything.

Last night Jake and I took our female friends to a large carnival that is in Albany. We sort of "let our hair down" and acted like kids - fun tho. We tried all the rides but I couldn't get a thrill out of anything - not after loops and snap rolls in a PT-17.

My gal is a darn spunky little blonde by the name of

Jeanette Vaughn. Her hair is so light blonde, she is nick-named "Cotton." Don't worry Sis - I'm a good little boy (just in case you're wondering). It does us good to have dates - it gets our minds off flying. They give us open post often here. We need the relaxation it gives and that's the reason they encourage us to get away from it all whenever we can. They caution us not to do much drinking tho - that isn't any trouble for me!

Well I'm still hanging on in this flying game. Boy! There is nothing that can compare with flying. It's no cinch flying for the army tho! It's work and more work! They gave us a little joy ride the first time up but that's all. It would take a book to tell what I have already learned.

I soloed last week. My instructor got out of the plane and nonchalantly told me to take her up. I made nine pretty good landings that day. My next hurdle is a 20-hour progress check that everyone gets at that time. I now have 14 hours and 47 minutes in the air. Two and 1/2 hours of that is solo time. It's a lot of hard work and very tiring. I'm going to try but none of us knows how long we can stay with it. At this time 35% have been eliminated - mostly because they couldn't solo in the required 12 hours. If I do wash out it will hurt my pride mostly I guess. It must be the Emerson in me (Ha).

Darr Aero Tech has about 100 planes in the air every day and to this day it has a record of no fatal accidents. Just thought I'd tell you.

Love, Donald
XX - A kiss each for Beverly & Bonnie.

XX— A kiss each for Beverly and Bonnie. My two older sisters; I was sure they would remember something about Donald and the war.

But when I asked Beverly, she couldn't remember anything about Donald, and her memories of the war were very vague. She remembered bringing money to school to buy stamps — it had something to do with helping fight the war. And she remembered it as a time when Mom was always crying.

And Bonnie? Could she still remember Donald, or remember being in the room when that phone call came from Uncle John? She remembered none of it. The only memory she had about the war was of being told it was over, and then she had said, "Good. Now we can get a bike."

May 1, 1943

Dear Folks & Bro. John,

It's a beautiful Sat. morning - just enough wind to keep it from getting too hot. It's getting pretty darn warm here and they say we haven't seen anything yet.

Since I wrote you last, I have really been putting in the flying time. Starting Monday of this week, I have flown an average of three hours each day. When you practice acrobatics for 3 hours straight, it really leaves you pooped! It's quite a mental strain cause you have to be on your toes so much. We fly two hours solo for every hour of dual instruction. We accomplish most when we are up alone. The purpose of acrobatics in primary flight training is to get us to fly automatically. Such maneuvers as "lazy eights," "pylon eights" and slow rolls, etc.

I passed my 20-hour progress check without any trouble at all. I now have in 29 hours, 10 minutes time. My next check will be the 40-hour check. We no sooner "sweat out" one check and there is another one staring us in the face. When we started there was 205 of us and now there are 125 left. Figure it out for yourself. The 20-hour check got a number of the fellows. No kidding! This is a tough racket. I'm not just saying this to make an excuse for myself should I wash out later on. You may think it's funny that so many can't make it. There is some logic to it tho - if we can't handle a simple PT-17 exceptionally well, what chance would we have in a hot P-51 or P-38, etc. Grab me?

I'm going to relate to you a personal experience that I had Wednesday which is typical of what most everyone goes thru occasionally. I was practicing 180 degree approach landings with my instructor and I suddenly lost my touch on landings and made two in a row that were so bad they could have been dangerous. This may sound a little silly to you, but I felt so sick and mad that I got tears in my eyes and it was all I could do to keep from bawling in front of Mr. Jesse, my instructor. Jesse talked to me and told me it must be my off-day and that I wouldn't need to go up alone if I didn't want to. It was somewhat of a temptation to take him up on it and stay on the ground but I forced myself to get in the plane and take off alone. I climbed to 500 feet and came right in again to land. I was thinking I better land this dam crate or else. To make a long story short I made a perfect three-point landing and that was all I needed to regain my confidence. I felt so good I poured the coal to her and took off again. I climbed to 5,000 feet and pointed the nose straight up until she stalled and then put her into a spin and pulled out at 3,000 feet. I guess I just wanted to prove to the plane that I wasn't afraid of it. Yes this flying is a funny game and don't confuse army flying with private pleasure flying cause there is no comparison!

There is no news other than what I have been writing about. We live, eat and sleep flying so you'll have to pardon my letters.

I don't know what I'll be doing this weekend. We haven't any plans. Jake and I are cooking up something for next weekend tho. If Alice (Jake's girl) can talk her folks into it she is going to have Jeanette and us come out to the plantation in the country. Oh boy!

Love, Donald

May 11, 1943

Dear Dad, Mom & Bro. John,

I guess it's time I got busy and scribbled you a letter. I got your letter yesterday Dad. Also received letters from Mom and John last week. Your faith and expectations in me at home scares me a little. Of course I'm doing everything I can to not let you down and then it means everything to me also. Sometimes even our best efforts aren't enough when it comes to flying the way the army insists. Out of the 205 who originally started here in our class, there are only 85 of us left. They say our class is worse than the average that have attended Darr Aero Tech.

I now have 40 hours of flying time. If I were back in civilian life, that would give me a private flying license which would allow me to take other people up for rides. I would have taken my 40-hour check ride this morning but the weather is not fit for flying. I think I can pass the check O.K. I've come this far and should be able to keep on. We are now practicing advanced acrobatics in earnest, such as slow rolls, snap rolls, loops and flying upside down, etc.

Next week we will start cross-country flying. This is to give us practice in navigation. We have a working knowledge of navigation from ground school but haven't put it to practical use before. We get a total of 65 hours in Primary, then we will move on to Basic and start all over again.

I spent quite a weekend. Took my gal to a show Sunday afternoon. Jake's girl was sick so we didn't have a car.

Love, Donald

P.S. Thanks for the pocket testament you sent me, Mom.

May 27, 1943

Dear Folks & Bro. John,

We finished up with ground school and flying on Tuesday so we are enjoying a four day vacation as we don't ship out of here until Saturday night. We are going to a basic flying field at Courtland, Alabama. It's in northern Alabama, close to Tennessee. I'm glad we are moving back north a little cause they say the heat gets unbearable here in July. The air gets very humid here because of the many swamps close by. This part of Georgia is known for its swamps. About 75 miles southeast of here is the Oki Finoki swamp which is supposed to be the worst in the U.S.

The day after I passed my 60-hour check, I was a little tired of practicing acrobatics so I took off on a little excursion. I flew a compass course of 140 degrees and kept going 'til I got over a wicked looking swamp. I flew around at low altitude trying to spot a crocodile. I didn't keep that up for long tho cause I figured that was a dam poor place to be if I should have engine failure. On the way home I buzzed every farm house I flew over. I saw a guy on an "A" or "B" John Deere in a large field. I put my PT-17 into a shallow power glide and touched my front wheel on the field beside the tractor going at 150 M.P.H. with full throttle. I pulled up and left the farmer in a cloud of dust from my prop wash. When I looked back he had stopped the tractor and was no doubt cussing me to h___. I guess it's human nature to get a kick out of doing things that aren't supposed to be done.

Well I'm half-way on the road to getting my wings but the next four months will be plenty tough. We know how to fly now so what comes next is learning how to handle heavier planes and formation flying, night flying and flying by instruments and radio, etc.

We are going out to Radium Springs this afternoon and soak up some sunshine. We can stay out 'til 12 every night and don't need to get up in the morning until we feel like it. Jake's girl came from Washington, D.C. to see him so he is enjoying this vacation immensely! All the boys whose homes are close to here got three-day passes to go home. I envy them dam it! We are scheduled to arrive at Courtland sometime on Sunday. I'll write as soon as I can so you'll get my new address.

Loads of Love, Donald

Alistair Cooke. That's who Grandpa reminded me of — Alistair Cooke on a tractor. It was too bad he had to leave college, I thought; he would have been more at home in a threadbare-tweed, suede-elbow-patch world. My mother thought he went to college long enough — got out just in time, she said; he had come close to believing the theory of evolution.

I had many memories of Grandpa — he lived to be 93 — but none connecting him to Donald in any way. I could still see him tapping out his thoughts on his typewriter, or taking a break from the heat at midday to read from his stacks of newspapers and magazines. And I remembered watching him as he sat under the bridge near our farm one time, so absorbed by whatever he was writing in his little notebook that he never did see me. But where had he been on all those Memorial Days — the only times I ever saw Grandma close to tears from remembering Donald?

The American Legion awarded a Gold Star Citation to the surviving kin of any member of the armed forces who died during the war; this had made Grandma a Gold Star Mother. Memorial Day services were held in the Karlstad High School gymnasium; a special place of honor was reserved for all of the Gold Star Mothers. When an Auxiliary member pinned on Grandma's poppy corsage, she'd stand with her head up and look straight ahead. Face stiff, mouth tight, eyes shiny. Visible pride. Lousy trade, I always thought: a gold star in exchange for a son.

After the memorial service we'd go out to the cemetery, sometimes walking alongside the marching Legionnaires and the high school band. When we got there we'd gather at the far end of the graveyard where a dozen or so small white wooden crosses stood in symbolic testimony to the local war dead. When I was little I had thought Donald's grave was under the one stenciled with his name, but later I learned he was buried far away in Holland, near the place where he had died.

I could remember hearing the thankful, somber prayers about patriotism and supreme sacrifice — and the horrific, obligatory rifle fire ripping through the tree tops — and the mournful trumpets playing and echoing "Taps."

But I still couldn't remember seeing Grandpa there. "Where was he?" I asked my mother.

"Oh, my dad was always there, too," she answered. "Don't you remember?"

"No. I just remember the fuss made over Grandma because she was a Gold Star Mother. Why didn't anybody call Grandpa a Gold Star Father? That didn't seem right."

"I don't know — it wasn't right, but he was always there."

"I've been trying to remember something — anything about Grandpa remembering Donald, but I can't. I don't think he ever talked to me about him."

"He was different than Mama that way," she said. "When he was sad, he'd get real quiet, keep to himself. Mama said he took it very hard when their first baby died, too. He could never understand why such things happened. I remember once, not long after Donald died, we were talking about it. My dad said he didn't know why there had to be wars, and he wondered when people would learn to live in peace. I reminded him that the Bible says there will always be wars. 'You will hear of wars and rumors of wars,' I told him. He didn't say anything then — just got a real pained look on his face and turned away. He wrote a poem in memory of Donald, you know. I'm sure that's there with the rest of his stuff."

Then I remembered, and I could see him standing tall and straight at Grandma's side, white hair neatly trimmed and combed, gray suit. His stoic silence on what had seemed to be Gold Star Mother's Day had made him nearly invisible to me, but of course he had been there every time.

In later years it became clear that whatever difficulties he had had in understanding life along the way, at some stage he had arrived at acceptance, and near the end of his days he could often be heard serenely reflecting on all the changes and technological advances he had witnessed in his near-century of living. His final assessment never varied. "It's a wonderful world," he would say in conclusion. "A wonderful world."

Alistair Cooke in his armchair.

ARMY AIR FORCES BASIC FLYING SCHOOL
Courtland, Alabama

May 31, 1943

Dear Folks & Bro. John,

Just a few lines to let you know I have arrived here and to give you my new address. We left by Greyhound buses from Darr Aero Tech Saturday evening and got here yesterday (Sunday) afternoon. I don't know just where Courtland is located but it's somewhere in the northern part of Alabama. We haven't started anything as yet so won't be able to give you the lowdown on this place until later. All I know is that the food couldn't be better and that we are back in the army again. I can see already that this place is run like Maxwell Field and that ain't good!

I'm looking forward to getting into one of those silver BT-13s. They have a 450 H.P. Pratt and Whitney engine and have a cruising speed of about 140 M.P.H. Cruising speed is about half throttle or a speed that is best for the engine. These BT-13s use 91 octane gasoline. The PT-17s used 73 octane. This is for your benefit Johnny. If you would like to know anything in particular about the planes or engines just ask me.

I imagine you're still darn busy with the spring work. Your little brother is kept pretty busy too. In fact dam busy. I guess I can take it tho. It would just about kill me to wash out at this stage of the game.

I'll write again as soon as possible. I just wanted you to get my address so I'll hear from you.

Love, Donald

P.S. I guess Courtland, Alabama is about 500 miles closer to home than Albany, Georgia was.

Sunday afternoon

Dear Bro. John, Mom & Dad,

It's so hot I'm almost too lazy to write but of course I have to send one letter home a week at least. I imagine you get tired of hearing how hard we have to work but our schedule here doesn't leave any spare time. If we get five minutes to ourselves we consider it a furlough! The weather here is very hot and humid. We do have good flying conditions tho - we have only lost one day on account of rain.

I received your letter one day this week and somehow it made me quite homesick. I can understand why Warren H. likes to get on the tractor when he gets home. I'm pretty sure I won't get a furlough during the summer months. It will be the last of September before I graduate and of course I can't get a furlough until then unless I get sick and that isn't likely. I now weigh 144 with my uniform on and that is the most I've *ever weighed.*

I have quite a bit to tell you so this will probably turn out to be a long letter. First of all, maybe you are wondering why I'm not on open post instead of writing letters on Sunday afternoon. Well, I've been a bad boy! I was a victim of circumstances but that didn't alter anything. It so happened that another cadet by the name of Edward Walden and I were assigned to a plane to go up together on what we refer to as "buddy rides." These basic trainers have radio receiving and transmitting sets in them which are used mainly to control traffic by the tower. Also they have the interphone system with which the instructor can talk to the students. This is to explain how I got in hot water. As soon as we were in the air and clear of landing and take-off traffic we switched the radio to interphone so we could talk to each other without broadcasting what we said.

Well talk we did and we weren't very careful what we said! What we didn't know was that the radio switch was loose and so left the radio set for receiving and broadcasting. I think you can understand how that complicated matters cause every radio tuned to our frequency heard what we said. That included all the radios in the 240 planes at this field and in the main control tower. Now there is a federal law that says swearing over the radio is punishable by a $500 fine and we did a very good job of violating that law!! To make a long story short we were partially pardoned due to the mechanical malfunction in the radio controls but we were both confined to the post for the durations of our stay here at this field which is <u>six</u> more weeks. Oh I'm not proud of it but a guy can't be perfect all the time.

One thing good - I'll have time to write letters while the rest of the guys go to town and I'll save money too. Ha. Ha. We only get every other weekend off here anyway. We flew last Sunday. I guess I'd better not tell Eleanor we have to fly on Sundays (Ha).

Life here is pretty fast - at least there is never a dull

moment around here. With some 200 BT-13s operating day and night with stupid cadets as pilots, well - sometimes things happen. We are flying one big plane now and it's no toy! You don't need to worry about me doing anything foolish like I told you about at Primary. There is a law here that says all pilots caught flying below 1,000 feet, except when landing and taking off, will be given a dishonorable discharge and that's bad for a man's reputation.

Something happened last week that made things very clear to us on that point. A 2nd Lt. instructor and a cadet decided to do a little low flying one day. Now we are only 15 miles from Muscle Shoals and a large aluminum factory so there are numerous high tension power lines around. This instructor flew the plane into a 110,000 volt line, wrecking the plane and tearing down the power line. Nobody was badly hurt but they put all the blame on the instructor and gave him a dishonorable discharge plus a $1,000 fine. He got off easy tho cause that power line supplied power for three defense plants which were without power for three hours.

I'm pretty well acquainted with the BT-13 now so I can tell you more about it. It's an all metal job with a 450 horsepower engine and weighs a little over two tons. It has a Hamilton Standard adjustable pitch propeller and has landing flaps and all instruments for blind flying such as artificial horizon, turn and bank indicator and a gyro compass. The plane is "redlined" at a speed of 250 M.P.H. and has a cruising range of 700 miles with a fuel capacity of 120 gallons plus a 17 gal. reserve. This plane is not hard to fly but there is a lot of cockpit procedure and we have to know what to do or else.

Our first few hours were spent in learning the cockpit procedure for landing and takeoff. Before we could solo we had to do everything in a blindfold test. I am quite proud to tell you that I was the second man in our "flight" of 50 cadets to solo. We also had to learn the stalling speeds of the plane and be able to bring it out of a spin before we could solo the ship.

I have a lot of time and I'd like to give you the procedure we have to do when taking this plane up. I'll start from the beginning and takeoff and make a square pattern around the field and land.

1. Check general condition of plane for tire inflation, nicked propeller blades, loose engine cowlings, etc.

2. Fill out the flight record which is a record of the plane and engine time.

3. Put on parachute and adjust the plane's seat to the right height.

4. Fasten the safety belt and adjust the rudder pedals for correct leg length.

5. Turn on the radio and plug in the headset, call the tower to be sure the radio is working.

6. Set the fuel cock to the fullest tank (one of three).

7. Unlock the controls (elevator, rudder and ailerons).

8. Zero all trim tabs.

9. Make sure the flaps are up.

10. Check the heat controls for the carburetor and oil tank.

11. Set the altimeter to field elevation (680')

12. Crack the throttle and adjust the mixture to full rich.

13. Make sure prop is in high pitch. (There is a good reason for this but it's too long to explain.)

14. Lock the brakes and ask the mechanic if the prop is clear.

15. Energize the electric inertia starter.

16. Operate the hand wobble pump to build up the fuel pressure.

17. Prime the engine and engage starter.

18. Put the prop in low pitch and warm up the engine checking the fuel pressure, oil pressure and heat and the cylinder head temp.

19. Call the control tower for clearance and taxi and takeoff instruction (which direction and runway to use, etc.).

20. Taxi out to runway and check magnetos at full throttle and make sure engine revs up to at least 1850 R.P.M. (brakes

locked.)

21. Check everything mentioned all over again and roll down 30 degree flaps and make sure prop is in low pitch which allows high engine speed like low in a car.

22. Give her the coal in a steady movement of the throttle and take off holding plenty of right rudder to compensate for engine torque. Plane will leave the runway at 90 M.P.H. We can pull it off at less speed but then there is danger of stalling.

23. Climb at 800 ft. per min. at engine speed of 2150 R.P.M. AND PROP IN LOW PITCH.

24. Level off at desired altitude and put prop in high pitch and roll up the flaps - cruise at 150 M.P.H. at 1900 engine R.P.M.

Landing Procedure

1. Call tower for landing directions and what runway to use and what type of air pattern to use.

2. Glide down to 700 ft. and change to low prop pitch and roll down 30 degree of flaps. Fly a course 90 degree to the landing runway and cut throttle when 45 degrees from spot on which we want to land.

3. Turn parallel to runway and glide in at 90 M.P.H. At this point we are really busy! We are "crabbing" to correct for any side wind drift and rolling down all the flaps and holding that 90 M.P.H. glide. As we near the runway we slow down the glide to about 85 M.P.H. and point the nose slightly up and when the plane stalls out at about 70 M.P.H. it will set down three point (we hope). The BT-13 will land at about 100 M.P.H. without flaps and that's too dam fast. That will give you some idea of how to pilot a BT-13.

The training here consists of night flying, blind flying under the hood and formation flying, also cross-country. In ground school we study radio code, advanced navigation, aircraft identification and a rather extensive course in meteorology. Naturally weather is important to a pilot and we have to be able to predict what's ahead of us so as to avoid storm and icing conditions, etc. Better brush up on your weather predictions, Johnny, or your little brother will outdo you (Ha). By the way I can tell what weather you are having at Pembina by the teletype reports that come in from all stations to make up the national weather map each 6 hours. I know more about that station now than when I was home!

Love, Don

P.S. Are the William Barrons at home? I never did get their address so couldn't write them.

June 15, 1943

Dearest Sis,

I've let this go so long I hate to start cause I'm ashamed of being so slow. I have only one excuse and that is lack of time. I wrote a letter home on Sunday and intended to write to you too but I let a couple guys talk me into seeing a show and it was bed time when we got back. Well, better late than never and you can expect a letter from me every week hereafter.

I suppose the happy event will soon happen. I don't suppose you look forward to it too much tho. Just remember your little brother is pulling for you!

I think that picture you sent of Glenn is real good. Looking at it, I can't imagine him going into battle and shooting anybody. Come to think of it, I can't imagine myself doing that. If it comes to that I'd rather be in the air than on the ground tho!

Loads of love, Donald

P.S. I'm sending you another picture taken just before I left Darr Aero Tech. I'm terribly tanned up so my face is pretty dark.

John Mitchellweis, Jr., was the 4th Fighter Group's first pilot accidentally killed during non-operational flying of the Thunderbolt, followed by Garret King and Vincent Castle; James Wilkinson was wounded — when his fractured spine had healed sufficiently, he flew with another fighter group and was then killed in action. Of the eight P-47 flyers lost during combat in the first half of the year, Frank Smolinsky crashed and died as he tried to land; the rest were shot down by enemy aircraft. William Morgan survived his wounds to become a POW; Stanley Anderson, Richard McMinn, John Lutz, Robert Boock, Leland MacFarlane and Gordon Whitlow all died.

Red River Valley farmers were looking ahead to abundant crops, and Hot was hired by his brother-in-law John to help with the harvest. Lela would be coming back to help Mabel again — though there had been a brief scare when a neighbor lady tried to lure her from the Emersons' employ with a salary guarantee of $35 per month. ("Who does that [name deleted] think she is, anyway?" Donald had retorted upon hearing about the offer. "Personally," he said, "I wouldn't spit on the best part of her!")

With the hope of a profitable yield, Mabel was spurred into lobbying for their first big winter trip. They were the only Emersons left in North Dakota now, and she wanted to visit the rest of Frank's family on the west coast. His sister Elspeth (Elsie) and her husband William (Jim) Ferguson had an insurance business in Seattle, and brother Ray and his wife Hilda (Swanson) had moved out there too; Ray worked as a carpenter, and Hilda was a registered nurse.

In anticipation of Cousin Max's annual visit, the farm was spruced up and all the buildings given another coat of paint. Eleanor and Hot's expected arrival, of a more permanent sort, was delivered by Dr. Waldron, Jr., at St. Elizabeth's Hospital in Drayton, North Dakota, on June 24th — the first of their children not born at home. "Virgil" soon lost its appeal as a name for the baby, however, and discussions to find one more appropriate resumed. When the Torkelson's new daughter was a couple of months old, she would be christened Sandra Dawn — her middle name chosen to honor her Uncle Donald.

June 27, 1943

Dear Mom, Dad and Bro. John,

Here I sit on Sunday afternoon while the others are on "open post." If it wasn't for the fact that I'm confined, I don't know if I'd ever get any letters written though. I just finished one of the best meals one could imagine. We had fried

chicken, sweet potatoes, corn on the cob, sweet peas, iced tea
and ripe peaches with ice cream. The food here is wonderful.
The Cadet Mess seems to be very well managed. Occasionally
they hand out a package of cigarettes to each man cause
they can't use up all our ration money for food. Too bad I
don't smoke, eh?

It's starting to rain at this particular moment. Another
one of the thunder showers that come up so quickly around
here. I came back from a short cross country hop one day
last week and when I arrived at the field it was under a nice
thunder head. They radioed for me to stay up until it was
past so I circled at 10,000 feet for almost 30 minutes. I had
plenty of gas and had an interesting view of a thunderstorm
going on below me.

We started instrument flying last week. We always fly dual
when on instruments. We are in the back seat under the hood
and the instructor or another cadet is in the front seat to
prevent head on collisions etc. With some 200 planes
operating off this field we have to be on our toes to prevent
that kind of accident. This blind flying is harder than one
would expect. We have all the modern instrument aids to blind
flying but there is a knack in using them. At first one has a
tendency to not believe in the instruments and to try to fly by
the seat of our pants but that just don't work. One can be in
a steep bank and swear that he is flying straight and level.
You see when a plane is in a bank the pilot corresponds to
water in a pail that is being swung around on a string.
Yesterday I flew to Corinth under the hood, a distance of
about 100 miles. All I had to go by was a compass heading
figured out in advance. I was very surprised to hit my
destination right on the nose. We even take off under the
hood. I can't understand how we keep from knocking down all
the runway lights. Flying under the hood is preparation for
night flying which will start soon. In Link trainers we have been
learning to fly the radio beam. Flying a commercial plane would
be a picnic as far as navigation is concerned when they have

the beam to follow. I was looking at an aeronautical map of the Pembina section and the north twilight zone of the beam is directly over our house. That's why north bound transports usually pass over the way they do. Of course the beam is very narrow at that point so it doesn't make much difference which direction the planes are going.

I wish I could get away from writing this technical type of letter but we live, eat and sleep flying so you will have to pardon me.

The class that I finished here yesterday held a competitive review of everything they had learned here. All went O.K. until they started to make spot landings. In this they try to hit a certain spot when landing and are not allowed to use the throttle after once retarding it. Yesterday a cadet competing in this event tried to stretch his glide in an attempt to land farther on. This made him stall when still about 50 feet up. He attempted to regain gliding speed by shaving the nose down and ran the plane right into the ground. The plane was completely wrecked but the cadet was barely scratched. We have a saying that any landing is a good landing when we can walk away from it (Ha). The fact that a $40,000 plane is wrecked is of small importance. That figure may seem large but that's what these trainers cost.

I don't suppose these letters are of much interest to you, Mom, but I haven't had a letter from you for some time. I didn't tell Eleanor to write you what she did and I personally think it's a lot of foolishment! Just remember I take everything with a grain of salt and don't jump to conclusions!

Love, Donald

P.S. Hello Lela - I'll write to you later, maybe yet today. I bet the mail box will be full since you arrived there. Just make sure nobody else reads your mail! (Ha.)

P.P.S. Eleanor's boy should have arrived by this time.

6-29-43

Dearest Sis,

As I sit down to write this there is some very good band music coming over the radio. I can't remember if I told you before or not but we have a table model combination radio and record player in our room. My roommate had it sent from his home in California.

I received your card yesterday. I wasn't too surprised but didn't think it would be another girl. It's a good thing Harold likes girls. I bet he did want a boy this time tho. I imagine Beverly and Bonnie are all excited and have seen their new sister by this time. I suppose the folks have been down to see you too. No doubt you are confronted by that old name problem again. You have about run out of girl names haven't you?

It has been raining the past two days so we haven't done much flying. When it rains like this we spend our regular flying hours at the Link Trainer Dept. A Link Trainer is an ingenious mechanical mock-up of a plane in which we can practice instrument flying without leaving the ground. Clever, eh?

I saw a very good show here at the post theater last night. It was "The Amazing Mrs. Haliday," with Deanna Durbin.

I haven't much news, but I hope this will reach you at the hospital before you leave there.

Much love to you and the "Youngun"
Donald

July 4, 1943

Dear John, Mom & Dad,

Well here it is the Fourth of July. At this time a year ago I was a "rookie" at Fort Snelling. I don't regret this year in the army. It's been a lot of work but I've learned a lot. They sure keep us on the jump, but whenever we fly at night they give us at least 7 ½ hours sleep.

This night flying scares heck out of a guy the first time. Imagine driving a car at 150 miles per hour at night without lights - of course there is no road to run off of but we have to watch so we don't run into other planes. You look out and all you can see are the wing clearance lights. All sense of direction is lost and of course you can't see the ground. Of course the magnetic and gyro compasses and the altimeter aren't just decorations on the instrument panel! We learn three types of night landings. 1. Landing by use of runway floodlights. 2. Wing landing lights alone and 3. Black-out landings where all we got to go by are the dim runway clearance lights. This is a heck of a letter - I hope you can follow me.

Our daytime flying consists of navigational cross-country and formation flying. We average about 400 miles a day. Formation flying is a real strain. Each plane is spaced three feet apart in the air - we have to be so darn careful not to creep up on the next plane and chew his tail off with our prop. We'll have a night cross-country coming up soon. We all wish it was over cause it's darn easy to get lost at night.

Today this field is open to the public. I wish you could be here - it reminds me of the county fair. Civilians are about overrunning the place. We are being told to fly around close to the field and do what we want to. At 4:00 our instructors are going to put on an air show for the benefit of the public. This is sort of a drive to get more young guys in the cadets so they want us to make it look good for them. Then at 6:00 all the cadets will put on a dress parade. It's quite a fancy affair. We will wear our white belts and white gloves which we wear only on special occasions. Well I hope the public enjoys it cause it won't be much fun for us to parade in the hot sun.

I suppose you were over to Drayton to see Eleanor and the new girl. Too bad it couldn't have been a boy!

I got your letter Johnny. I'm glad to hear things are looking good on the farm. I sure hope you can pick up another combine. It would be a big help. I guess we should have gotten a bigger one in the first place. I'd sure like to be there this fall to help you but I suppose I'll be flying a P-38 or something by then. It all depends on which advanced school they send me to the end of this month.

I want to go to single engine advanced school but what the army says may be different. If they need a large quota of men at twin engine school for bomber pilots well that's where we go. That junk about small men going to single engine and the large cautious men going to twin engine is a lot of bunk. I've seen men smaller than me as pilots of a B-17, and the P-47 will take a large man in the pilot's cockpit. I used to think I wanted to fly the heavy bombers but not anymore. I want to be a "pea-shooter" pilot and not an "arm chair" pilot as the bomber pilots are called. I want to fly a plane that can be made to do things and not fly straight and level in a bomber. A bomber pilot is just a stooge. All he does is take off and land. The navigator keeps the plane on course by the automatic gyro pilot, and the bombardier has control of the ship when over the target, the gunners do all the shooting and the radio operator takes care of all the communications. Hence the name "arm-chair pilots." Now take a single seater or "pea-shooter" pilot. He's got to be a darn good flyer plus gunner, navigator, & radio operator.

Oh, I'll gladly be an arm-chair pilot if they say so but I would like to fly one of the following: P-47, P-38, P-51, P-70 (A-20). If I had my outright choice I'd take the F-5 which is the P-38 stripped of armorment with cameras in place of guns plus two 100 gallon belly gas tanks and used as a long range fighter reconnaissance plane. Every month they give us preference sheets to fill out and they do try to give us our choice if it's convenient to the needs of the army. Last month the graduating class from here were all sent to twin-engine school so maybe we'll get single engine.

Maybe you wouldn't think so the way I write but I do realize the grimness of it all but that's what the army is spending $27,000 to train me for. The motto of the Southeast Training Command is "Prepare for Combat" and the air forces are going to play a darn big part in this scramble. The war news sounds pretty encouraging. Now if we can only keep it up.

I get a big kick out of [neighbor's name deleted] idea of good flying. A guy could have 1000 hours in a light plane and still not know half of what a cadet has to learn at Primary. When you realize that we only get a total of 225 hours of training altogether you see how intensive our training must be. They are always throwing something new at us. I now have 110 hours in plus 20 hours of Link Trainer time. Link Trainer time costs $25.00 an hour in commercial schools so the average fellow in civilian life couldn't afford it.

By the way, very few get washed out at Basic or advanced schools. They weed out the poor ones at Primary. No I guess I'd better dry up.

Love, Don

July 18, 1943

Dear Folks & Bro. John,

It's Sunday evening and hot as usual. I have spent most of the day in bed, but for a very good reason. We flew last night over at the Muscle Shoals airport and I didn't get back here 'til 5:30 this morning. I finished the last phase of night flying so I'm through with that now except for a 300 mile night cross-country coming up soon. I was in the plane for three full hours last night - two hours circling in my zone and one hour practicing black-out landings. These are done without the aid of any lights except the flare pots outlining the landing runway. It isn't quite as hard as it sounds - we really get "cats' eyes" after a couple hours of circling in the dark. We used the Muscle Shoals airport for practice at a strange field. It's a good government airport with 4,000 ft. oiled runways. Our runways here at Courtland are concrete and 5,000 ft. long. We only need 1,000 ft. to land the BT-13 in and it can take off in a minimum of 600 ft. and 15 seconds. This plane gains a speed of 90 M.P.H. How's that for acceleration - it beats a car all hollow!

Getting back to Muscle Shoals, we were assigned a definite zone and altitude in which to fly. My zone was right above the Wilson Dam, the Muscle Shoals Nitrate Plant and the Reynolds Aluminum Factory. I done a little dreaming and imagined what a lot of damage I could do if I were in an enemy bomber. I'll know pretty soon if I'm destined to be a bomber or fighter pilot. We leave here for the advanced schools the 28th of this month. Gosh how time flies. In two short months I'll have realized my ambition. I'm pretty sure of myself now. At this stage of the game they don't like to wash out anybody.

It costs "Uncle" about $100 for every hour we spend in a training plane considering everything and at that rate they have already sunk about $14,000 in us so... The training I have yet to get at this field is as follows: One more day cross-country, a night's cross-country, four short instrument cross-countrys, five more hours of regular instrument flying, three more hours of formation flying and four hours of acrobatics. You can see that we don't just go up and fly around - we learn something new every day! Acrobatics are not stressed in basic or advanced schools. They gave us a lot of it in primary because it gives one a good feel of the plane and of being in unusual positions. Contrary to popular belief, acrobatics are not used in combat.

In advanced training we will get a lot of formation flying and cross-country navigational flights. We will also get aerial gunnery. This will be fixed or flexible depending again on which type of school I get sent to. Even a bomber pilot is a full-fledged gunner to take care of any circumstance. Well I guess that takes care of what I have been doing for this time. Not getting out on Open Post I don't have anything else to write about. Most of the fellows don't go out anyway. We all look forward to these all too few Sundays as a day of rest. Brother we need it - they sort of run us ragged! I guess you're pretty darn busy at home too.

Speaking of home, I realize now what wonderful flying country it is. One could make a forced landing in almost any field. It's different here with the small fields and rather hilly country. I could set down in the alfalfa field at home with no trouble at all. In fact, we are required to use only a specified 1000 ft. section of the runway to increase our accuracy in short field landings.

Love, Don

Monday night
July 26th

Dear Folks & Bro John,

I guess it's about time I was writing home. I owe everybody a letter but they can wait 'til I get to my advanced school.

We have finished ground school now and are flying both morning and afternoon to finish up. It sort of gets one down - like driving a car all day long. I am practically thru now. All I have left is one hour of instrument flying and a final instru- ment check. Half of our flying here the past month has been under the instrument hood. It's pretty important cause naturally we can't be "fair weather pilots" in the army.

Well I got my choice - I'm going to single engine fighter advanced school at Craig Field, Alabama. Only 20% of the class are going to single engine. The rest go to twin-engine bomber school. I was one of the few to get what I wanted. The shipping orders came from Maxwell Field and nobody knows how we were picked. My instructor congratulated me and said I was a lucky guy. He went to Craig Field for advanced himself and he says it's a swell place. We will fly the army single engine advance trainer, the AT-6. It has a 600 H.P. super- charged engine with a constant speed prop (automatic pitch). It has retractable landing gear and a 30 Cal. machine gun firing thru the prop.

The next two months should be a lot of fun. We will do a lot of tight formation flying and learn combat maneuvers. My instructor said they turn us loose at advanced and let us do about what we want to, like low fly and having dog fights with each other, etc. About midway in the course we will go down to Florida for gunnery school. When that is over the fun commences! We start flying P-40s - 1200 H.P. under the nose and no chance for dual instruction. That doesn't mean we will be flying P-40s after we graduate. It's just part of the training. The P-40 is a good ship but it's getting a little out-dated. I eventually hope to end up flying a twin engine fighter such as the P-38 or A-20. The boys that go to twin-engine advanced school get the heavy planes like the B-17 & B-24 and Boy! - They can have them. That straight and level flying in a heavy bomber don't appeal to me at all.

A new version of the P-51 landed here this afternoon en route from California. Instead of the regular 1250 H.P. engine and three-blade prop, this has a new Packard made Rolls-Royce Merlin 1600 H.P. engine with a four-bladed prop. That's the first in line engine to have a four-bladed prop - that is, in this country. The British Spitfire has had it for a long time. This new P-51 is really a flying engine with all that horse power. The P-47 may have more H.P. but it's also twice as heavy. The P-51 is a very small plane. I'd fit in it very nicely (Ha). It has a little sign in the cockpit which says - "Do not exceed air speed of 500 M.P.H." Hot Dog!

I'll leave here sometime the end of this week. I'll send you my new address as soon as I get there.

We are having our graduation ball this Wed. night. It's being held in the American Legion Hall in the city of Florence. They are letting us confinees out for that (Ha). There are about 15 of us now. Confinement is the prize form of punishment here.

If Max is there say hello for me.

                          Love, Donald

I did write to Uncle John again. I thought he had to remember — the way everyone remembered horrible happenings — those moments scorched forever on the brain. Where he was...what he was doing...who was with him...who gave him the news...what time of day it was...what the weather was like...

Like the way I remembered exactly where I was when I heard on my car radio that the Challenger Space Shuttle had exploded — I thought of it every time I drove down Highland Parkway in St. Paul. Or the way I remembered my daughter's phone call to me one night while I was working at the hospital, telling me that Uncle Glenn and his second wife, Hellen, had been killed in a car accident.

Or the way I remembered turning on the television set shortly after I was married, just in time to hear that President Kennedy had been assassinated. Seconds later there had been a knock at the door; I opened it and let in the caretaker and a Realtor who wanted to look at the apartment building.

"DID YOU HEAR?" I shrieked at the two men. "THE PRESIDENT WAS JUST SHOT!"

"Yeah, yeah, we heard," they said, brushing past me. "How many rooms in this unit?"

Or the way I remembered hearing that my cousin Keith Hodne, Aunt Alice and Uncle Hardin's oldest son, had died in Nebraska, where he was stationed with the Air Force.

I was at the First Lutheran Church in Karlstad, a warm Sunday morning, September twenty-first, 1958. Sometime during the worship service the telephone in the pastor's office began ringing — an uncommon occurrence. An usher ducked out to answer it, coming back in minutes to urgently whisper something to Mrs. Sam Hodne, Keith's aunt, who was sitting a couple of pews ahead of us; she got up immediately and exited the church.

I didn't think of the brief distraction until later, when the Sunday School class that followed was almost over. I was standing with the rest of the kids, shifting restlessly from foot to foot as we waited to be freed by the closing devotions; we were eager to get outside where we could swap social notes concerning the night before. The leader began, as usual, by ad-libbing the customary prayers of thanks and current concerns, and it was at the end of this segment that she asked that God "...help us to remember in our prayers the family of Keith Hodne, who was killed early this morning in a car accident. Our Father, who art in heaven..."

I wanted to run up and grab her — shake her, and scream that there must be some mistake. Poor woman. New in the community, she didn't know Keith's mother was a Torkelson, and hadn't realized she was breaking the news to anyone closely related. Dumbstruck, as my mind flashed back to the usher's mysterious whisperings to "Mrs. Sam," which now gave supporting evidence, I lurched forward and somehow made it outside to the car where my parents were waiting to tell me it was true.

My mother said it was worse, even, than when Donald died. There was no way to prepare yourself for something like that — a tragic accident, an act of God. When soldiers went off to war, you knew there was a chance they might never come back. War was not an accident. War was never an act of God.

Having boys as first cousins was as close as I would ever get to having brothers. I knew I would remember everything if my brother died.

Chapter Five

The Fascist Italian regime of Mussolini was crumbling and appeared ripe for defeat. Early in July of 1943, a half million Allied soldiers of Patton's and Montgomery's armies landed in Sicily, taking it by mid-August. The Italian people were becoming increasingly disillusioned with the war and Mussolini, and began preparations to change military alliances. As Hitler at one time noted, "The Italians never lose a war...they always end up on the winning side." Mussolini's resignation was demanded and his successor then signed a secret armistice with the Allies. The Germans fighting there, however, held on to northern Italy until the war was nearly over and provided a haven for the ousted Italian leader.

North Dakota's war deaths numbered 144 so far, but that didn't stop the young — or the not so young — from marching off to it. Five sons of Mr. and Mrs. Robert Crotty of Pembina had joined the army and, as the press reported, were "doing their best to get this war over so they can settle down to real living." Mayor Albert Christopher, a WWI combat veteran, resigned his post and left his business to enlist in the U.S. Navy. At the same time, a very disappointed, unidentified 15-year-old boy was on his way back home to Fargo; the army had discharged him when his sister sent a copy of his birth certificate to his commanding officer. The Pembina paper also printed a blurb about Aviation Cadet Donald R. Emerson's transfer to Advanced Flying School. The news item was supplied by the Craig Field Public Relations

Department, and Donald sure hoped nobody thought he put it in
himself!

**AVIATION CADET ADVANCED
TRAINING GROUP
CRAIG FIELD
Selma, Alabama**

August 4, 1943

Dearest Sis Eleanor,

I got your last letter yesterday. It was transferred to me
from Courtland. No doubt you received the card I sent you
when I first got here. I suppose you are a little dismayed to
hear I'm at an advanced fighter school. Well Sis, I asked for
this and I would have been very much disappointed if they had
sent me to a bomber school. Flying one of those slow-flying
"box cars" don't appeal to me at all. You have to be a better
pilot to fly a fast fighter and that's one reason why I want to
fly one. Not one of the guys I palled around with at Courtland
came with me. They all went to a twin engine school at
Columbia, Miss. Only 20% of our class came here.

The next day after we got here, they took us over to the
tailor shop where we were measured from head to foot for our
uniforms. Everything is tailor-made including the blouse,
pants, shirts, overcoat, etc. We have to buy a specified
amount of officer's uniforms before we can graduate and it all
comes to about $300. Fortunately the army gives us $250
for this and the rest comes out of our own pocket.

Mom wrote and told me about their proposed trip to
Seattle this fall. I'm all for it and pray they can go. They both
deserve it and it would do Mom a world of good. Something
like that does her more good than a dozen doctors.

Your dreams of a new home sound good to me too. I know
the place you mentioned and it would be grand if you could own
it some day. We are fighting so such dreams can come true. I
have a few dreams myself.

We are building up an enormous air force and our bombers

have already gotten results! Bombers need fighter escorts and that's where I'll come in. I knew you wouldn't like the idea of me being a fighter pilot but it has its good points too.

I hope it's cool enough the first of October back there to wear a winter uniform. It's beautiful! Do you feel better now? I haven't told anybody else yet and I'm not going to for awhile. I thought you'd appreciate knowing this.

Love, Don

P.S. Hello to H.O.T.

Craig Field's population had a decidedly international flavor, and Donald enjoyed its cultural and ethnic mix. Among those training with the cadets were one Chinese, three escaped Dutchmen, and a couple hundred Frenchmen from the Free French Army in North Africa. Their excellent and highly respected instructor was from India.

Here the cadets would get up at 5:00 AM seven days a week for ground school and then fly until 7:30 at night practicing formation flying, aerobatics and hedgehopping in an AT-6. Although they sometimes would go as high as 20,000 feet with the use of oxygen, Donald liked best the sensation of speed felt when flying low at 200 M.P.H. The AT-6 was a beautiful ship to fly, he said — perfect training for the real thing.

The real thing they'd be flying in their final month was the latest model P-40, the P-40N, a modern combat plane with a liquid-cooled 1200 horse power V-12 engine, which Donald said would do 480 miles per hour in a dive without the wings coming off. He wrote home of dramatic instances demonstrating how a simple but foolish mistake made by a pilot could sometimes be his last. Two of his fellow cadets had crashed their planes — one fatally. "Military flying is no place for a dumb guy even if I do say so myself," he said. Then, far too late to ease a mother's mind he added, "Don't let it worry you, Mom."

The only thing that could prevent him from graduating as a fighter pilot would be his getting a very poor grade in air gunnery. "A fighter pilot is no good if he can't shoot!" He explained. He'd spend about a week in the western part of Florida for gunnery training.

Eglin Field bordered the Gulf of Mexico, where the soil was a fine white powder and the only thing that grew was a scrubby type of pine tree. The Yankee farm boy was not too impressed, and as soon as he got there remarked, "Well I've seen another southern state and it stinks like all the rest of them... I guess Florida is okay in spots but I sure don't think much of this part of it."

Eglin Field proper was the armament testing and proving grounds for the Army Air Forces, with many interesting and classified experiments being conducted there. The entire Eglin Military Reservation covered about 600 square miles and was made up of ground gunnery ranges, practice bombing ranges, aerial ranges and six airports.

All gunnery practice at Craig Field had been with gun cameras, which just took pictures of where their bullets would have gone. Now the pilots would be shooting live ammunition for the first time — 3,000 rounds altogether — most of it while flying over the ocean so they couldn't possibly hit anybody on the ground. They'd fire at two types of targets. One was a 4' X 6' stationary ground type which they'd dive down and fire at when they were 300 yards away; when they'd pull up they'd clear the target by about 30 ft. ("Some fun!" Donald declared.) In aerial gunnery they'd fire at a 4' X 20' target being towed by another plane. Shooting at moving targets at 90 degree angles took a little science, he said, but he'd explain all about deflection shooting when he got home.

Sept. 27, 1943

Dearest Sis,

I guess you will be waiting for this letter to find out exactly when I expect to get home.

We graduate Friday morning Oct. 1st, and I expect to catch a 3:50 PM train out of Selma which will get me to Chicago at 2:35 PM the next day (Oct. 2nd). At 4:00 PM I'll get on the Burlington Streamliner which will get me to St. Paul at 10:30 PM that night. From St. Paul I expect to continue on the Northern Greyhound Bus which will get me home at around 3:00 PM Sunday afternoon. If I can't make that bus connection I will have to wait in St. Paul 'til 8:00 Sun. morning for the Great Northern R.R. which will get me home Sunday evening.

I don't much look forward to that 50 hour train ride but it will be worth it to see you all again. There are several of us from North Dakota and we will be together most of the way.

We finished flying the P-40s on Saturday and we are just finishing up the loose ends now in the AT-6. I have only five more hours to get in which I expect to do tomorrow.

On Thursday night I get an honorable discharge from the regular army and on Friday morning I get sworn in again as a commissioned officer. From then on I rate a salute and live and eat at the Officers' Club.

Be seeing you.

Love, Don

On the morning of October 1, 1943, the new pilots received their officers' commissions and temporary appointments as Second Lieutenants. Immediately after that it was back to the barracks to put on their new "pinks and greens," the worsted wool dress uniform of loden green jacket and light taupe shirt, tie and pants. After a short turn around the area to receive some of the salutes that they had been giving over the past several months, they hurriedly finished packing, cleared the base and headed for home and a few days of impressing family, friends and the girls with the new uniform and "Wings" — and no doubt most, like Donald, made front page news there as well.

Donald made this notation in his stateside logbook:

Completed Advanced Flying
School Oct. 1, 1943
Received Wings & bars
Oh happy day!

The war continued to go in the Allies' favor as 1943 drew to a close. The Germans had been crushed by the British in North Africa, and the Russians were over-powering them and taking back their homeland. In the Philippines the Allied invasion had begun, and Gen. MacArthur's pledge to return was at last set in motion.

The Eighth Air Force spent most of its first year of active participation learning first-hand what the British already knew and had tried to impress on them, that daylight bombing was too costly. The plan to wear down the enemy by bombing both day and night was effective, but as their offensive missions pushed more deeply into enemy territory their fighter escorts — or "little friends," as they were called, had to turn back and head for home before running out of fuel.

An auxiliary fuel tank strapped to the belly of the P-47 had extended its protective reach, but still not enough for it to accompany the bombers to farther-flung targets. When left alone to lumber through the skies, the slow-moving B-17s and B-24s became easy pickings for the German fighters. The bombers were jumped from above by Messerschmitt 109 and Focke Wulf 190 single-engined planes and attacked from below by twin-engined Messerschmitt 110s, and the numbers of unescorted heavies downed and aircrew lost during 1943 were appalling.

TALLAHASSEE, FLORIDA
DALE MABRY FIELD

Oct. 14, 1943

Dear Folks & Bro. John,

Well after four days on the road I finally got here at 4:30 this afternoon. The train connections to this place were terrible. I rode seven different trains and none of them ran on time. Even the old faithful N.P. let me down. Somewhere below Detroit Lakes the engine developed valve trouble and we limped along with only one cylinder delivering power. We got to St. Paul three hours late and missed all the night trains for Chicago. I was 24 hours late getting here but I had wired ahead that I would be, so it was O.K.

As I told you before this is a replacement center for pilots and we won't stay here over two weeks - maybe less. We already know what's what though and I'm more than satisfied. I'm going to fly the new P-51 with the 1650 H.P. Rolls-Royce engine and the four blade prop. I'll have a lot of fun in that baby cause it's a low altitude fighter used mostly for ground strafing and light bombing. I consider myself lucky cause most of the boys got P-40s. None of us got P-47s like we expected. We know pretty well what our program is and even though you might not like it, there is no sense in not telling you now. In about two weeks we will go down to Bartow Field, Florida, for six weeks of training in P-51s. Then we come back to this field and wait for overseas shipping orders. That doesn't mean combat that soon but what further training we get will be over there. The first of the year will most likely see us leaving out of here. I told you I'd probably have another furlough but that's out too. Now you know what's what and I think that's the best way. We all feel, the sooner the better, as long as it's got to be that way.

I guess we won't do any flying at this field. We will get a bunch of lectures etc. I don't care much for Tallahassee or the surrounding country - it's all woods and swamps.

This letter is short and to the point cause I'm darn tired. I'll write again soon but I want you to get my address. Use the return address on the envelope.

Love, Donald

"They had to be the best," my mother always said. "They only took the best."

But as proud as she was of her brother's perfection, when trouble spots erupted in the world and other conflicts threatened, she made a habit of mentally gauging the chances of going off to war for those close to her. One was too old, right? Another was too young. And of Lee, she said, regarding my own youngest son, "They'd never take him, would they — because of his eye?"

"No," I answered, with unashamed relief. A congenital cataract classified him legally blind in one eye.

My mother was relieved, too; the young grandson who had

*once pleased her so by choosing to build a little model of a P-51
Mustang could never qualify to fly one in combat, the way
Donald had.*

*"They had to be the best," she said again. "They only took
the best. And Donald was the best — at least I know he was the
best one of us."*

The need for a fighter escort to provide long-range, high altitude
protection was urgent, but the solution had already been found.
Developments improving and refining the North American P-51
Mustang had finally produced a fighter plane which satisfied this
demand. Although the early model Allison-engined P-51A had
already proved itself worthy, it could not compete with the P-47's
performance at high altitudes.

Originally developed for the British in 1940, and in
production the following year, the sleekly designed Mustang was
used primarily for low-level photographic reconnaissance
missions and for giving close support to ground forces. Late in
1942 the RAF refitted it with a Rolls-Royce Merlin engine
converting it to a very able high-altitude, long-range fighter.

Now the U.S. Army Air Forces were giving it a try. Their
new P-51B, with a Packard-built Rolls-Royce Merlin engine gave
them a speedier, more maneuverable high-altitude fighter than
the distance-limited P-47. At only about half the weight of the
Jug, its superior fuel efficiency made it the vehicle of choice for
long-distance flying. With some further refinements the later
P-51D model Mustang would be considered by many to be the
finest fighter plane of the war.

HILLSBOROUGH ARMY FIELD
TAMPA, FLORIDA

Monday, Nov. 1st

Dearest Sis,

Every time I wait so long to write like this I feel sort of
guilty and wish I didn't have to write at all. I got here a week
and two days ago. The day after I had to go to the hospital
with an infection in my foot. I didn't pay much attention to it
at first but my foot started to swell up and was a little more

serious than I thought. They kept me in the hospital for six days and grounded me for another five days so I won't be able to fly 'til the day after tomorrow. The other boys have been flying all this time and they have nothing but praise for this P-51. It's a very easy ship to fly but a little tricky to land. A couple days ago my roommate, William Dunwoody, landed so hard he blew out all three tires. This Dunwoody is a very nice guy. He is 24 years old and was married not quite a year ago. He has his wife staying in Tampa.

This is a small field and that makes it nice cause everyone knows everybody else. Morale is high here - the older officers are all men who have already been in combat. We get the best instructions possible cause they know what it's all about. This used to be called Henderson Field before the army took it over. It is located just outside of Tampa which is a pretty nice city of 100,000 population. This is a good time of the year to be in southern Florida. It's pretty warm in the daytime but cools down enough at night to wear our winter uniform.

Yes, I did have a very nice time when I was at Bemidji. To tell everything would take ten pages so I won't even begin. I was with Jennie almost constantly from 6:00 Friday evening 'til late Saturday night. Avis H. and Margie S. were with us Saturday afternoon and a very nice time was enjoyed by all. Now I'm not talking anymore!

It's time to eat lunch so I'm going to close. Use the return address I put on this envelope. It's the correct one for this field.

All my love, Donald

"The Battle of Berlin" began in late November when RAF bombers launched a series of nightly raids on cities throughout the Third Reich, nearly half of them on Germany's capital. Very soon American bombers would have fighter planes to escort them on their daylight raids all the way to Berlin.

Because they were the first in the USAAF to be equipped with P-51Bs, the Ninth Air Force's newly-formed 354th Fighter Group, led by Col. Kenneth Martin, was called "The Pioneer

Mustang Group." The Mustangs arrived at their base near Colchester, England, on November 11, 1943, scheduled to be operational for combat by December 1.

November 19, 1943

Dear Folks & Bro. John,

It's 8:30 in the evening and I just got back from the Link Trainer Dept. where I spent an hour practicing radio and instrument procedure. We get about three hours in the Link trainer each week. In the air we are doing a lot of tactical formation work and aerial gunnery.

I love to fly the P-51 - it's a good airplane. I was on a high altitude mission one morning and at 20,000 ft. I got 390 M.P.H. out of it in straight and level flight, or "on the deck" as we call it. When I was alone, a formation of four P-40s jumped me and started simulated combat. As yet we don't have much experience in combat tactics but I stayed in there with them and did manage to get on the tail of two of them. Of course I was outnumbered and probably would have been shot down had we been playing for keeps. The P-40 can turn in a tighter circle but the P-51 has it when it comes to climbing and diving speed. In simulated combat a person is "blacked out" half the time due to the tight maneuvering. Leaning way over on the stick helps a lot though.

I like this P-51 more every hour I put in it. I sure get a kick out of landing this plane. The tires fairly squeal as they hit the runway at better than 100 M.P.H.

On Tuesday which was my day off, I went over to McDill Field, which is a bomber base, and went up in a B-17 Flying Fortress. The "armchair pilots" can keep their bombers - I'll stick to the fighters!

Last night I went along with Capt. Langhorn, our Sqd. Flight Surgeon, to a football game. "Doc" is a swell guy - I got to know him pretty well when I was in the hospital.

Tomorrow morning we all have to take part in a formal review. It's in honor of Major Griffith who has been our commanding officer. He is going back to combat the second time after spending some time here as head instructor.

I'll write again soon.

Love, Donald

In view of the fact that the 354th Fighter Group had no combat experience, a skilled leader was needed to get them started. Major Donald J.M. Blakeslee of the 4th Fighter Group was rapidly making a name for himself as possibly the best leader ever in aerial combat, and though not yet his group's commander, he more often led their missions than anyone else. Reciprocity between the air forces allowed the talents of the peerless Blakeslee to be borrowed from the 4th to lead the "Pioneer Mustang Group's" first few missions.

Donald sent home for safe keeping a small oil painting of a Mustang painted by George Klim, one of his roommates. On the back of it Donald wrote: "P-51B — Sweetest thing on wings."

November 24, 1943

Dear Folks & Bro. John,

I'm pretty tired but I'm going to write this before I go to bed. We didn't have any ground school today so we spent all our time flying. This morning I was on a 650 mile cross country navigation flight. I spent most of the afternoon doing acrobatics at 30,000 ft. Planes handle a lot different at high altitudes so we go upstairs and put the ships through the "mill" to get the feel of it. When I was tired of acrobatics I rolled over on my back and pointed the nose straight down in a full power on vertical dive. When I started to recover at 20,000 feet, I was doing 630 M.P.H. Just call me "speed" from now on (ha). I guess I'll wait 'til some Jap gets on my tail before I go any faster. The P-51 will pick up speed in a dive faster than any other plane although the P-47 & P-38 will go just as fast in a more prolonged dive.

I got my finished pictures yesterday and the studio is mailing them for me. I'm sending two of the small ones to you and you can send them on to Max and Ray Emersons. I don't know their addresses. I'm getting a couple small ones (5" X 7") black and white in paper folders which I'll send to Harts and

Art Barrons.

Incidently the picture studio asked my permission to put a large one like I sent to you, Sister and Roswells, in their display window. I'm not so crazy about my expression but I like the way my uniform shows up. In case you notice, that hat is my new "Hot Fighter Pilot's" style hat.

I got an invitation from the "girl friend" to eat Thanksgiving dinner at their place but unfortunately I can't go cause we have to fly tomorrow just like any other day. They are having a special dinner for us at the Officers' Mess though. I hope you have a pleasant Thanksgiving Day! I guess we have a few things to be thankful for even if things aren't perfect. I see in today's paper that R.A.F. and U.S. bombers have been giving Berlin hell the past two nights.

No, I can't write straight any longer so I'd better "log" some good old "sack time." Bye for now.

Love to you all,
Donald

Col. Anderson had moved on to another post in August, and Col. Chesley C. Peterson was now in charge of the 4th Fighter Group. For his service in the original Eagle Squadrons, and as the first American to command an RAF squadron, Peterson had been highly decorated by the British. When he was transferred to the U.S. Army he became, at 23, its youngest full colonel.

As their participation in combat increased later in 1943, the ratio of enemy planes destroyed to pilot losses improved, but attempts to attract and engage the Luftwaffe fighters found limited success. But even with the Germans often holding back their attacks until the fighter escorts turned around and headed for home, they did put up enough resistance to account for a majority of the 4th's pilots lost during that year. Joseph Matthews evaded capture in France and later made it back. Henry Ayres, Jr., Aubrey Stanhope, Frank Fink, Clyde Smith and Robert Patterson became POWs. A non-combat flying accident claimed the life of John McNabb; and Ward Wortman, Frederick Merritt, Dale Leaf, Frank Gallion and Ivan Moon were all killed in action.

Mon. Eve.
December 6th

Dear Dad & Bro. John,

I guess I owe both of you a letter. In fact I owe everybody a letter - I've been neglecting my letter writing lately. There is a certain girl in town who has been taking up too much of my spare time. She's a beautiful blonde and a nice girl but I'm afraid she's trying to hook me. It's good I'll be leaving here the end of this month so I'll be able to break off without any hard feelings.

I got a letter from Mom this morning and I'm glad to hear she's at Halma. Being over there usually does her a lot of good.

I hope you get a good market for the pigs. I guess you can put a feather in your hat, Pop, for those pigs. I do appreciate what you have done at home the past two years - I'd never make the farmer that you are, John. I don't mean that I have lost interest in the farm, but while I'm on the subject I'd like to clear up a few things. When I was home I'll admit I didn't show much interest in farming. I had too many places to go in too short a time. Then after a year of having flying pounded into my brain - well what I'm trying to say is that I think more along flying lines than anything else. Please believe me, the idea that I'm drifting away from you, or that I'm getting big headed, is erroneous and ridiculous! Contrary to most of the fellows in the army, I love my work and my role in uniform.

We are practicing aerial gunnery, ground strafing, dive bombing and skip bombing now. In dive bombing we peel off at 8,000 feet, drop the bombs and recover at about a 70 degree angle to the target and sight the target through the regular optical gun sight. It's not at all hard to make accurate hits. In skip bombing we fly toward the target at a very low altitude (25-50 ft.) and drop the bomb just in front of the target so it will skip, bounce or skid right into it. Very accurate and lots of fun. In aerial gunnery and ground strafing we fire four .50 cal. machine guns at the same time which gives a combined fire power of about fifty to sixty .50 cal. slugs per second. This morning when we were dive bombing one of the boys dropped a 100 lb. practice bomb in a farmer's pasture. About an hour later the farmer was over at the field and mad as a wet hen. The pilot said he didn't mean to do it but I have other ideas (Ha).

Bye for now,
Love, Donald

Within weeks Donald and his Craig Field classmates were bumping along on a northbound train, destination unknown. He made one last notation in his pilot's log:

Completed Fighter Combat
training Dec. 26, 1943
Headed for Overseas

Because I had no memories of Donald, I thought compiling his biography would be a painless job for me. How very wrong I was. After first reading and then typing all of Donald's letters, I felt I knew him very well. Studying what soon became a very personal war made me sick, but I couldn't stop until I had figured out his exact place in the whole thing. I had never really understood much about it except that Hitler was the bad guy and pretty much started it all. What never sank in before was the enormous number of lives that were lost — thousands of people could die on either side in a single battle, and the loss would be acceptable if the number were a lot smaller than that of the enemy. Had we really covered this in high school? I must have been looking out the window. It was all absolutely, overwhelmingly sickening. And each one killed was some family's Donald — one more box of stuff sent home to be sifted through and treasured, or to be stashed away in a musty attic and forgotten. Whoever first said "War is hell" deserved to be quoted. One more thing for me to look up! It was said by William Tecumseh Sherman over 100 years ago; there was just no better way to describe it. And the simple Christmas wish for peace on earth began taking on new meaning. Why had I — who wouldn't buy

*toy guns — let my boys have those little green plastic army men?
Jay and Lee played war by flinging fistfuls of them at each other.
Lose a bunch in the grass? Dog chew up a few? Kick some
under the couch? Here's a dollar — go to the store and buy
another bag.*

*The WWII section at the Highland branch library became one of
my haunts; I had stopped reading novels. Who needs fiction?*

 *"This is the third time you have renewed these books. Please
try to finish them this time."*

 "Okay, I will."

 *"We're really only supposed to allow one renewal, you know.
If there had been a request out for these titles I would have been
forced to take them from you now."*

 *"Ooooo — that could have been ugly. Thanks for not doing
that."*

 "Merry Christmas."

 "Same to you."

 *Crazy lady. Had she really thought she could intimidate
someone who was in the middle of the bloodiest war in the
history of the world with a puny little threat of hand-to-hand
combat with an unarmed librarian? HA!*

Chapter Six

It was early January, 1944, when the new pilots checked in at Fort Hamilton in Brooklyn, New York. The location of troops was classified information, but Donald got around this minor technicality and let his family know where he was by mentioning one of their gutsiest and most talented cousins, Evelyn Roswell. Liberated well ahead of her time, she had dared dream big, with career goals that catapulted her out of Halma, Minnesota — about the smallest speck on any map — all the way to New York City.

January 8, 1944

Dear Folks & Bro. John,

I haven't been able to write for some time and there is not much that I can tell you now. I am still in this country and somewhere on the east coast. We are under strict censorship and I can't tell you anything. You may have received my temporary A.P.O. number from the war department. If not, it is on the return address of this letter. You can write to me at that address until you get my permanent A.P.O. number from me. Incidently as soon as I let you know that I am overseas it would be better for you to use V-Mail when writing to me. The letters you will receive from me will be V-Mail also.

I look forward to this little trip and please don't worry about me. Just remember I'm not the first one to go over and

I wouldn't feel right to stay behind.

It's cold as heck here and we really feel it after being used to warmer weather. If I had Evelyn's address I'd go see her. I can't remember her married name or the name of the hotel so I'm out of luck. I think I'll be gone before you can get an answer back to me too. There is so little I can write about that I may as well close.

Love to all,
Don

Once the aviators were encamped to await shipping orders, the city's popular tourist attractions beckoned. Leery of getting lost, a passel of them stuck together and braved the New York subway system — first stop: the Empire State Building, where they went straight to the top for that desired bird's eye view of the urban landscape, and then it was on to Madison Square Garden.

Bob Planck was among this party of young officers that night, and he remembered that Donald "...met a girl there, with whom he spent some time." Irving Reedy remembered her, too. "A striking girl," he said.

The girl Donald met wasn't just any girl. She turned out to be that one special girl: Elinor Lindemann, from New York. She was the one who made him forget all the other girls he may have ever thought he cared about, or ever knew. He also, apparently, forgot his recently declared resolution not to "...do anything so foolish as to fall for some girl."

On the evening of January 8, 1944, the thrill-seeking fighter pilots got to the ice rink at Madison Square Garden and elected to do some skating — a skill not possessed by all. As Donald struggled to stay on his feet, he approached a young girl who was skating there — a very petite brunette with big brown eyes shaded by the longest, thickest eyelashes he'd ever seen. Whomp-on-the-head beautiful, and about 15 years old, he judged. He suggested that if she would skate with him, it might improve his chances of remaining upright. To his surprise he discovered that they were the same age; she was equally astounded to learn that the stumbling young lieutenant had grown up in North Dakota — didn't they live on ice there?

The instant chemistry between them was almost palpable. From the first moment of that initial encounter, it was as if they'd known each other forever somehow. For the rest of the evening they talked easily together as they slid and skidded around the rink. Though slipping, falling and grasping to hold each other up, they skated quite effortlessly into a most ardent acquaintance.

Their conversation and relationship quickly took on that certain ease enjoyed only by loving couples long-bonded by time, or by soul mates magically united, and from the very start they spoke very openly about everything.

Until Pearl Harbor, Elinor had been a carefree college student in Florida, with a steady boyfriend. When the war broke out, both education and romance were disrupted. The boyfriend left school to join the army, and Elinor moved back to New York with her family and took a job with an insurance company.

Donald told Elinor everything about his life, too — except for any part about girlfriends.

He arranged to meet her every single day until he shipped out — she never knew just when or where he'd turn up, and for six days running they saw the sights and took in shows. Elinor brought him home to meet her parents, two sisters, and Mr. Chips, the Lindemanns' little Scottie dog. Her big-hearted mother was such an excellent cook, and so ready to fill an extra plate, that Donald became a regular dinner guest.

They liked rum and Coke, he called her "Princess," and their song was "I'll Be Seeing You." Donald would thereafter refer to this time spent together as a week, and Elinor would teasingly remind him that it had been only six days.

The overwhelming passion he felt for her had hit Donald so suddenly that he had been mentally knocked off his feet as well, but he kept these feelings from his family until he had sorted them out and regained his equilibrium. This process may have been somewhat slowed by the transatlantic cruise, because he didn't tell anyone about her until he was once again on land.

V-MAIL

January 30, 1944

My Dear Sis Eleanor,

There are two Eleanors in my life now and I love to write to each of you. The other Elinor (that's the way she spells her name) is a girl from New York whom I met when I was in the "big city." I met her at Madison Square Garden where I went ice skating. I never believed in love at first sight before but I do now! We saw each other every night for one week and that was enough. As soon as I can get some air mail paper and envelopes I'll write you a regular letter and tell you all about her. I just have to tell somebody and you're the one whom I like to confide in the most. Nothing new today so bye until next letter.

Love, Donald

(My love to the girls.)

Donald had said goodbye to Elinor, and with the rabbit's foot she gave him for good luck, sailed to Europe on the Ile de France, one of several luxury ocean liners that had been converted to carry troops during the war.

This adventurous voyage might have been even more exciting, remembered Don Patchen, another Craig Field classmate, but they weren't smart enough to be scared. They didn't learn until later that the already rocky, storm-tossed crossing had been greatly exacerbated by the ship's all-out efforts to elude enemy U-boats. Any residual appetite for food was then tempered by the food itself — or as Patchen delicately put it, "Gaining weight on the trip was not a problem, as it was an English-manned ship serving two meals a day, with smoked herring for breakfast — among other things — that no American farm boy was used to facing that early in the day."

In the U.K. they spent a few weeks in additional training with the 496th Fighter Group at Goxhill, where they were billeted in prefabricated housing made of corrugated metal, similar to Quonset buildings. Though these huts were equipped with premade beds, the heat from the stoves was seldom enough to

No.

CENSORS STAMP

Mrs. Harold Torkelson
Strandquist,
Minnesota.
U.S.A.

Lt. D. R. Emerson
SENDERS NAME
A.P.O. 15689
SENDERS ADDRESS
% Postmaster
New York, N.Y.
DATE Jan. 30th

FEB 1 1944

(My love to the girls)

England
Jan. 30 1944

My dear Sis Eleanor

There are two Eleanors in my life now and I love to write to each of you. The other Elinor (that's the way she spells her name) is a girl from New York whom I met when I was in the "big city." I met her at Madison Square Garden where I went ice skating. I never believed in love at first sight before but I do now! We saw each other every night for one week and that was enough. As soon as I can get some air mail pages and envelopes I'll write you a regular letter and tell you all about her. I just have to tell somebody and you're the one whom I like to confide in the most. Nothing new today so Bye until my next letter.

Love Donald

V—MAIL

*V-Mail to Eleanor
regarding Elinor*

*Lucky Rabbit's Foot
[C. Konsler]*

Elinor & "Mr. Chips"

CRAIG FIELD CLASSMATES

Donald

Don Patchen

Bob Planck

Leonard Pierce

ward off England's biting dankness, and to keep warm the men crawled between the cotton sheets, still dressed in their fleece-lined flying gear.

February 6, 1944

Dear Folks & Bro. John,

It's Sunday afternoon and I have just finished eating dinner. We get Sundays off so I didn't get up 'til 11:00 O'clock. We aren't working very hard, reason number one being the English weather doesn't give us a chance. I haven't seen the sun since I came here. The English people all have rather pale complexions and it's not hard to understand why. Incidently the winter uniform is worn the year around here. It doesn't warm up enough in the summer to wear light clothing. The average temperature variation between summer and winter is only about 30 degrees. Looking at a map it seems funny that England isn't a lot colder - it has about the same latitude as northern Canada. I guess it's the Gulf Stream that keeps it warm.

I'm going to town in a few minutes. The thing that's hard to get used to are the completely blacked-out streets. Just think - there are kids growing up over here that have never seen lighted streets. Must close.

Love, Don

February 13, 1944

Dear Folks & Bro. John,

This has been a rather quiet Sunday. I flew one hour this morning and had the rest of the day off. I meant to go back to the barracks and write letters but when I got here I laid down on the bed, flying clothes and all, and slept all afternoon.

We aren't working too hard, just learning how to fly in the world's worst weather. One cannot be a "fair weather pilot" over here. The visibility is usually very low and conditions change very rapidly. One morning we had all the different kinds of weather in the book - high winds, calm, fog, rain, hail, snow, sleet and sunshine. The sunshine made it an unusual morning itself. It's a rare day indeed that the sun comes out for even a short period. The British have worked out this bad weather and instrument flying procedures pretty well and we are learning a lot from them that we didn't get in flying school. The R.A.F. has to be given a lot of credit for what they have accomplished since this war began. Their methods of flying are the best possible and the U.S. air forces over here use their methods also. This of course would be necessary because the R.A.F. and the A.A.F. work together so much.

Unfortunately there is very little I can tell you for reasons of security. Incidently you may be curious to know why I sign my name and rank on the lower left corner of the envelopes. An officer is allowed to censor his own mail and that signature is the same as giving your word of honor that you have not violated censorship tho so some of my mail may get opened. We often get the unpleasant job of censoring the enlisted men's mail. Doing that makes one very security minded himself so I don't think my letters will ever contain anything that would be useful to the enemy. I hope to get some mail soon! Please write often.

Love, Don

The darkened streets of the nearby villages and towns offered many forms of entertainment, but before being turned loose to explore, the new replacement pilots were instructed in British customs and given some tips to help interpret what was supposed to be their common language. Donald and William Dunwoody, from the Bronx — his best pal since Jake — promptly found an ice rink and became more proficient skaters.

Though the British had always been extremely hospitable, the incredible influx of uniformed Yankees was a major source of irritation to the English men because of the unwelcome competition for their women. And many suspected that there was a direct correlation between the ladies' attraction to American servicemen and the size of their paychecks. With U.S. officers earning more than three times that of their RAF comrades, American flyboys were prime choice. Donald told his brother, only half in jest, that some of the English girls chased after them so hard they practically tripped and knocked them down. Warranted or not, the resentment toward their allied rivals caused the begrudging Brits to coin a rather notorious phrase neatly summarizing their complaints about their guests: "The only trouble with Americans," they said, "is that they're overpaid, oversexed, and over here!"

February 17, 1944

Dearest Sis & Harold,

Boy I feel fresh as a daisy - I just came back from the Officers' Club where I had a hot bath in a bath tub! Not bad when you can be in a theater of war and still enjoy a bath tub. One nice thing about being here in England, the living conditions aren't too bad. Of course being a pilot I get a break in that we don't have to live in field conditions.

I saw a fairly good U.S.O. show last night. I've seen several since I came here. James Cagney is in London getting ready to tour the "Yank" stations here in England and I hope I get to see him. We see movies from home all the time - even the English theaters show those.

I got another V-Mail from you, sent January 12th, and I got a regular letter mailed the same time so I guess V-Mail isn't too much faster. The trouble with V-Mail is that it has to be processed on both sides of the ocean which of course takes time. I don't like this excuse for writing paper but it's the only thing we can get.

Love, Don

Col. Donald J.M. Blakeslee rose to take command of the 4th Fighter Group on January 1, 1944 — a promotion thought by many to be long overdue. Extremely modest and taciturn, he sported no victory crosses or decoration on his personal airplane, and as a leader was never one to heap praise on his pilots. In fact, the men who flew with him have said the highest compliment he ever paid them was to say nothing at all.

Far from being the best shot, Blakeslee's skill lay in his leadership instincts and zeal for the hunt. Air combat to him was "a grand sport," and he preferred that his team's players be unmarried; he believed marriage would dull a pilot's eagerness for combat, even though there were several in the Group who soundly disproved this. (Blakeslee, himself, would become one of them when he got married later that year.)

He was big and tough, and so strong willed and tireless that he refused to go home on leave until after more than three and a half years in combat. At age 26 they called him "Old Man River," because he just kept rolling along. He would become the most experienced American pilot in the war, having flown several hundred missions...how many even Blakeslee doesn't know, because he doctored his logbooks to keep the brass from grounding him for flying too many missions.

His command now official, he was ripe to challenge the only other air commander ever argued to be his equal. Col. Hubert "Hub" Zemke and his "Wolfpack" had already racked up 300 victories — double the number of the 4th — putting the 56th Fighter Group in first place, and Col. Blakeslee was literally gunning for the title.

The 4th Fighter Group got its first U.S. trained fighter pilots on January 26th; three days later they were flying combat missions in escort and support of the heavy bombers hitting enemy targets in the Netherlands, Belgium, France and Germany.

The most enemy aircraft destroyed by the group in any mission in the early part of 1944 was eight; on February 10th they made that mark for the third time. At first they didn't know it had been accomplished without any cost to themselves, because one of their trusty pilots was reported missing.

Robert Wehrman, part of the group since September 1943, spotted two Me 109s on the return trip from Germany and broke away to attack. As he closed in on one of them he saw red, flashing tracer bullets hitting the left wing of his P-47 from a third 109 lurking behind him. While he twisted and turned and radioed for help, a 20mm shell burst through the cockpit, inches from his head, smashing the instrument panel. Fate was kind; the shell misfired and did not explode on impact. Seriously wounded by gunfire in his left leg, Bob hastily prepared to bail out as the Luftwaffe pilot closed in for the kill. Fortunately, mere seconds before the German could strike, Louis "Red" Norley came zooming to Bob's aid and shot down the 109. Just in time Norley had recognized the panicked voice responsible for the somewhat garbled and confused call for help. After shooting down the enemy attacker, Norley completely lost sight of Wehrman and assumed he'd been shot down too. But his dependable P-47 was still flying full throttle at about 110 mph, barely above stall speed, and even though he'd jettisoned his canopy and radio-equipped helmet, Bob decided to stick with his plane and try to fly it back to the English coast.

The era of the Thunderbolt was nearly over for the 4th, but before the long-awaited Mustangs arrived and were operational, six more of their pilots were shot down by German aircraft. Edwin Mead and Hubert Ballew survived to become prisoners of the Germans. Burton Wyman, William Cox, Richard Reed and Joseph Sullivan all died during battle.

Sunday, Feb. 20th

Dear Folks & Bro. John,

I am writing this in our Officers' Club with a big cheerful log fire in the fireplace. The fire feels good because as usual it's cold and damp outside. I swear that if I ever have a home of my own it will have a fireplace in it! I just came from the Mess Hall where I had a good steak dinner. Just in case you folks think we are roughing it over here, you're mistaken.

Believe it or not Jack Benny is on the radio. The overseas short wave service works swell and we get the U.S. programs very good. There are several R.A.F. officers in the Club and they are getting a big kick out of Jack B. If you are listening, Jack is bear hunting in Maine. The program just ended and it was a recording of the March 19th broadcast so you won't remember.

It has been some time since my trip over here so I can tell you something about it without giving away any information that would help "Jerry." As you probably guessed I made the trip by boat. I had hopes of flying over but no such luck. It wasn't a bad trip tho as we were on one of the world's four largest ocean liners. We sailed alone, depending upon our speed for safety. We hit a bit of bad weather and the seas

got pretty heavy. I didn't get seasick but probably would have
in a smaller ship. To get seasick is one of the worst things
there is. First one gets so sick he is afraid he's going to die.
Then he feels so terrible he begins to wish he would die.

After being in this country I can see why the Pilgrims left.
Who would want to live in this climate is beyond me. They say
it gets better in the summer tho. Then it gets daylight at
four in the morning and doesn't get dark 'til 12:00 at night. In
regards to my bonds and insurance - the insurance has a
second beneficiary which is Dad so you don't need to worry
about that.

I'll see the special service officer and see what I can do
about the bonds. I could make out a will - I didn't before cause
I didn't think I needed one as I have nothing in my name. Let
me know if you have received any of the $50 bonds which I
subscribed for starting with the month of Sept. By the way
have you received my latest insurance policy? We had to make
out a new one after we were commissioned so that old one is
no good.

Mom, you can go ahead and get rid of any of my clothes
that you want to. I'll never wear any of them when I get back!
Take good care of the military clothing that I send home tho.

I got a letter from Lela the other day. I enjoy her letters a
lot. I wasn't too surprised to hear that Dave & Elma are
engaged. Hearing about Milfred Hart getting hitched did
surprise me tho. I'm going to write Max a letter this
afternoon too.

There is a recording of a National Barn Dance program on
the radio now. It sure does sound good to our ears. The
English programs are very flat - they don't go for the
slapstick humor as we do.

John, I know what you would like to have me write but I
can't very well do that. Listen to the news - you know the
plane I fly.

Love, Donald

With a loud "THANK GOD!" and silent thanks to Republic Aircraft for the beautifully built Thunderbolt, Bob Wehrman had tied his silk neck scarf around his bleeding leg and aimed his P-47 toward England. With no working instruments except needle and ball indicator, he dodged another 109 in the clouds, relying entirely on "the old reliable training method of 'needle, ball and airspeed,' " to see him through. When he landed safely at another American base, it was without a working right flap and with a useless left leg. After six weeks in a field hospital he came back to the 4th Fighter Group, still bragging about the P-47 Thunderbolt, and calling it the best fighter plane in the world! "The joke was on me!" he said, because he found out the 4th Fighter Group had already been flying the P-51 Mustang for a month.

Blakeslee's first three P-51B Mustangs were delivered to the Group on February 14th. He ordered his pilots to get checked out in them between missions, and by February 26th, all three squadrons were Mustang equipped and Mustang ready.

Though the P-51 did have some definite advantages over the P-47, a variety of mechanical problems soon cropped up to shake the pilots' original expectations. In the two weeks of flying before it was grounded for further adjustments, the 4th lost 15 Mustang pilots — easily 1/3 or more of them were downed because of engine trouble; the rest by enemy intervention.

Steve "The Greek" Pisanos, unable to get out of his P-51, crash-landed in France; he lived to evade capture and returned to Debden six months later. Vermont Garrison, Phillip "Pappy" Dunn, Paul Ellington, Hugh Ward, Robert Messenger, Cecil Manning, Henry Mills and Selden Edner bailed out and became guests of the Germans. Robert Frazer was killed in a flying accident; George Villinger, Glenn Herter, George Barnes, Robert Richards, and Edmund Whalen died while flying in combat.

Limey Land
March 7, 1944

Dear Folks & Bro. John,

I received your letter today Johnny old boy and enjoyed its contents. It seems to take on the average of three weeks for letters to reach us but it doesn't make much difference.

V-Mail is a little faster but as you said they are no better than postcards.

Today was one of those unusual sunny days which we get about once a month over here. We had the afternoon off so three of us went bike riding which I enjoy doing very much over here. Incidently all officers and most of the enlisted men get issued a bike. They are very handy to use around the field and they help save on "petrol."

As I said before, I enjoy riding around the English countryside. The towns are very close together and there is always something to see which is odd and quaint compared to what we have in the States. I was quite interested today in noticing that there was threshing going on at several farms. One of the fellows I was with was a farm boy also and having a common interest we stopped at one place and saw how they go about it. The middle of the winter seems a funny time of the year to be threshing but I imagine you have already guessed what the story is. They stack all the grain when it's cut and then thresh it when they can. I noticed that the grain was not tied in bundles but stacked loose. I guess they don't even use binders. The separators themselves are small and of fairly modern design but they are built of wood and have no straw blower. They have another unit with an endless chain type of carrier to remove the straw. They use Fordsons for power - they are the only tractors I have seen in the United Kingdom.

Everything over here is done on a smaller scale than back home. All the cars are slightly larger than our Crosleys & Bantom cars and have a narrow tread. The railroads have narrow gauge tracks and the engines aren't the size of ours. The freight cars are almost comical. They are known as "goods wagons" and are only about 10 feet long. The passenger trains run about every hour. This country is so densely populated and the towns so close together the trains act as street cars for people going to work, etc.

Something else I saw this afternoon of interest was an old

stone castle built 1,000 years ago. I had seen it from the air and was curious to get a closer look at it.

I'm going to get in touch with Phil Kiner soon. Be sort of nice to see an old familiar face in place of the "Limeys" for a change. Limey means men of the sea.

All for now - Love, Donald

I read such horrible things — so many people had suffered in such unbelievable ways. They died in freak training accidents, or ordinary plane crashes in bad weather; others were killed by their own bombs or shot down by their own gunners. Foot soldiers had to look into the faces of those they fought to the death; paratroopers could drift off target and land in swamps and drown, strangled by their own chutes. I read of bombers making it back to base, but so badly shot up that what was left of some crew members had to be flushed out with high-powered hoses. Prisoners of war were often starved and ill-treated, even tortured. One prisoner of the Japanese reported being forced at gunpoint to bury his buddy. Alive. The saddest of all were those who somehow lived through the war, only to come home so wounded in body, mind or spirit that for them the war would last forever.

I felt almost guilty for my thoughts, but I began to think that even though Donald died in the war, compared to many others, he was one of the lucky ones. He didn't have to see the people he killed, and when he died, he probably hadn't suffered too much. It was quick. It must have been over in minutes.

I said all of this to my mother. She agreed, and then she remembered something else.

"Did you know we had a cousin who got shot down in one of those big bombers?" she asked. "Just a day or so after Donald? It went down over an ocean. They were about the same age, too, I think."

"Was he in the Eighth Air Force too?" I asked.

"No — couldn't have been," she answered. "He was one of the Canadian Emersons. Ralph Waldo."

"RALPH WALDO?"

"Yes. That was his name. His body was never recovered. At least we have Donald."

Classmates were being scattered and friends parted company as assignments to the various fighter groups were handed out. Bob Planck and William Dunwoody were headed for the 354th — the "Pioneer Mustang Group," and Irving Reedy went off to the 355th. Honored to draw duty with the prestigious 4th, along with Donald, were Don Patchen, Leonard Pierce, William Hawkins, Robert Kenyon, and Warren Johnson. Of these men, Patchen, Johnson and Donald were assigned to 336 Squadron; Kenyon and Pierce went to 334, and Hawkins to 335. Other pilots assigned to the 4th at that time were Lloyd Henry and William Newell to 335, and Oscar Lejeunesse to 336.

England, roughly two-thirds the size of Minnesota in land area, had only a few permanent air bases before the war. To make room for dozens of additional temporary airfields, estates and farms were taken over and many homes and other privately owned buildings were acquisitioned by the government for military use.

The 4th Fighter Group's base at Debden, in Essex County, was situated on what was once farmland owned by A.C. Kettley. In 1934, as England began preparing for war, Kettley was forced to sell his farm to the Royal Air Force for use as an airdrome, and when the 4th Fighter Group was mobilized in autumn of 1942, the RAF turned it over to them.

March 10, 1944

Dear Folks & Bro. John,

I have just arrived at a new station and I'll scribble you a few lines tonight so you'll get my new address soon. I have written you a V-Mail also which you may get before this.

I consider myself a very lucky guy to land in this Squadron. It's the oldest American fighter unit in England. It was the famed "Eagle Sqd." I don't think I need to say more. These boys really know their business and they are a swell bunch. This squadron just started using the plane I fly so I have a lot more time in the plane than the older boys but there is a he__ of a lot I can learn from them on other things. By the way, I do hope you have the radio working or have a newspaper cause we are making history over here and if you can hear reports on what "my plane" is doing you will get a picture of my activities.

This station is known as the best in England as far as personal comforts go. We live in regular hotels with steam heat, bathrooms, etc. Our mess hall has the air of a banquet hall - white linen tablecloths and more silverware than I quite know how to use. We also have pretty civilian girl waitresses which adds spice to things (Ha).

I'll write again very soon and give you more detail. Right now that big soft bed in my room looks very inviting. We rode all day on the train. I had the misfortune of being placed in charge of the group and it was my duty to see that we caught the right trains, etc. We only changed trains nine times so you can see the job I had. The English do things backwards and their method of train travel is no exception. No, I'm tired!

Bye for now,
Love to all, Don

Donald was joining the Fourth just as it was about to achieve fame as the highest-scoring fighter group in the war. Between March 5th and April 24th, their destruction of 323 enemy aircraft would earn them a Distinguished Unit Citation.

The combat exploits of a number of its aces were elevating them to near star status, and while Gentile, Godfrey, Goodson, Hofer and Beeson were elbowing each other for the top spots, many others — such as Glover, McKennon, Montgomery, Carpenter, Norley, Anderson, Megura, Millikan, Schlegel and Hively — were hot on their heels.

If the pilots of the 4th were acquiring the reputation of being "snotty prima donnas" it was entirely understandable. As the oldest American fighter group, "the spearhead of the world's mightiest air force," they were constantly in the spotlight and popular with the news media. Visited by an incessant parade of royalty, high-ranking dignitaries and Hollywood entertainers — including Bob Hope! — the boys ensconced in the "Country Club of the Air Force" were the darlings of the ETO.

March 13, 1944

Dear Folks & Bro. John,

It's 8:00 in the evening and I just returned from the Mess after eating dinner. We had ice cream for dessert. Things aren't too bad when we can still enjoy America's favorite dish.

Incidently dessert in English circles is known as a "sweet." The first time a waitress in our Mess asked me if I wanted my "sweet now," I didn't know what the heck she was talking about. Not wanting to show my ignorance or embarrass her, I simply said "yes" and found out soon enough what "sweet" was.

I am in a district of larger scale farming than I've seen before in England. Tractors and power machinery are quite prevalent and I am seriously considering offering my services to some farmer when I get a leave. They could use the help and I'd rather enjoy it. It's not an original idea as others have been doing it.

I guess I told you in my other letter what a wonderful station this is. This is a comparatively old air station built on peacetime standards for the R.A.F. When the "Eagle Squadron" of volunteer Americans was formed, they were very welcome guests and as such were given one of the nicest air fields in England to operate off of. Since then the Eagle Sqd. has exchanged their R.A.F. uniforms for U.S. army uniforms and has become a part of the 8th Air Force. Those boys still wear their R.A.F. cloth wings along with our silver wings. The small number of us who just were assigned to this outfit are slightly conspicuous because we are the first American pilots here and of course we don't wear the R.A.F. wings. We were given a very hearty welcome when we got here and they made us feel right at home. After they found out we had a lot of time and training in "Mustangs" they asked us questions about the plane, etc. They are all a swell bunch and darned good pilots or they wouldn't be here cause they are all veterans of a good many combat missions. In those days we didn't have air supremacy over Europe that we have now. I am *enclosing a clipping that I cut from today's "Yank" about our commanding officer. As I said before, I'm a lucky pilot to get in such an outfit as this.*

My love to you all,
Your Son & Bro., Donald

P.S. We have eggs (fresh) for breakfast every morning. Eggs are rare indeed in England but this place has its own chicken farm. I think that's one for the books!

Mr. Kettley's farm had become something of a self-contained municipality, now populated by well over a thousand humans and several dogs. There were more than two hundred officers — between 100 and 125 of them pilots, and except for a few civilian employees the rest were enlisted military personnel on permanent assignment.

Debden had its own theater, where touring USO shows and stage plays were performed and the latest American films were shown. And out on the airfield each of the three squadrons had its own huge hangar, runway and maintenance buildings; pilots could always be found in the dispersal hut — swapping war stories, or just reading and relaxing, while a big console phonograph perpetually droned out plaintive melodies.

The stately brick Officers' Club in the center of the grounds was the hub of the more discriminate socializing, and within its high-ceilinged, gleaming wood-trimmed walls, the pilots were treated like members of an exclusive fraternity, which they indeed were. The large parlor with its open fireplace was next to a beautiful formal dining room where all meals were served, and in this posh atmosphere the newly appointed rubbed shoulders with seasoned Eagles and Top Brass, and juggled the profusion of china and silver essential to the art of gracious dining.

Down the hall were a lounge and a game room, where they'd mingle more casually after dinner. At the bar they could listen to the old hands reliving perilous forays, and join them in rousing toasts to victories, or respectfully raise their glasses in solemn salutes to those who hadn't made it back.

If they were lucky, Mac, the honky-tonk piano player-in-residence might be in the mood to entertain. Pierce McKennon, a classically trained pianist turned fighter pilot, had been musically transformed at Debden, and except for his soulful early morning overtures of "The Old Rugged Cross" before flying off on missions, he stuck pretty faithfully to plunking out the best boogie-woogie and blues heard in all of Limeyland.

Chuck Konsler, a 334 pilot, remembered there was usually a poker game or two going on until the wee hours of the morning, along with an incidental dice game. The frequent announcement over the loudspeaker, "THERE WILL BE A SMALL GAME IN THE GAME ROOM," meant they were looking for a few players to shoot craps. (And he distinctly remembered looking down at the thumbprint-sized mole on the back of the neck of the dice-throwing Don Emerson.)

March 15, 1944

Dear Sis Eleanor,

To give you an idea of what nice living quarters we have I'll just describe my room. I have a room to myself which I like. I like privacy occasionally - for instance I can write a much better letter when there is no one around to bother me. About my room - I have a very comfortable bed with a thick mattress and sheets, etc. I have a dresser with a large mirror and plenty of drawers. I also have a wall closet with more room than necessary for my clothes. I have a nice writing desk and a wash basin with a mirror above it also. The room has steam heat and carpeting on the floor. Just across the hall is a complete bathroom. A civilian caretaker, called a "batman" comes in and keeps the place clean. He gently wakes us up in the morning and shines our shoes, makes the bed up, etc. This applies only to officers' quarters of course but the enlisted men have nice brick barracks to live in which is a heck of a lot better than the "Nissen huts" and tents that most of our men over here have to live in. Outside of the fact that we are in combat, to say that we have it nice would be putting it mildly.

You know it seems as if I've been getting the "breaks" ever

since I got in the army. With God's help let's hope I still keep
getting them!

Love, Donald

Donald and Don Patchen, by then best buddies, had acquired a
pair of English bikes, speeding their sight-seeing treks during the
almost leisurely first few days spent at Debden. The pace was
about to change. In just a matter of days they would be flying
into combat, and then they'd find out for themselves how fast
they "could work up a sweat in 25 degree weather," as Patchen
vividly told it, "by going down the runway with a full load of
ammo and an overload of fuel, and telling the 'ole girl' it was
time to spread her wings and fly because the right hand turn at
the end of the runway was fast approaching!"

They had been at Debden a whole week before their first
squadron mate was lost. Without seeing any action themselves,
their crash course in combat began, and the tarnished flip side of
the lustrous life of a fighter pilot was exposed. During a bomber
escort mission the Group came out on top during a mammoth
shoot-out in the sky with the Germans, smartly out-scoring them
thirteen to one. But this game was for keeps, and Ernest Skilton
lost his life when the Germans shot him down.

March 17, 1944

Dear Folks & Bro. John,

Well big brother, I received a letter from you today so I
guess that calls for an answer. Incidently the letter was
dated Feb. 28th.

You asked me to confirm a little information that you had
picked up on the P-51. Well it has extremely long range but
firepower was not sacrificed to accomplish this. True it
doesn't have quite the firepower of the P-47 but we spout lead
at the rate of 3200 .50 cal. slugs a minute. It may interest
you to know that we carry 62 barrels of fuel. It's a dream of a
plane and it would take pages to tell you why and not being a
pilot there are many points that you wouldn't fully appreciate.

I spent a lot of time in the air today. It's the policy of our
squadron to fly as much as possible. The more time spent

practice flying the better the results. Instrument flying is
very important cause we are in the clouds half the time.
Maybe you will hesitate to believe this but we do fly formations
in clouds. It makes you sweat like hell and takes plenty of
nerve but it's done by flying so darn close (3-5 ft.) that you
can still see the silhouette of the wing of the other plane. The
reason we have to do this is because we usually have to climb
up through 5-10,000 ft. of clouds before breaking out on top
and if we didn't stay together we would be scattered all over
and probably not find each other again. You know of course
that fighters work in groups and stay together at all times.

Love to all, Don

The status of a missing pilot was not always immediately known,
and until it was, he was simply listed NYR — not yet returned.
If there were no eyewitness or radioed reports, the possibilities
were many. He could be alive and well, wounded or dead. Did
he end up somewhere else okay — or did he crash? If he had a
chance to bail out, did he make it out safely, or was he injured or
killed? Downed over water, would he be spotted in time and
rescued, or drown? Landing in Nazi-controlled territory, he
might be able to evade the enemy, but most probably he'd be
captured and taken prisoner by them — or worse yet, he might be
caught and executed by bomb-battered, nerve-shattered German
civilians.

If he were harbored by allies, or in the hands of enemies who
played by the rules, word of his fate should eventually trickle
back via the Red Cross. If not, his military unit and family might
never know.

In the meantime, the business of war continued, and before
too much time passed, a cold, terse telegram would be sent to his
next of kin stating at least that he was MIA — missing in action,
and his personal effects would be packed up and shipped home.
And soon another fresh-faced young pilot would come to take his
place at the table, and sleep in his empty bed.

On Donald's first mission, March 18th, the Group put on quite a
show. Encountering more than 60 enemy fighters jumping the

American bombers, they destroyed a total of 12 German planes that day, for a loss of only two of their own. His squadron's participation alone must have given him quite a jolt. Goodson and Carlson swooped down to strafe some German bombers on the ground, and Blakeslee and Gentile locked horns with six enemy fighters, shooting down two of them. Of the 336 Squadron pilots who returned to England after the mission, Donald was the last straggler. More than half an hour after Blakeslee landed at Debden, Donald set down at another airfield. No explanation was noted.

Woodrow Sooman had to turn back due to engine problems, but was still in Germany when he was forced to bail out and become a POW. Edward Freeburger died when he was shot down by a German pilot.

Donald's second mission, a fighter sweep into Germany, was less eventful. Zero destroyed. Zero lost. But on the third, a fighter sweep of German airfields in France, 20 enemy aircraft were destroyed to a loss of seven of the Group's own. Along with that expected mayhem, Lt. Emerson was able to confirm Lt. Braley's claim of strafing a hangar, and scaring a horse and wagon out of it. It was also reported with some relief that the horse appeared to be okay.

Though wounded, James Dye got back to the base. Seven others were lost, mostly due to flak. William Hawkins bailed out and was able to evade the enemy; Alexander Rafalovich, Kenneth Smith, Robert Williams and Earle Carlow all bailed out and were taken to prison camp — Carlow later escaped and made it back to England. James Brandenburg and Joseph Goetz were both killed.

March 21, 1944

Dear Folks & Bro. John,

I've been a darn busy pilot since I came to this squadron. We are on the go every day and our missions last as long as six hours and better. That's a long time to be strapped in one position! The old seat starts to hurt at the end of 3-4 hours and after that it gets numb and you don't feel anything. I'd like to give you details but to do so would take a book length letter and a lot of it would come under the heading of confidential stuff. That's sort of an excuse on my part but not altogether. Today I covered land in the country that Tom was in but we were about 500 miles south of where he was. We usually do what long-range fighters were intended to do but not today. When we get back to the base everyone gets a double shot of whiskey. I'm not a drinking man (boy) but that's one time I accept it and not because I want to get intoxicated!

Love, Don

By the end of Donald's first week in active combat, he had gone on fighter sweep missions in France — where his Uncle Tom Roswell had served during World War One, had been on Blakeslee-led escort missions all the way to Berlin, as well as to Schweinfurt, where American bombers steadily pounded the center of Germany's ball bearing production. It was believed the war rolled on ball bearings and the destruction of these factories would stop Germany in its tracks.

This intensive on-the-job training was giving the new pilots a good look at some of the air war's highlights. Flak, the armour-piercing fire from anti-aircraft guns on the ground was ever present; at altitude its innocuous appearance as soft and colorful, fluffy puffballs belied its lethal impact. Frequently Axis and Allied airplanes could be seen crashing or exploding in mid-air, then spiraling or plunging to earth. They'd pray all airmen would have a chance to escape, and then they'd see those who broke free tumble from their disabled craft, some softly drifting earthward like pale, silken blossoms, and others, nipped in the bud, plummeting unopened.

On March 27th, on his sixth mission, Donald drilled his first enemy target. After the escorted bombers dumped their loads on a German airdrome in France, the fighters dropped down to strafe a large number of planes left on the ground, demolishing 23 of them. He and Maj. Jim Clark shared the credit for one of the Ju88s destroyed. An anti-aircraft gunner's flak brought down one of the 4th's pilots. Archie Chatterley bailed out over enemy territory and was captured.

By the end of March, four additional pilots were lost. Glenn

Smart safely bailed out when his engine died; he was rescued from the North Sea. Raymond Clotfelter, Kenneth Peterson and William Newell were shot out of the sky — all three bailed out safely and surrendered to the Germans; Peter Lehman, scion of the New York banking family, was killed in a flying accident. And one of the Group's most tragic losses occurred when Edward Brettell, its first POW, was executed by the Germans. One of 76 prisoners involved in "The Great Escape" from Stalag Luft III, he was among the 50 recaptured officers shot by a firing squad.

April 1, 1944

Dearest Mom, Dad & Bro. John,

I have forgotten when I wrote to you last as it's quite a few days ago. I haven't written anybody so I just have to scribble a few lines tonight. I'm on the go darn steady and usually don't feel one bit like writing. Getting enough sleep is very important - to go on a mission feeling drowsy is next to suicide. These long trips are pretty rough. When I got back to England today I landed at the first air drome I came to with only ten minutes of gas left. We must have run into some strong head winds on the way home from Germany cause it took us longer than usual.

I guess you will be interested in knowing that I got my first "Jerry" on the 27th of March. It was "Junkers 88" which is a twin engine combination fighter and light bomber. I fired 320 rounds of ammunition before it started to burn like the devil. I won $40 on that too. All of us who didn't have any destroyed to their credit contributed to a pool to be won by the first guy to get a "destroyed." Incidently this group set a new record over here this month by destroying 154 German planes and damaging a great many more. I couldn't have possibly landed in a better fighter group than this!

I was in London on business one day and got a general idea of the city. There is a sharp contrast to our cities in that there are no buildings higher than 10 stories. It struck me as a depressing place but of course it's very old and it was a very dull day. By the way - I saw Berlin before I really saw London!

You see in local flying over here we stay away from the London area for various reasons.

I am getting your letters regular - the latest one dated March 18th, which is pretty fast service considering. Keep them coming - every one of them helps my morale a heap. My morale is not very low tho - I'm quite happy even if I am working harder than I have for some time.

I wrote to Phil Kiner and got an answer the other day. He's attached to the air corps at a field and if I get the chance I'll take my "kite" and fly over to see him.

I sent home $600.00 today. It will reach you in the form of a war department check and is made out direct to you John. Put it in your account. I have no "will" so I don't want an account of my own. Feel free to dig into it if you need it. Spring is just around the corner and I remember how cash seems to be scarce about that time.

I'll write whenever I can but that may not be too often.

Love to you all, Don

P.S. I wish I could send you something for Mother's Day, Mom. I send you my love tho and wish you the best of everything!

Phil Kiner's letter to Donald had revealed where he was stationed as a radio repairman with the Ninth Air Force. Army censors had caught this indiscretion and Phil was disciplined for the disclosure. In any event, Donald's participation in combat was becoming so taxing that he never did get around to dropping in on Phil.

During missions in April, the Group was racking up some stunning daily totals, with as many as 20, 30, even 40 and more planes destroyed in a single day, but nine more of their own were lost before Donald wrote home again.

Charles Carr, Allan Bunte, Robert Hughes, Howard Moulton, David Van Epps and Duane Beeson — one of the finest pilots in the war, and the first in the 4th FG to become an ace — would all sit out the rest of the war in prison camp. Frank Boyles and Robert Claus were both killed during a big air fight over Germany, and squadron mate Robert Hobert was downed in the cold North Sea. After several hours Hobert was found and rescued but, extremely debilitated, later died from the exposure.

April 9, 1944

Dear Folks & Bro. John,

I guess it's about time I scribbled off a few lines to you again. We have been taking it easy all day for a change. We were supposed to go out again this morning but something came up and the mission was canceled. That didn't make me a bit unhappy cause I wanted to go to Easter chapel service anyway. We have been at it pretty steady - hardly miss a day.

One of these days you will be reading about a new fighter ace who just lately boosted his score to a record high of 30 German planes destroyed. He is Capt. Don Gentile and I'm proud to be flying in the same squadron with him. He had 14 to his credit when I came here and has really been going to town lately. The news-reel cameramen have been here all day taking pictures of him. I am sending a clipping taken from a London paper telling about a little expedition we went on the other day. This Gentile got five Jerry planes that day. I was flying with him and didn't do so bad myself. I destroyed two and damaged a couple others. Our squadron hit this airdrome and left just about every plane on it in flames. Incidently a plane destroyed on the ground counts as much as one in the air. Altogether I have three to my credit now.

I'm glad to hear Lela is going to help you again this summer. Incidently I got an Easter card from her this morning. Sort of a coincidence that I should receive it on exactly the right day. I haven't any other news. I would like to give you more details on my activities but I might say too much.

Love to you all, Don

On April 11th, Eisenhower, along with Gen. James Doolittle and other honchos from the Eighth Air Force, arrived at Debden. Ike personally decorated Don Blakeslee and Don Gentile, awarding each a DSC — the Distinguished Service Cross, the highest award after the Medal of Honor — for heroic achievements and prowess in combat — Blakeslee for leading the top fighter group, and Gentile for destroying 30 enemy planes.

Two days later, as he came over the field after a mission, Gentile could not resist making a little curtain call for the still-rolling cameras of the press. Unfortunately, he bowed a little too deep, caught the ground with his Mustang's propeller and smashed up the plane.

Blakeslee forgave no one — not even his star ace — for "pranging a kite," and in another two weeks, his stellar combat career over, Gentile was on his way back to the States, where he'd team up again with Johnny Godfrey — this time for the purpose of touting the Army Air Forces on an extensive publicity tour.

There was no pause in the offensive action for the reception of guests — however distinguished — and in the five missions surrounding all this hoopla, the 4th destroyed 59 more enemy aircraft, most of them in massive strafing attacks on airfields, averaging the loss of just one pilot per mission. Joseph Bennett broke his shoulder when he ran into something in a cloud; he jumped out and was rescued from the North Sea. Vasseure Wynn was shot down in a dogfight and Raymond Care had to bail out; both survived and were imprisoned. Clemens Fiedler was shot down in France, Ralph Saunders went down in Holland, and Robert Seifert had to jump out over the North Sea; all three of these men died.

On April 18th, following a bomber support mission to Berlin, and through flak that was reported to be "very rough," numerous fighters went down to strafe several German air dromes on the way back. Millikan, VanWyk, Emerson and Logan "fired on many ships" — 190s and 109s at Wenzendorf, and along with Bob Nelson, who destroyed a 109 near Genthin, they accounted for their squadron's share of the enemy aircraft claimed that day.

The 109 Donald destroyed had exploded beneath him, blowing jagged fragments of aluminum sheeting and its factory nameplate into his Mustang; he had to fly another P-51 on the next day's mission while his plane was picked clean of the metal debris.

Grover Hall, public relations officer for the 4th, wasted no time in alerting the press, and Donald's home town area newspapers had the story of the "Pembina man," and the "North Dakota Flier" in print the following week, complete with this quote from Lt. Emerson: "He blew up in a hundred pieces! One lodged in my air scoop and I brought it home with me."

The Group destroyed 19 that day — some in the air and some on the ground. At least two of its three pilots lost were downed while dogfighting. George Carpenter shot down two before being shot down himself, to be captured by the Germans. Victor France died when his plane hit the ground while chasing a 109, and Lloyd Henry was shot down and killed sometime during the action.

Of necessity, the pilots soon became hardened to reality, and victories and losses were reported as well as received with increasingly taut levels of emotion. Combat duties had adversely affected Donald's bent for letter writing, and now with Elinor in the picture, what letter-writing loyalties and energies he had left were divided. As his letters home became less frequent, his mother began corresponding with Elinor, and in anxious tones begged her for any additional crumbs of information.

During the last 12 days of April, 52 enemy aircraft were destroyed to a loss of just eight. On a fighter sweep into Germany on April 22, the Group pounced down on more than 20 German 109s at 8,000 ft., with 336 Sqd. being credited with 14 of the 17 downed that day. Willard Millikan got four single-handedly, Johnny Godfrey shot down three, Louis Norley and Blakeslee got two apiece, and Donald and Kendall Carlson shared credit for one. Even though this was his first aerial victory, Donald took his time in writing home about it.

Only one of their own pilots was brought down that day. Robert Nelson bailed out and landed in a tree after his engine failed during a skirmish. He evaded the enemy for four days, living off the land, so to speak, until he was captured. When his fellow inmates learned what he had eaten to sustain himself, they began calling him "Buffalo Grass."

Others downed and taken prisoner of war during April's last days were Milton Scarbrough, Paul Riley, John Barden and Pete Kennedy. Forced by flak to bail out over German-occupied France, Fred Glover got back to England with the help of the

French Resistance Forces. Charles Anderson and Thomas Biel were both shot down and killed.

April 29th

Dear Folks & Bro. John,

It's so long since I last wrote that I imagine you will be a little worried by the time you receive this. I don't feel much like writing tonight either but I just have to scribble you and Sis a few lines. I usually go to bed at night as soon as possible but most of the time that isn't too early. It's daylight here now 'til 10:30 in the evening and we can and do fly that late. I'm sure that from what you hear in the news that you can realize what the air force is being called upon to do over here at the present time. I do not wish to be guilty of disclosing military information so I can't give you any detail. I know that the newspapers seem to give a lot of information on our activities but the army frowns upon anything of that nature written in letters - and I'm not going to argue! Incidently officers' mail is subject to spot censorship - just for curiosity's sake, have any of my letters been opened?

I got the paper and birthday card you sent. Thanks ever so much! I hope you won't mind if I use it mostly to write to "her" with. She's probably wondering what's happened to me also cause I just haven't done any letter writing lately at all.

I imagine you'll soon be making the dust fly at spring work. The other day I was just thinking of all the farm work I could do with all that H.P. in the nose of my plane. I just had a new engine put in - after so many hours we change engines even if the old one still seems to be in good condition.

Bye for now,

All my love,

Don

UNDER THE EAGLE SQUADRON SCOREBOARD
Col. Blakeslee (standing) with (from left) Tussey, Patchen, Benjamin, Emerson,
Goodson, Hobert and MacCarteney [D. Groomer]

Hughes, Carlson, Emerson, Patchen & Gentile in front of Godfrey's Mustang
[E. Houston]

"The Blakeslee Briefing" [D. Groomer]

Bob Wehrman

Frank Speer

Sy Koenig &
Chuck Konsler

Bob Nelson with Frank Blankschaen & "Pip Squeak"

Escape Kit photo for use in forging ID

Prisoner-taking practice [F. Grove]

DISPERSAL HUT SCENES

Reading & relaxing (Godfrey leaning against wall, Nelson slouched in chair)

Goodson holding forth (Donald far right, Gentile & Patchen at table)

Aces Beeson, Megura, Gentile, Godfrey & Goodson playing cards

Don Pierini

Doug Groshong

Joe Joiner

Pierini & Joiner at 336 Ops.

Francis "Lefty" Grove

May opened with Donald leading a section for the first time. His squadron sent up 15 planes that day, making the last of its four sections — the Green, led by Donald — one short; Joe Higgins flew as his #2 and Don Patchen was #3. Protecting bombers from a squadron of German fighters on the attack, the Group countered by chasing down and destroying four of them at no cost to themselves.

Deplorable weather limited the fighters' participation for the next few days, and a flying accident a few miles from base was the cause of their only loss in the first week of May. Ralph Boyce died when he crashed trying to land after a training flight.

Donald's third month at Debden began with a ground-strafing mission in France on May 9th; four pilots went down. Lloyd Waterman, Robert Sherman, Vernon Burroughs and Herbert Blanchfield all became German prisoners of war. Within a few days a second squadron friend, Robert Tussey, was forced to bail out into the North Sea, and although he was quickly fished out, he died from his injuries.

Hobert and Tussey had both been either section or flight leaders, leaving a couple of big holes to be filled, and Donald was ready to advance. C.J. Hein, 336 Squadron's Adjutant, said that while he and the other permanent personnel made a conscious effort to keep an emotional distance from the pilots "...because they could be gone overnight," he remembered one thing about Donald — that although new pilots did not often gain immediate acceptance from the Group, word was soon out that Emerson would be a good one, because he was a very good pilot and he liked combat flying.

On May 13th, when the Group's job was to give bomber support in the area of Poznan, Poland, the first of Donald's Craig Field classmates lost his life. How his plane became disabled is unknown, but Leonard "Pappy" Pierce bailed out over the North Sea. He was spotted struggling in the water with his parachute, but drowned before he could reach his dinghy and be picked up by rescuers.

Emerson and Patchen had both been on the mission when Pappy Pierce was lost, and war's wretchedness was hitting ever closer to their hearts. After completing about 30 missions apiece they were badly in need of a break. They spent the following weekend in London, "celebrating" Donald's 21st birthday. In some ways this holiday was not so very different from their lark in New York; they were still wide-eyed country boys looking over one of the world's largest cities, but now both tourists and sites were war scarred, and somewhat lacking in gaiety and innocence.

They found London rather frightening, and were glad to get back "home" to Debden. Don Patchen flew with the Group on bomber escort duty to Berlin on May 19th, a mission that did not include Donald. The flak was reported as "very bad" 30,000 ft. over Berlin, and some of it punctured the engine of Patchen's Mustang. He was last seen bailing out over Hanover, and appeared to have hit the ground okay.

Patchen didn't know exactly what happened, or how he escaped death. He just remembered the sounds of his plane's dying engine and the wind, and his seemingly futile efforts to get out. The next thing he knew everything was beautifully quiet, and he could see the earth below dressed in its spring finery as he floated in his chute, rip cord in hand, his plane in flames on the ground.

Although a telegram reporting Lt. Patchen MIA was received by his mother after about a week, and in another month she'd have word that her son was alive and a prisoner of war, news of his plight did not make it back to all of his comrades. His assistant crew chief, George Anderson, believed he had been killed — until he met up with him at a reunion many years after the war.

Also thinking that Patchen was probably dead, Donald took the loss very hard and stayed off operational flying for a couple more days. He used this time to prepare his friend's personal belongings for shipment home to Patchen's mother in Bainbridge, New York, sending along some photographs of 336 Squadron showing the two friends together.

May 21st

Dear Mom, Dad & Bro. John,

It's high time I was writing again. Somehow I'm getting so I detest letter writing. I usually don't feel much like it and then there isn't too much to write about. I have written a lot more to you in my letters than I really should have. It may seem quite harmless but we are not supposed to write anything which would give away our activity.

I just came back from London where Lt. Patchen, a friend of mine, and I spent a three-day leave. It was the first leave from duty which we have had since we came here. We stayed at a hotel, saw the sights and in general took life easy. We have been going pretty strong and the rest was welcome.

London does not appeal to me as a city in the least. Except for the bomb damage, I would say the city looks now as it did 100 years ago. One afternoon we hired a guide and had an enjoyable time sight-seeing. We saw and visited Buckingham Palace, St. Paul's Cathedral, the parliament buildings, Westminster Abbey, London Tower - also "The Eagle Hut" which Tom told me he stayed at for a couple of weeks in 1917 - and many other places and buildings with interesting backgrounds.

In this letter I am enclosing a clipping from a British magazine telling a little about this outfit. They gave us a rather impressive write-up but it's not exaggerated. The picture of the drop fuel tanks may interest you too.

Also I am enclosing a piece of scrap metal which is a very small part of what I brought home with me one day. Refer to the piece in the Grand Forks Herald about me.

When I came back from London I found out I had been promoted to 1st Lieutenant. I was recommended for it some time ago and after going through the official channels it came thru.

The last letter I got from you was dated May 7th.

Bye for now-

Love, Don

P.S. The increase in rank gives me $40 more pay per month.

After landing unhurt near a Wehrmacht Army outpost, Don Patchen would be unexpectedly grateful to be captured by German soldiers. He hadn't noticed that the excited band of farmers — whom he'd at first guilelessly thought were running toward him to offer food and refuge — had expressions and intentions as steely and deadly as the long-tined pitchforks they were brandishing, and they meant to retaliate for the demolition of a perfectly good crop of wheat. He had time for only a flicker of fear before he was plucked from the angry mob by the more sportsmanly professionals — rescued by his captors.

Other than that, he did not remember being afraid of the Germans at any time, and he gave no thought just then to the loss of freedom or the general deprivation he'd surely suffer as a prisoner. Their interrogation of him was not harsh — almost dispassionate, since he hadn't been around long enough to have any information they didn't already know. But as a typical fighter pilot he had taken such great pride in his job as escort and protector, and was so eagerly awaiting his anticipated part in the imminent invasion of France, that what he remembered most about his capture was hearing the beautiful voices of the German soldiers joined in harmonious singing as they drilled outside... while he languished under lock and key, feeling sorely dis- appointed he'd been taken out of the fight, and so very sorry he'd let everybody down.

He would spend the remainder of the war in various German prison camps, the main one Stalag Luft III in Sagan, where he'd meet up with other 4th Fighter Group pilots — including the recently captured Maj. Carpenter, who would be his barracks commander. Already checked in next door was Craig Field classmate, Bob Planck, who had been brought down the month before by cannon fire from an Me 109. When he had attempted to bail out of his Mustang, his foot got caught in the cockpit. He was riding the plane down in a fatal dive when, miraculously, he got loose without a second to spare. His parachute had barely opened before he hit the ground, and the bone-bruising impact seriously injured his legs.

On Donald's first mission after the loss of his friend, Col. Blakeslee led the Group, with Donald flying in his section. After this six and a half hour flight, Donald appeared to be back to normal, but something about him had changed. It was soon noticed by those closest to him that his natural aggressiveness was now tinged with a more meaningful and vengeful purpose, and with renewed dedication he meant to hunt down and destroy the enemy.

In the next two weeks his group's efforts were very productive, with the number of enemy aircraft destroyed four times that of their losses. Willard Millikan and Sam Young were captured after their planes collided and crashed while dodging flak. Three pilots were shot down by Allied aircrew gunners: Nicholas "Cowboy" Megura became an internee in Sweden, Carroll McElroy a POW, and Robert Homuth died. Elliot Shapleigh evaded after bailing out when his plane developed mechanical problems, and Robert Kackerback crashed and died during routine training. Thomas McDill and Joseph Bennett were downed in a dogfight over France and were taken prisoner; the same happened to Aubrey Hewatt in Germany. Strafing attacks made flak victims of Frank Speer and William Hunt. Speer evaded capture for several days, and months later would escape. Hunt did not survive. Richard Bopp also went down to become a POW, and Harry Jennings and Mark Kolter were killed in the skies over Germany.

I kept a smaller black and white photograph of Donald on my desk; I looked at it whenever I tried to write about him. It was not the posed picture I remembered looking at as a child, but I liked it even more.

He had just landed after a mission, thrown back the canopy of his Mustang and ripped off his oxygen mask and headgear. Still strapped inside the cockpit, he was writing in his logbook; he had looked up as the camera caught him off guard. His hair was tousled and his face creased from the mask. He no longer looked quite so young and innocent, and there was evidence of a worldly weariness in eyes that now looked straight at me.

My three grown children would sometimes wander in and out while I worked. Their reactions were as varied as their person-alities.

"Still writing about Donald?" or "How's it going?" they would ask.

"Um-hmm," I'd mumble in answer. "I wonder if I'll ever be finished."

"What's it going to be — a book? A screenplay?"

"She's writing a war book."

"It is NOT a war book!" I said rather defensively. "It's just about my uncle—"

"Yeah, your uncle who was in the war. A WAR BOOK! I'm surprised at you — I thought if you ever wrote anything, it would be something like Bombeck."

"What more is there to be said about laundry?" I asked.

"What more is there to be said about war?" they countered.

"IT IS NOT A WAR BOOK!"

"I can see it all now — you'll go really weird on us — start running around in military uniforms, camouflage fatigues—"

"I do have that plastic army helmet I bought at a garage sale," I considered.

"Is this him sitting in the plane?"

"Uh-huh, he's writing in his log book after a mission."

"He was a good looking guy — nice mouth, great lips! WHY COULDN'T I HAVE GOTTEN LIPS LIKE THAT?"

"Life's a grab bag," I philosophized. "You might have his nose, sort of."

"Say...is that a leather bomber jacket he's wearing?"

"Not here; he had one, though, I'm sure. Grandma has the 'Donald Duck' patch that was on it."

"Really? Do you suppose the jacket could still be around somewhere with the rest of his stuff?"

"I don't think so."

Grave robbers. One kid wanted his jacket, and another one wanted his lips.

Boy, Donald, your story is getting written just in time; you were one generation away from oblivion. Your brother's and sister's stories have been secured for another three generations — both Ma and Uncle John have great-grandchildren. I guess I wanted to find a way of giving you a little more life somehow, even if it could only be on paper.

Hmmmmmm... a screenplay, huh? I'd want Candice Bergen to play me — unless it's a musical — then, maybe Bette Midler.

I AM SUCH AN IDIOT! I was barely in this story. My part would be played by some bald-headed, long-legged baby.

I was getting ahead of myself, too. I had no idea what I was writing; I only knew it was NOT going to be a war book.

Chapter Seven   *D-Day, Donald Duck & the DFC*

The Allies continued their advances in the Pacific, and the bombing offensive against Germany was rapidly gaining momentum. With the protection of their long-range fighter escorts, the heavy bombers were moving farther into enemy territory to strike new targets, and by the summer of 1944, the Allies had achieved air superiority over the Germans.

The plan to take back France had now been delayed more than two years. The enormous amount of preparation needed to accumulate the necessary material and manpower and to coordinate activities of the land, sea and air forces made the invasion the high point of the war. The date for this operation, code named "Overlord," was finally set, and Eisenhower was again chosen to command. With 11,000 aircraft from the Allied countries ready to take part, Ike assured the ground troops that any planes seen overhead that day would be ours.

Capt. Otey Glass arrived at Debden's gate the evening of June 5th. He had grown tired of his Stateside job as a flight instructor and had jumped at the chance to get into the real action. Riding in the back seat of a plane with fledgling birdmen at the controls could be a task with catastrophic consequences — increasing the appeal of combat flying, and when a call went out for volunteers, Otey had signed up for overseas duty. Then, leaving his wife and baby daughter back home in Virginia, he came with a large group of former instructors to England as replacement pilots. The army was preparing for the possibility of heavy losses surrounding

D-Day and after.

All aspects of the planned invasion were surrounded by strictest security. When Otey's detachment was met by troops with machine guns, he knew something was up, and then he saw the ground crews painting the broad black and white invasion stripes on the wings and fuselages of the group's Mustangs.

At 2000 hours (8 PM) Col. Blakeslee briefed his pilots, telling them that he was prepared to lose the entire Group. At 3 AM they were ready to go, and twenty minutes later Donald had taken flight on the first of the Group's numerous fighter sweep, patrol, and bombing missions for that "longest day." By late evening the Allied invaders had established a foothold on the beaches of Normandy, and the contest for France was on.

Although D-Day was supposedly the turning point in the war, it proved to be surprisingly anti-climactic for the fighter pilots of the 4th. Expecting to encounter all-out opposition from enemy fighters, they instead found very little, and the Group destroyed only four enemy planes the first day.

Of their own ten pilots who were downed, Harold Fredericks made it back to England; Thomas Fraser and Oscar Lejeunesse were taken POW. The other seven lost their lives. Cecil Garbey, Bernard McGrattan, Harold Ross, Jr. and Walter Smith — 335 Squadron's entire Blue Section — were caught in low clouds and killed when they were shot down by enemy aircraft. The fatal elements in the loss of Michael McPharlin, Mike "The Pole" Sobanski and Edward Steppe were unclear.

The Group continued its air support of the invasion, and Donald would log eight missions during D-Day operations — two the first day. The third day, June 8th, he was given one of the new P-51D model Mustangs which had just begun arriving: serial #44-13317. On a fighter bomber escort mission to LeMans, France, his squadron targeted a transformer station at LeTheil. He made a direct hit.

June 9th

Dear Folks & Bro. John,

I have heard that our mail home has been held up so I don't imagine you have heard from me for some time. Come to think of it, it is some time since I have written too - around May 20th, I believe. I'm getting so I hate letter writing cause I usually haven't the time or energy. From the news I'm sure you know how intense our activity has been the past month. In the month of May I put in over 100 hours of combat time over Europe and I was off duty five days on "leave." Due to present activities we are usually near the point of exhaustion when night comes but I don't mind as long as I can take it physically cause I feel we can't do too much to help the boys who are slugging it out on the ground. Your imagination or the news would tell you what our job is at the moment. We took off in the dark that first morning and were over France before daybreak. I'm glad I was able to take part in that long-awaited day. Colossal is about the best word to describe it.

Mom is right about the money I'm sending home. I do not want it sunk in war bonds or anything like that. If you do not wish to put it in with your account you may put it in a safety box as you suggested. By all means cash the checks - I don't think they're any good after a year. Since my promotion to 1st Lt. I am making close to $300 a month, but there are certain expenses taken out and also the $37.50 for the war bond.

The 29th of last month I shot down a German plane which was in the act of attacking a box of bombers so I have six destroyed. Due to our work now, the chance to shoot down enemy planes may not present itself as often. Incidently I am not and never was out to make a record along that line. Naturally whenever the opportunity presents itself, I make the best of it cause that's our job and it's always best for a fighter pilot to be on the offensive and never give the enemy a chance to attack you first. A couple weeks ago I had a new responsibility given me which involves quite a bit of extra work. Each squadron is divided into two flights of 15 pilots each. I have been made a "Flight Commander" and am in charge of one of the flights. I guess there is no harm in putting my best foot forward and I think I have applied myself well since I came here.   As always,

Love, Don

For the day's first mission on June 10, Donald flew his old P-51B #6889 for the last time. His chief mechanic Larry Jones and crew were fine-tuning the P-51D, and distinguishing artwork was being added to personalize it. That afternoon, Frank Caple flew #6889 on his very first mission. He crash-landed somewhere in France, and just four days after his arrival, he became a prisoner of war.

Hundreds of American warplanes had been painted with distinctive designs, making the sky an almost surrealistic gallery of mobile pop art. The front-end sections of bombers and fighters were blank canvasses, willing to accept any conceivable illustration. Disney artists were responsible for some of this "nose art," including the 4th Fighter Group's Eagle logo, but most of the monikers, patriotic emblems, cartoon characters, voluptuous babes, vicious threats, snarling epithets, and ribald remarks embellishing the majority were expressed by the less famous but equally talented artists found among the ground crew.

There were some pilots in the 4th who shunned such ornamentation as frippery, but throughout the Group's service, it accumulated some very interesting examples of nose art. Along with the usual nicknames, sweethearts and wives, there was a parodied preacher, a boxing mule, a kicking jackass, a wild boar, a fighting bumble bee, a termite outfitted for battle, and a few others sporting somewhat less than proper terms and slogans.

There had been two Dons all in favor of such frippery: Emerson and Patchen. As newcomers they had watched a third, Don Allen, a chief mechanic, decorate the new red-nosed P-51Bs of the seasoned pilots, and as soon as they were assigned planes of their own, they put him to work on theirs. Patchen went with the nickname his nieces and nephews called him back home, "Uncle Dunkle." He couldn't remember what Emerson had painted on his, because there hadn't been time to step back and admire it. Before the paint dried they heard from a fourth Don; it seems their creative expressions were premature. Don Blakeslee could ignore — or at least tolerate — the use of nose art by his proven professional pilots, but not by his rookies. Nose art was a privilege they had not yet earned, and the colonel made them remove it.

No one remembered why Donald chose the emblem he had painted on his new plane, but the seed of inspiration may have been planted at the Lindemann home. When her older sister had come home during one of his first visits, Elinor met her at the door to caution her that she was entertaining a suitor in the next room.

"DONALD!" her sister had exclaimed, loudly enough to be heard through a thick wall. "His name is DONALD? That always makes me think of Donald Duck!"

Now, with five shared kills and nearly four dozen combat missions under his belt, Donald's right to nose art was no longer in question. The incomparable Don Allen personalized the new Mustang with Donald's name, the appropriate number of victory crosses, and the fearless image of his cartoon namesake: Donald Duck, dukes up and fighting mad. This bit of whimsy may have been one of the last visible signs of the boy within Donald the man, but his morally starched sister was eternally grateful and proud that he chose a cute cartoon character — instead of a naked lady — for his artistic statement.

With the Luftwaffe in hiding, the Group's missions in the first two weeks of D-Day operations consisted mainly of bombing and strafing of railroads, marshaling yards, truck convoys and bridges in France — the destruction of which, although as important as destroying enemy aircraft, boosted nobody's score. These low-level attacks were extremely dangerous, and despite the absence of enemy fighter intervention, 13 more of their pilots were casualties due to ground fire or flying accidents. George Bowyer, though shot in the arm, made it back. Bob Dickmeyer had a very close call while strafing a train; when on his second, lower pass to finish it off, a boxcar concealing a "buzz bomb" exploded, but he flew out of it unscathed. Eacott Allen and James Glynn evaded capture; Osce Jones, Frank Caple and Robert Little were imprisoned by the Germans; Kenneth Smith, James Scott, James Byrd, Conrad Netting, Harry Noon, Leon Cole, Harvie Arnold and Dean Hill all died.

June 16th

Dear Folks & Bro. John,

Just another note to let you know I'm O.K. The picture I'm
enclosing was taken by a photographer from a British
magazine similar to our "Look." I have no news, at least none
that I can tell. I haven't heard from you since I last wrote. I
may not be able to write again for some time - how long I don't
know. Just don't worry if you don't hear from me.

Love, Donald

Not until June 20th on a target withdrawal support mission into
Germany itself did the Group again encounter enemy fighters. In
an air battle with over 50 fighters, followed by a strafing attack
on an airdrome, they destroyed 15 and lost two of their own. Vol
Harris and Jim Goodson were both shot down and taken prisoner.

Major James A. Goodson was the commanding officer of 336
Squadron. Raven-haired and mustached, this witty sophisticate
was described by Grover Hall, the 4th FG public relations officer,
as having eyebrows arched, physically and mentally. Called
"Goody" by his friends, and dubbed "King of the Strafers" by the
press, the former Eagle Squadron member had destroyed at least
30 enemy aircraft.

Expecting that day's mission to be rather routine, Goodson
recalled that he originally had planned to stay home, allowing
Emerson — now second in command of 336 — his first chance
to lead the squadron. But for some reason Donald hadn't felt
quite up to it, and was concerned that he might let his comrades
down. After talking with him, Goodson had decided to lead the
squadron himself, with Donald taking the #1 position in the Blue
Section.

Whatever Donald's misgivings may have been, he quickly
recovered, because during this mission he shot down a FW 190
— he saw its pilot bail out — and then, while Goodson and
others went down to strafe an airdrome at Neubrandenburg, he
guided the bombers from the target to the coast. Heavy flak
brought down two of the Liberators. No chutes were seen.

But flak brought down Goodson, too, and at age 23, he would
be serving the war in a new capacity. As an imprisoned

American officer, he was to become Camp Adjutant in one of the compounds of Stalag Luft III, in charge of 2,000 men.

The next day, June 21st, Col. Blakeslee would be leading the first Russia shuttle mission. While a thousand bombers diverted Nazi attention by flying over Berlin, three 16-plane squadrons from the 4th and one from the 352nd Fighter Group would provide escort for 104 heavy bombers as they hit German targets between England and Russia. After refueling and rearming at Russian bases, they would bomb targets in Poland on their way to bases in Italy. From Italy they would fly missions over France and Hungary before heading back home to Debden.

By combining efforts, personnel and equipment with those of other air forces and utilizing this multi-pronged attack, the Allies could pounce on Germany from three countries and three directions at once. Col. Blakeslee said the whole operation was for show. This was true. It would irrefutably show the Germans who ruled the skies.

Only 48 of the 4th's 125 qualified pilots were chosen for this special mission. To service the Mustangs at foreign bases, crew chiefs and mechanics went along flying as gunners on the bombers. Major Howard "Deacon" Hively, 334 Sq. CO, another former Eagle Squadron member, described the enthusiasm of the group for this avant-garde mission best by noting that although it might seem odd to the layman "...of the 125 guys available, 126 were chomping at the bit to risk their lives on a damned difficult and dangerous do."

On the first leg of the shuttle, enemy fighters attacked the bombers, forcing Goodson's crew chief, Bob Gilbert to bail out. He spent over a month fighting the Germans with Polish/Russian guerrillas before making it back to Debden. Kidd Hofer, whose boyish exuberance sometimes compelled him to disregard orders and go off on shows of his own — even in combat — was at first thought to be missing in action, but turned up later at another base. Pilot Frank Sibbett was killed when his P-51 was hit by flak.

The accommodations in Russia were crude, but their hosts were cordial and the vodka plentiful. Some of the food offered them, however, was questionable. Not wanting to offend the

Russians, they went eyeball to eyeball with the "dead fishes" on their plates and did their best with it. Eventually they were served an unidentifiable but delicious American lend-lease concoction — small rolls containing some sort of amalgamated meat product. After ingesting the repellent fare they'd had earlier, it was "like dining at the Waldorf," commented pilot Joe Higgins.

During the first night, while most of the airmen were asleep, the Luftwaffe showed up to bomb and strafe their planes, destroying a good number of bombers and damaging 15 Mustangs on the ground. The Americans scurried off to relocate at other, even less comfortable Russian bases.

A few days later they took off for Italy and some flying and socializing with the Fifteenth Air Force. Joe Higgins had the happy occasion of finding his brother Walt, a navigator with a bomber group, and surprising him by walking into his tent. This was the last time Joe saw his brother alive; three weeks later Walt's entire squadron would be shot down by German fighters. The B-17s had been flying without any fighter support.

In Italy the participation by the fighters was hampered by the pervasive Mediterranean dust which choked their unfiltered Mustangs, causing a number of them to abort. On July 2nd there were just over 20 of them making a fighter sweep from Italy to Hungary when 50 to 75 Me 109s burst through the skies to attack the bombers. Donald, lucky enough to be still flying, spotted one next to him. As the German plane attempted to escape in a steep climb, Donald attacked from one side and Joe Higgins blasted away at it from the other. The Me 109 soon lost a wing and it went spinning to earth. Donald and Joe would receive equal credit for this victory.

When it was all over the fighters had destroyed eight and lost five of their own. J.C. Norris and George Stanford were taken POW. Grover Siems was so seriously wounded by a mortar hit in his neck that he was thought to be dead and "posthumously" was awarded the Purple Heart. Minus a few pints of blood, he woke up in an Italian morgue, completely covered by a sheet and unable to move or make a sound. He focused his last shred of moribund energy on showing some sign of life, and when the attendant came back in the room he managed to move his little finger before again losing consciousness. The course of his treatment was quickly reversed, and the next time he awakened, Madeleine Carroll, the movie actress, was sitting at his bedside, holding his hand.

Thomas Sharp and Ralph Hofer were both killed in action near Budapest. The irrepressible "Kidd" Hofer, a former Golden Gloves boxing champ, had made his way to Debden via the Royal Canadian Air Force. On his very first mission he had shot down an enemy plane; this was but a harbinger of his astonishing combat career. On any list of aces his name is always among the top four of the 4th FG's highest scorers.

July 8th

Dear Folks & Bro. John,

I just got back and I 'm going to scribble you a few lines as I imagine you're a bit anxious. If you have followed the news and put two and two together you may have a good idea of what I have been doing. Later on I will be able to tell you the whole story - it's quite interesting.

There were 17 letters here for me - several from you at home and Eleanor (Sis). Of course there were others too (Ha). I won't attempt to answer your letters tonight - I'll write a longer letter soon.

Sure glad to hear about the rain and good crops - I guess you'll soon be in the harvest grind. More work, right? I'm plenty busy myself. Since I last wrote I have moved up another step and am now operations officer of the squadron. Besides several other duties I'm second in command and lead the squadron on missions when the commanding officer stays home.

I must write a couple other notes also. Incidently Mom dear, go easy on that New York correspondence. Remember we are not engaged so be careful not to cause any embarrassing situations O.K.?

Love, Don

After returning from Russia, Donald usually led either a flight or his squadron on their missions. On July 7th, he led 336 for the first time when Capt. VanWyk became ill and had to turn back. They were escorting Liberators to Bernburg when the beleaguered Luftwaffe, rather surprisingly, managed to send up more than 100 fighters to attack the bombers head-on. John Scally of 334 Squadron collided with an Me 410; he survived and was taken POW.

At least seven Liberators were knocked down by the Germans that day — the same number of Mustangs lost by the 4th during the rest of the month; in this same time they destroyed 11 more enemy aircraft. Curtis Simpson and Lester Godwin were able to evade the Germans, but James Hanrahan and Wilson Edwards were taken prisoner. Lloyd Kingham and Kermit Dahlen both died; Kingham crashed shortly after taking off on a mission, and Dahlen's airplane exploded during a dogfight with Me 109s.

July 21st

Dear Folks & Bro. John,

I suppose you received the short letter I wrote you after returning from our little "excursion." I don't believe I need to give you the story because "Public Relations" informed me that they had sent it to my home town newspaper. You may think it funny that they can publish such when I cannot write it in my letters but that's the army.

Nothing much new - if you follow 8th Air Force activity you will have an idea what I'm doing. I've got nearly 80 missions under my belt now and seven destroyed with another which I'm not sure of. About two weeks ago I was awarded the Distinguished Flying Cross and an Oak Leaf Cluster to it at the same time. The citation dealt with my destruction of German planes and some other bull. The D.F.C. is one of our higher decorations and I'm a bit proud of it. The Air Medal is more or less automatically earned by combat pilots who complete a certain number of missions or hours. Incidently when you're awarded the same decorations more than once a bronze oak leaf cluster is added to the original medal. I have three clusters to the air medal and one to the D.F.C.

I got a letter from Sis yesterday written while visiting you.

The picture of the girls sort of surprised me. Beverly isn't going to be a big girl - she looks sort of small on the picture. Bonnie's features seemed to have changed a little - I think she'll be darned cute. I think Sandra looks like Hardin's oldest boy.

My letter writing ambitions ain't what they need to be so you'll have to excuse my not writing so often.

Say hello to Lela - tell her if she writes me a letter I'll read it. Oh boy! I can see her eyes now when you tell her that - MURDER!

The bar is open so I'm going to finish this and go and visit it. Now don't get excited - I mean the snack bar. They put out a little help yourself lunch for us at around bedtime. I sort of like a little to eat such as cake, coffee and lots of sour pickles - you have the most horrible dreams! Guess maybe I'm getting "flak-happy" the way I'm writing tonite.

Love, Don

Defensive and offensive measures are meant, by definition, to be employed against an enemy. But in a world run amok, this is at best an ideal. It is not uncommon in war to kill your own. Accidents were bound to happen when nervous gunners in the air and on the ground had only split seconds to identify airplanes coming at them as friends or foes, and to further complicate matters, the silhouettes of the Allied Spitfires and Mustangs closely resembled 109s, and Thunderbolts could be easily mistaken for 190s. In addition, Germans had been known to invade by flying captured Allied planes; therefore it was not unthinkable to shoot down a correctly identified friendly plane if it appeared menacing. And even when armed with the best intelligence information, targeted enemy trains and installations might contain Allied POWs, and with Nazi and Allied lines of defense nearly abutting in places, the Allies' stated objective of precision bombing was not always the reality.

One of the most publicized of these incidents happened during a bombing raid by U.S. bombers near St. Lo, France, on July 25th. Bombs were accidentally dropped on American troops, killing over 100 and wounding nearly 500 more.

Alarmed by this ghastly error, Maj. Gen. William Kepner, head of the Eighth AF Fighter Corps, asked Col. Blakeslee to send him a couple of his pilots to escort him on an aerial inspection of the area.

The colonel tapped Donald for this mission. Donald then went out to the Parade Grounds, where the nightly softball game was in progress, and pulled Otey Glass in from center field to go with him. The pair then flew to Fighter Command Headquarters and spent the night. But in the morning they were informed by one of Kepner's aides that the plans had been canceled — without explanation — and they returned to Debden, without seeing the General at that time.

Bomber escort missions took up the first half of August, often coupled with beat-ups on trains, tracks, and marshaling yards. The Group lost nearly as many as it destroyed, and flak was responsible for most of the losses. Maj. Leon Blanding suffered severe head wounds from broken canopy glass, but somehow made it back to England; Donald Malmsten was injured when he crashed in enemy territory, but successfully evaded and returned; Fonzo Smith, Sidney Wadsworth and Thomas Underwood were captured by the Germans. Gerald Chapman, Robert Fischer and Frank Jones were killed by flak; and Stephen Boren died when his plane crashed after clipping a wing in a tree.

August eighth was Elinor Lindemann's twenty-first birthday. Donald was on a Blakeslee-led mission to escort RAF Beaufighters to attack German ships on the coast of Norway; Elinor was taking a short vacation in the mountains. Delivered to her home that day were two dozen long-stemmed red roses, a large bouquet of gladiolas, and a package containing the Distinguished Flying Cross from Captain Donald Emerson — the new rank in front of his name on the return address her only clue to his recent promotion. Elinor's father brought the gifts to her the next day. She said she'd never had a nicer birthday. She was so proud of Donald that she told him if he kept this up, she'd have to get a bigger hat.

On August 15, 1944, on his 77th mission, Donald led his squadron for the seventh time; he was also leading the entire 4th Fighter Group for the first and only time. They escorted

Liberators to Zwischenahner Lake in Germany, strafing an airdrome on the way back. Norman Achen's plane went down that day, and he became a prisoner of war.

This was Donald's last mission before going home on furlough. It was also to be the last mission he would fly the "Donald Duck" Mustang. After he left, his favorite P-51 would be flown by several other pilots before being assigned to Harry Davis. Donald and "the duck" had flown 28 of their missions together.

Three days later, the Group targeted German convoys bringing supplies to the front lines in France. While they were bombing and strafing trucks and railroads, several squadrons of Me 109s jumped them, exacting a toll of nine.

The luckiest of the lost were Arthur Cwiklinski and Otey Glass. Cwiklinski was able to bail out, but Glass was flying too low and crash-landed in a wheat field. Otey's luck held; he was unhurt, and the civilians he encountered were friendly; a French family hid and fed him, sharing their meager provisions with him. Cwiklinski also successfully evaded capture, and both pilots returned to Debden when the First Canadian Army overran the area a few weeks later.

Dean Lange bailed out, but was taken prisoner by the Germans. The other six — Leo Dailey, Robert Cooper, John Conley, Bernard Rosenson, Donald Smith, and C.G. Howard were all killed.

A couple of days after this, Johnny Godfrey, just recently back from publicity touring in the States, was accidentally shot by his wingman. He went down over Germany, where he'd eventually be corraled with many of his old friends already imprisoned in Stalag Luft III.

August 19, 1944

Dear Sis,

I've just finished writing a few lines to the folks and while I'm in the mood I'll get a letter off to you also. I really should write you more often to keep you from getting anxious but like I told the folks we have been pretty busy and I just don't feel like writing. You don't have to apologize for not writing often enough - it should be the other way around. Even my Elle doesn't get letters from me very often. She is a darling tho and hardly misses a day in writing to me.

I was glad to hear Harold got rid of that bus and got a car instead. I never did think that bus driving business was worth the effort considering what you got out of it. Mom wrote that Harold was out there helping harvest now.

I wasn't much surprised to hear Glenn was in France but his job is sort of unusual! Dead animals don't shoot back tho - that's one consolation.

I was officially presented the D.F.C. by Gen. Auton on August 3rd. The picture enclosed shows how impressed I was by the occasion. By the serious look on my pan one would almost think I was ready to burst into tears any minute.

I have been a Captain since July 27th. I've had a rather rapid promotion but I've worked for it and no one thinks I don't deserve it. It's $350 per month now.

I guess this will be all for now. Give my love and a big hug to Beverly & Bonnie. If this war don't hurry up and end they will be young ladies before I will be able to hug them myself.

Your loving bro., Don

By month's end, six more pilots had been shot down. Pierce McKennon bailed out safely and was hidden by the French underground; he made his way back to the base a month later. Archibald Thomson also became an evader in France, but Kenneth Rudkin was captured. Ferris Harris, Herbert Vandervate, and Albert Schlegel were killed.

Both Donald and Colonel Blakeslee were on their way to Stateside furloughs. In Blakeslee's absence, first Lt. Col. Jim Clark and then Lt. Col. Claiborne Kinnard would be the 4th's acting commanders, with leadership during missions shared by them and several other top pilots: Van Wyk, Brown, Hively, Norley, Glover, McFarlane, Blanding, Montgomery, McKennon, and Monroe.

Gen. Auton officially presenting Capt. Emerson with the DFC
(Col. Blakeslee extreme left)

Donald's "Donald Duck" Mustang (Photo taken from an escorted bomber)

Otey Glass

Joe Higgins

READY FOR RUSSIA
Standing: Neil Van Wyck, Harry Dugan, Ferris Harris, Charles Shilke, Richard Corbett & Col. Ben Kelsey Front: Gilbert "Mike" Hunt, Joe Patteeuw, George Logan & George Smith

Donald, home from Russia, and

АМЕРИКАНСКИЕ
ВОЗДУШНЫЕ СИЛЫ

летчик   а-813134

1st. Lt. Donald B. Emerson

I AM AN AMERICAN.	Я АМЕРИКАНЕЦ.	YA AMERICANYETSS.
I AM HUNGRY.	Я ГОЛОДЕН.	YA GOLODYENN
I AM THIRSTY.	ХОЧЕТСЯ ПИТЬ.	KHOTCHETSYA PIT.
I AM WOUNDED.	Я РАНЕН	YA RANYEN.
BREAD . WATER	ХЛЕБ. ВОДА.	KHLEB. VODA.
SHELTER	УБЕЖИЩЕ.	OUBEJISTCHYE.
WHERE CAN I HIDE.	ГДЕ МНЕ СПРЯТАТЬСЯ.	GDYE MNYE SPRYATATSSYA
WHERE IS THE SOVIET FRONT	ГДЕ СОВЕТСКИЙ ФРОНТ.	GDYE SOVIETSSKY FRONT
NORTH . SOUTH	СЕВЕР. ЮГ	SEVER . YOUGG.
EAST . WEST	ВОСТОК. ЗАПАД.	VOSSTOK . ZAPADD.
WHERE ARE THE SOVIET AUTHORITIES	ГДЕ СОВЕТСКИЕ ВЛАСТИ	GDYE SOVIETSSKYA VLASTY

Russian/English phrase card

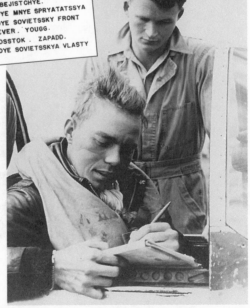

Crew Chief Larry
Jones [Ed Richie]

Elinor Lindemann with birthday gifts from Donald

Beverly, Sandra & Bonnie

All that Uncle John had added to his account of the day he got the tragic telegram was that it had been delivered one afternoon, when he was all alone at the farm.

It was becoming clear that my letter writing was not going to provoke the response I wanted, so I decided to save the rest of my many questions until I could talk to him in person. But by the time I did see him again I had come to understand how remembering can hurt — even when the memories are not your own, and I was beginning to lose my zealous need to melt every frozen memory and pry up every piece of buried truth. I hadn't yet heard that long ago, when it happened, he had cried so much he said he never wanted to cry again, and later he was determined never to let himself even think about Donald.

We met at my parents' home in Karlstad, the big pink stucco house at the south end of Main Street. My mother had told Uncle John that I would be there; he'd better be there, too — her version of a command performance. Although he was happy to see me and greeted me warmly with a hug and a kiss, he appeared to be somewhat guarded, as if bracing himself for the inquisition he was sure would come.

A couple of times my mother made a comment designed to prod him into making some statement of encouragement to me regarding my project, but the best he could do was nod his head. I knew I had his approval. He didn't have to say anything; I'd never try to make him talk about Donald.

He talked freely, though, about a variety of other subjects. He liked to read, and he had been watching a lot of educational television since he retired. He especially liked nature shows and remembered a good number of surprising details. Betty interrupted him once to say she was sure I wasn't interested in the mating habits of all those animals, but I insisted it wasn't so — in fact I never had quite figured out chickens.

"CHICKENS?" he said, as he went on to tell a story graphically illustrating the incredible stamina of a lone rooster tossed in with an entire flock of hens.

"You can throw a rooster in with a big bunch of hens," he said in summation, "and he'll keep going all day!"

He began to relax, and started talking about a happy time we shared: August, 1959. Did I remember that summer I stayed with them during the wheat harvest?

Yes — the summer I was sixteen. Their two oldest boys, Donnie and Darryl, had been old enough to go with them out into the fields, but David was only two years old and needed watching. On days when the combining was going smoothly, I got to drive their new black Pontiac and bring the noon meal out to them, with little Davey in the front seat with me and the kettles of hot food in the back.

Did I remember all the badminton we played that summer?

Of course. After a rain, when the grain was too wet to harvest, the Oakes kids would come over and we'd play in Johnny and Betty's yard.

Did I remember how mad Ritchie got when I beat him?

"HE WAS SO DAMN MAD HE SMASHED HIS RACKET INTO THE GROUND AND BROKE IT!" Uncle John laughed. "Remember that time?"

Sure, I remembered, I told him — I'd never forget it.

But remembering that made me remember that place, and I wondered if the peonies and lilac bushes still separated the lawns of the two houses, and I could almost hear again the whistling summer breezes sifting through the grove of pine trees on the north side of the farm — like the sound of the wind whipping through a screen, right before a storm. And then I wondered, to myself, if Donald's clothesline might still be there behind the house where Grandma and Grandpa used to live.

* * * * *

WESTERN UNION

New York   N Y Sept 3
                    John G Emerson, RR
          Pembina N Dak.

Back home on leave. Expect to see you in
about ten days. Will let you know in
advance the date of expected arrival.
Please wire two hundred dollars to me in
care of Elinor Lindemann. Will be in New
York for about one week.

                              Capt. D R Emerson

Donald arrived in New York on Sunday, September 3rd. The next day he was waiting near Elinor's apartment at 840 Grand Concourse as she came walking down the street — just coming home after spending the Labor Day weekend in Tannersville. She did a double take when her young captain suddenly materialized, "...as though he came up from the sidewalk," she said. "I'll never forget that day as long as I live... I hadn't expected him home for a long while to come."

It is unknown exactly what transpired next, but Donald and Elinor clearly enjoyed Week Two of their relationship.

He made it home to Joliette by September 14th. The raft of relatives, friends and neighbors he called on all noticed he was now a different man. Very solemn. Some even said he seemed depressed. He said he despised the war and hated having to kill people, and he didn't like to speak of it to anyone. About all he would say was that he was going back for another tour of combat and had signed on with his old Group, rather than take his chances with a random assignment — which, he told his family, could mean going to fight in the Pacific.

Before he left home that last time, he insisted they have a family picture professionally taken. The five Emersons went to Hallock, Minnesota, to the nearest portrait studio and stiffly posed for the photograph, all in their Sunday best except for Donald who wore his army dress uniform. They all looked very solemn.

When it was time to go Donald requested that no one but his brother John go with him to the train station; he preferred saying his farewells in private, and he bid them individually. At his sister's house he was practically smothered by the females and their kisses as Eleanor and the two older girls virtually threw themselves on him in tearful goodbyes. Then he reached down to pick up the toddler, but she wriggled free of his grasp and ran away.

The part of the story I most hated to hear — when Donald went away for the last time. I always hoped my mother would forget to tell it, but she never did. "He tried so hard to get a kiss out of you, but you just wouldn't!" she always said.

It took me many years to work up the courage to elicit an explanation for my unforgivable behavior, but finally I had tremulously blurted, "Why wouldn't I kiss him goodbye?"

She had laughed then, completely astonished by my guilt-ridden query, and exclaimed. "YOU WERE JUST A BABY! — THAT'S HOW BABIES ARE! You didn't remember him."

Home on leave

*With Elinor in
New York*

Bonnie & Beverly sporting some of "Donald's Stuff"

Emerson Family Portrait

Bro. John, Sis Eleanor & Donald

Beverly, Sandra & Bonnie

Some of Hitler's own people had botched an assassination plot against him in July — the only known attempt made from within to rid the Reich of its fanatical leader. All those implicated in the conspiracy were quickly rounded up, skewered on meathooks and hung out for public viewing, scarcely disturbing the primary slaughter in progress.

The Allies were gradually gaining the upper hand in the Pacific, with each jungle island recaptured another potential air strip from which to launch their bombing attacks against Japan and its home islands. Heavy bombardment preceding the assaults by the amphibious forces was supposed to ease each conquest, but there was no surrender by the stubborn remnant of Japanese survivors who had to be peeled from the caves and coral mazes and taken on one at a time. The fighting there was particularly drawn out and vicious, and aviators dropping down to within 1500 feet of the Palau Islands were assailed by the stench of death from the thousands of bloated and rotting bodies in the tropical heat.

France was now free, and the Allied armies had moved well into Belgium and the lowlands and had reached Germany's western fortification at the Ardennes Forest. As Holland was being liberated, the most famous airborne operation of the war was taking place. In a daring plan called Market-Garden, British and American paratroopers were being dropped behind enemy lines in order to secure a series of river crossings all the way to the Rhine and into Germany itself. Although this operation was only partially successful, several bridges were secured before the Germans stopped them at Arnhem.

The 4th's Mustangs maintained their support in bombing raids on Germany, along with providing protective cover for the airdropped troops trudging through the Netherlands. The competition with Zemke's 56th FG was still tight, with the Wolfpack and the 4th alternately holding the record for the most enemy aircraft destroyed.

During September the Group destroyed more than 50 German planes, to their loss of 11. George Cooley was caught in the same dogfight as William Groseclose and Paul Iden; he bailed out and was taken by a heavy artillery unit to an evac hospital for removal of the shrapnel in his side and was back in Debden a few

days later. Groseclose, James Lane and Clifford Holske had also
bailed out okay — though Holske suffered burns, but Henry
Ingalls, Thomas Joyce and James Russell had to crash-land —
Russell, because the explosion that cut his head also damaged his
parachute; all six of these men were taken prisoner. Iden, Robert
White, Roy Patterson, William Smith, and Nicholas Vozzy were
killed.

Donald was back on the Lindemann's doorstep early in October.
They saw quite a lot of him this time through, but they had no
one but themselves to blame. The paramount desire to be near
Elinor had drawn him there, but the company of her erudite and
politically astute father and the warm reception extended by her
winsome mother served to broaden the attraction. Donald so
enjoyed the convivial atmosphere and stimulating conversation
found within their home that he was there at every opportunity,
and had begun to think of it as his own.

In the daytime while Elinor was at work, Donald filled the
hours by taking care of some business matters. He had been
giving a lot of thought to his life after the war, and he now began
doing the preparatory footwork. He said he was "...rapidly
finding out that in domestic life it's not so much what you know,
but who you know that counts most," and with that in mind, he
contacted National Air Lines, where Mr. Lindemann knew
several men from handling some of their banking. He also
visited the other major airlines to see what his prospects might
be; they all were in the process of expanding and were having a
hard time finding pilots. The outlook was encouraging, but he
knew that when the war was over there would be a mad scramble
for those positions and he wanted to get a jump on the
competition.

While he was out and about, he also got around to taking care
of a nagging family obligation by looking up his audacious
cousin Evelyn, who was reportedly married to a very successful
manager of a hotel. But when Donald got to their address, he
"declined to go in." The establishment was so far removed from
his mental picture of it he feared she might be embarrassed to be
seen in such a "crummy" place. He left without her even
knowing he'd been there, and got on with his shopping, going

first to Bonwit Teller.

Donald's worldly travels had honed his innate sense of taste for high quality goods, and he now truly appreciated fine fabrics and materials. He loved handling the exquisite glass and chinaware used to serve him, and he had grown accustomed to the heft and luster of precious metals. Wanting those he loved to share some of these same pleasures, he chose Christmas gifts for them accordingly.

For Elinor he selected a delicate pink quilted satin robe, and a gold ankle bracelet — engraved with "Elle" on one side and "Don" on the other. For sister Eleanor he found a splendid set of eight jewel-toned crystal water tumblers and had them etched with her initials; each one was the color of a different gemstone: diamond, ruby, emerald, sapphire, topaz, amethyst, aquamarine and smoky onyx. At the International Silver Company, for his parents' humble farm table, he purchased six place settings of sterling silver flatware, choosing the "Spring Glory" pattern. And then, with the florist, he placed an order for two dozen long-stemmed red roses, to be delivered to Miss Elinor Lindemann on January 8th, one year after they met.

In October, in the Battle of Leyte Gulf, the greatest naval battle in history, the Japanese Navy was finally crushed in the Philippines. Though temporarily halted, Japan was not finished. In a desperate, suicidal offensive, kamikaze planes heavily loaded with explosives were sent to crash into American and Allied ships. And thousands of young pilots — given just enough training to guide an antiquated airplane into a target, with barely enough fuel to reach it — paid the supreme sacrifice for their Emperor.

The German-launched V-1 rocket attacks against England were heating up, with several of these "buzz bombs" exploding very near the Debden base. And as the Mustang pilots began encountering more of the new German jet-propelled fighters, they started practicing how to best battle them by staging mock dogfights against English Gloster Meteor jets.

The Group's missions that month garnered nine destroyed and a loss of two. George Logan and Joseph Lang both died in combat. Logan spun out and crashed; Lang got separated from the group during a mission and ran into ten 109s — he got two before they got him.

Ordered to report at Trenton, New Jersey, by Wednesday, October 11th, Donald said goodbye to Elinor and New York. That night he called her from the Ritz-Carlton Hotel in Atlantic City; there would be about a week's delay in transport, and he was biding his time in one of the hotels being used by the army to house troops. Could she come down?

Since the twelfth was Columbus Day, Elinor had a holiday from work and was more than happy to make the 125-mile train trip to be with him for the day. She went back again for the weekend, further prolonging their extensive farewell.

Donald and Elinor had a lovely time together in Atlantic City, doing nothing special but walking up and down the boardwalks, looking into the numerous store windows, and stopping in all the Penny Arcades along the way. Mealtimes were spent in the sumptuous Officers' Mess set up in the hotel, where officers and their guests were lavishly served and royally entertained, all compliments of Uncle Sam.

Though he was happy to be there with her, Elinor said Donald was rather gloomy and restless, and seemed almost eager to get back to his job. He told her he wanted to complete one hundred missions.

Had I heard all my mother's memories — read all of Donald's letters? I could never be sure. Just when I thought I must have, she'd remember something else, or find a few more letters. Some of them had gotten mixed in with letters from other people and had been put in assorted bags and boxes and packed away. But one by one they came out from the closets, dresser drawers, piano bench, and pantry where they'd been stashed. And, like the letters, there were still a few pigeonholed memories left to emerge from her mind.

I was looking again through the box of Donald's stuff at the kitchen table. She was busy at her trusty ironing board — she loved to iron, and her ironing board and I were forever linked in her mind.

"Got this ironing board the summer you were born," she told me, for about the fortieth time.

And then, as I knew she would, she chanted the sing-song jingle that was on its label when it was new.

" 'Will not wiggle-wobble, jiggle-joggle, slip or slide.' Don't know why I never forget that silly little rhyme," she said, "but I never do."

Had she ever shown me this? She wondered aloud as she stopped ironing to reach into a cupboard drawer. She pulled out a small, homemade, nine-page booklet cut from old ledger paper. It was yellowed and lined with blue and red, and held together by a rubber band. On the front it said, "The Start of Billy Winkle and His Famous Cat! By Donald Emerson, age 10."

Donald had written and illustrated a story about Billy and his very intelligent cat. It began with the cat finding a cave filled with gold and precious gems while out hunting, and ended after they invented a conveyance to carry away all their newly claimed treasure. The book was all done in pencil; the story was quite clever and the drawing very good, very neat.

I was still examining it when she remembered to tell me something else I'd forgotten being told. Donald was also about that age when she was converted, she said — referring to the time when she, as a 19-year-old baptized Protestant, went into an itinerant evangelist's tent meeting and came out "born again." She had shared her new Christian perspective with Donald saying, "When we die and go to heaven, we'll meet old friends and walk hand in hand."

He had run to her with a big hug and cried, "Oh, Eleanor! Thank you for telling me that. I thought when we're dead, we're dead."

Late in the month, both Donald and Col. Blakeslee returned to England from the States, where the colonel had secretly wed his girl friend back home. Donald's courtship, though equally passionate, had not advanced quite that far.

Officers' Mess
November 23, 1944

Dear Folks & Bro John,

I have just finished eating a very delicious meal and I'm full
to the point of being uncomfortable. I don't remember what
date you are observing it but today is Thanksgiving Day for
the U.S. Army here in England and on the continent. Eating
dinner tonight in our very comfortable Mess I was thankful
that I am a pilot stationed here and not one of the foot
soldiers who are slugging it out in the mud and rain on the
front lines.

I got back in the saddle again soon after I got back. I
hadn't flown for nearly three months but after a couple hours
of practice flying I was right back in the groove. I won't have
to work as hard as I did last summer cause the daylight hours
are very short. One thing is worse this season tho and that
is the weather. Most of our flying is done under instrument
conditions - fog, rain, snow, etc.

I'm very glad to hear of your intentions to make that trip
out West this winter. I hope you don't change your plans this
time. If you're leaving on December 1st I don't know if this
letter will reach you or not by then. Send it on to them,
Johnny, if they have already left cause I don't know Ray's
address. Take it easy yourself this winter, brother John. That
shouldn't be too hard if you have someone to help with what
outside work there is to be done. I can't see how you are going
to eat tho - I just can't picture you doing any cooking.

I have gained considerable weight since I got back to the
station. It seems odd but I didn't gain a bit while I was in the
States. I guess the rather hectic schedule I maintained
wasn't conducive to recovering any lost pounds.

Don't look for any more bonds from the War Department
as I have discontinued having them deducted from my pay.
The last one will be dated August 31st. I'll send it all home in
the form of cash now and if I want any more bonds you can
buy them for me.

How long do you intend to stay out West? Send me an address so I can write direct to you.

Love, Donald

Col. Blakeslee was able to lead a few final missions before being permanently grounded; his friendly rival, Hub Zemke had just been captured by the Germans, and headquarters was afraid that the same would happen to him. Early in November he went back to the States for good, replaced by Lt. Col. Claiborne Kinnard.

By then Donald was back at Debden. He had spent a couple of weeks in an army rest camp before returning to combat, and in the interim, while he was being deemed fit for active duty, five more of his comrades had been lost. Russell Anderson, Earl Walsh, and Earl Quist were POWs; Charles Mead was killed in a flying accident; and John Childs died when he was shot down by an FW 190.

November 25, 1944

Dear Max,

You have probably heard through the folks that I was home on a month's leave in September. I am sorry it couldn't have been a month or two sooner so that I could have seen you. I was in the States for almost six weeks, got thoroughly rested and enjoyed every day of it, but even that gets tiresome and I didn't mind getting back here to work again.

I flew the Atlantic on the trip home and arrived in New York after a short 20-hour ride from Scotland. I have crossed the Atlantic three times now - twice by boat - and if I have my choice I would never do it again except by air. I have no doubt that post-war travel around the globe will be largely by air. At the present the British are devoting a lot of their newspaper space to the International Chicago Air Conference. They are very worried about us gaining too much control of the world commercial airways.

I have done a lot of thinking about my post-war career and if the opportunity presents itself I would consider being a commercial pilot. Flying is the only thing I have a good knowledge of. When I was home I visited several airline companies in New York and filed applications with them - but it will be first come, first served, and no one knows who will get released first.

The G.I. Bill of Rights does present a good opportunity for an education but I would want it to be something I could depend on to make a living. If possible I want to leave the farming to John. My main ambition which I have had for a long time is to stay in and make a career in the Air Force. I like the work and having picked up considerable first-hand knowledge - I think I could be an asset to the Force. The pay of a flying officer isn't too bad and it provides a security which most civil jobs don't offer. When I was home I asked several high-ranking officers about the possibilities of getting a permanent commission, but no one seems to know on what basis they will be given out. If they decide to keep a standing air force, that will call for more men than there are West Point boys available; I think I should have a chance. No doubt of course politics will play a big part in that and a man's record may not help him much. I don't wish to bother you, Max, but you may be able to give me some good pointers or ideas which I would appreciate very much.

A recent letter from the folks said they intended to make a trip out west. I'm glad to hear it because I think it's about time they got out a little and Mother will get away from the cold Dakota winter - which doesn't do her health any good.

Sincerely, Donald

Earl Quist wasn't flying his assigned Mustang the day he went down, and now his VF-B #5054 was turned over to Donald. No artwork or kill crosses were applied to this plane, but "Capt. Emerson" was hastily and crudely scratched on its side. Good enough. The glamour of combat had about worn off.

Donald's first mission back was a strafing attack on a German airdrome in Leipheim. The Group destroyed an even dozen Me 262 jets and one Me 109 on the ground — Donald got the 109. The Germans claimed one Mustang. Ralph Lewis was killed in the enemy's counterattack.

The next three weeks were spent in bomber escort runs to several industrial sites in Germany, with Donald leading either his squadron or a flight on about half of them. Five more pilots went down in that span of time. Michael Kennedy survived and evaded; Donald Bennett and George Klaus were captured by the Germans; and Leonard Werner and Carmen Delnero were killed.

December 8, 1944

Dear Bro. John,

I presume Mom and Dad are in Seattle by now - I hope nothing went wrong with their plans this time.

I got a letter from Sis the other day. Said Harold was getting quite a few mink. I understand you were going to hunt deer over there. I hope the weather got better; Sis said it was very wet.

I'm not working too hard. Usually something to do every day but the short daylight hours make it quite a bit easier than it was last summer. Flying two and three missions a day is what takes the sap out of you. The first mission after getting back here resulted in another destroyed Jerry kite to my credit. It was a ground strafing job.

I sent $500 to you a couple of days ago. According to my figures, that brings my cash balance in the account up to $1,400. I think it was $900 when I was home.

I'm glad Mom liked the silverware - all she needs now is a decent table (hint).

Take it easy brother - send Ray's address - if that's where Mom and Dad will be for a while.

Don

P.S. Shot hell out of three locomotives one day. Some fun!

Merry Xmas!

In the Pacific, the war raged on without sign of abatement. What the Japanese lacked in materials they made up for by their unflagging strength of purpose, and the U.S. Navy estimated that it could take another five years to defeat them. But in Europe, the once-powerful Nazi war machine was breaking down, and the Allies believed it would be just a matter of days before the Germans' surrender. For the first time since the war began, soldiers dared voice the hope of going home in time for Christmas. Donald's father had written Elinor Lindemann that he thought the whole world was "on the end of a shake-up," and in letters to the Emersons she agreed, but also wrote, "I have hopes that the European War will be over by Christmas. Somehow I have a feeling that it will."

Hitler still had no intention of ever giving up or admitting defeat, and on December 16th, Germany launched its most powerful counter-offensive since D-Day. Von Runstedt's Panzer forces smashed the Allied lines of defense and pushed into Belgium and Luxembourg through a 40-mile section of what was believed to be the impenetrable Ardennes Forest, causing a "bulge" to protrude 60 miles into Allied territory. The Battle of the Bulge would be called by many "America's greatest battle." In preparing his generals for this arduous fight, George S. Patton, commander of America's defending Fourth Armored Division, exhorted them saying, "If we live through this one, be forever grateful that you have brought with you one of life's greatest moments!"

The unexpected setback sent Donald's sister pacing in despair — not only at the never-ending bloodshed, but because she feared the effects a long time in battle might have on her beloved brother. In deep concern for his immortal soul, Eleanor slipped into her bedroom, and on her knees prayed fervently to God, asking that if Donald's life were meant to be sacrificed in this war, to please take him soon, before he became tainted or corrupted by it.

For the first week of the battle a dense fog covering much of Europe prevented the air forces from coming to the support of the troops fighting it out on the ground, and the free-lance fighter sweep and bomber escort missions attempted by the 4th Fighter Group on December 18th and 23rd were almost pointless. Still, somehow, they found a few enemy fighters in the clouds, destroying two, and giving up one to them. Charles Hewes died when he was shot down by a German.

December 19, 1944

Dear Mom & Dad,

I'm using this V-Mail in the hope that you will receive this soon. It seems to be taking regular mail three to four weeks to get through. I hope you got a letter from me before you left home. I would have written direct to you sooner but I didn't have Ray's address which I just got in one of the letters you wrote to me before you left. I told John to forward my letters on to you in case you left before they got there.

Nothing very much has happened to me since I got back. Of course I'm flying missions again, but that's old stuff to me by this time. I recently got an additional destroyed Jerry plane to my credit.

I hope you made the trip O.K. and are enjoying yourself. Greet everyone for me and a Merry Xmas to you all!

Love, Donald

The skies began to clear on the 24th, and in the largest air raid to date, over 2,000 bombers dropped more than 4,000 tons of bombs in the area of the bulge. The 4th escorted B-17s to German targets in that operation; Donald led a flight that day with Gilbert Kesler flying as his wingman, and Gil would long remember how well organized the mission was. For more than five hours he stuck with Donald as they escorted the bombers going out. Then turning around, they flew at a lower altitude to make their way through a heavily defended area known as "flak alley," hunting for targets of opportunity on the way home.

Because of impermeable skies over Debden, the pilots were forced to land at other bases. Like Donald, most had landed their Mustangs at Raydon, at an RAF airdrome used by the 353rd Fighter Group. After a cold night of little sleep in unheated Quonset huts, many of them took off early the next morning; as he had the day before, Doug Groshong flew in Donald's section. Led by new Group CO Harry Dayhuff, their mission was to protect the bombing Liberators near Kassel, Germany. At about noon more than 30 German fighters came on the attack. To thwart the Luftwaffe's designs on the bombers, the Mustangs pursued them, actively engaging them in a full-blown dogfight.

In the brutal free-for-all, the Americans were the victors, with the 4th Fighter Group bagging 12 enemy planes, and losing only two of their own. The 334 Squadron's contribution to the hunt pushed their total to an ETO record-setting 300 kills. But 336 Squadron got a fair share that day as well; Maj. Fred Glover, current squadron CO, shot down one, Van Chandler got two, and Donald, two. A German pilot shot down Charles Poage, who bailed out and became a POW. Donald Emerson was downed by anti-aircraft fire, and died of his wounds.

Donald had gotten separated from the Group and wound up taking on six FW 190s by himself. Pilots Joe Joiner and Don Pierini heard Donald's urgent call for help; in a voice without panic he said he was alone with the 190s — then they lost radio contact with him. But others heard his staccato, blow-by-blow commentary throughout much of his last fight; Kendall "Swede" Carlson — perhaps the closest of Donald's remaining long-time buddies by this time — knew he was nearby, but he was in the same kind of fix himself, and though he tried valiantly, the muddle of so many aircraft amid so many clouds kept him from finding Donald and coming to his aid. In spite of the odds, Donald shot down two of the German fighters before running out of ammunition and escaping under the clouds. His last message heard was that he was on the deck, and going home.

As Donald crossed over into Allied territory he was hit by flak. His plane was seen crash-landing near the Holland/Belgium border in an area occupied by the British Army, but by the time friendly hands reached him, his life was gone. The medical officer's report said Donald was killed by enemy gunfire while crossing over the Germans' lines, and his death was believed to have been instantaneous.

In Germany's Stalag Luft III, the mail had been allowed to accumulate for some time, ensuring that there would be something for each prisoner, and on Christmas Day it was joyously delivered to them by a Santa driving a mail wagon decked with sleigh bells, pulled by two men dressed as reindeer.

At their English bases, American servicemen were busy hosting holiday parties for the local children. Glesner "Weck"

Weckbacher, the chief mechanic who often had to pull the physically spent Capt. Emerson from the cockpit, would not take part. He sat out Christmas of 1944 on a case of ammunition in the blustery cold, waiting until dark for his pilot to return. And utterly disconsolate, Swede Carlson began days of deep brooding because he hadn't been able to help his friend.

With Donald's parents in Seattle, Emerson and Torkelson family members spent Christmas Day at Eleanor and Hot's home. So excited to have her young aunts as captive playmates, little Beverly climbed up on the cupboard to reach a deck of cards on its highest shelf — tipping the hutch over, and dumping Eleanor's beautiful new set of glassware from Donald on the floor. The crash left only one unbroken: the onyx black.

There were no plane-loads of body bags or flag-draped coffins brought home during this war. The war dead would be finally interred in specially designed caskets and cemeteries when it was over, but until then they were quickly buried in hundreds of temporary graveyards set up along the course of battle.

Donald was buried the next day near the village of Margraten, Holland, beside an old Roman road which had been established as a warpath — long before Hitler — by the armies of Napoleon. At about noon on the day after Christmas, still wearing his flying clothes, he was given a simple soldier's burial, the blanket he was wrapped in his body's only barrier from the earth.

It was said the sun was shining brightly at the time, and in addition to military personnel there were many sympathetic Dutch friends present. Cecil H. Lang, the nearest USAAF chaplain was summoned to administer the grave side rites. From personal effects found on Donald's body, Chaplain Lang determined that he was a Protestant and conducted a fitting and dignified service.

...For I am already at the point of being sacrificed; the time of my departure has come. I have fought the good fight, I have finished the race, I have kept the faith.
                                        II Timothy 4:6-8

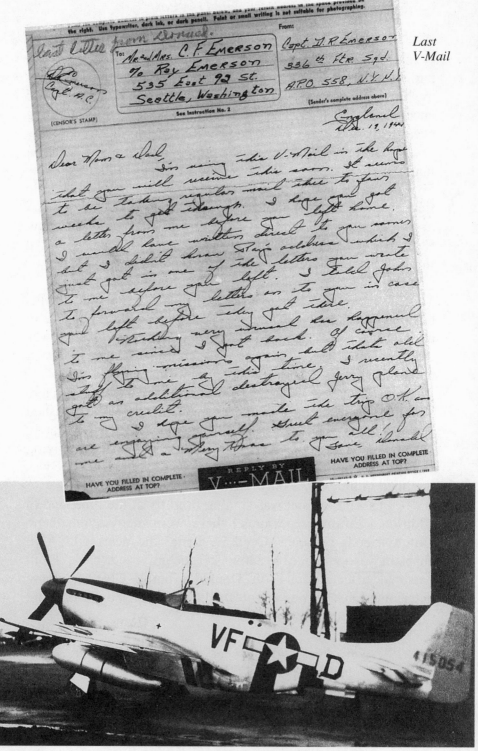

Last V-Mail

Last Mustang

Donald in cockpit

Temporary Grave Marker

W ar news in the European Theater over the holidays was the stabilization of "the Bulge." On Christmas Day *The Stars and Stripes*, the army newspaper, proclaimed massive Allied bombing raids had put a stop to the Germans' counter attack.

A short column farther down the page reported Major Glenn Miller missing; it was believed his plane had gone down in the English Channel. The popular band leader, too old for the draft, had joined the Air Corps anyway; his job was entertaining the troops, and the band he created performed all over England and the Continent.

At the Eighth Air Force's Fighter Command Headquarters, a smaller arena where the loss of a stalwart captain might be noteworthy, Donald's demise was upstaged by the revelation that a renowned major in the 352nd FG had been shot down by Allied anti-aircraft gunners. George Preddy, "Top Mustang Ace" of the war, died the same day as Donald.

Word of Donald's death was relayed back to Debden — where he was known by almost everyone — the next day, and prayers were offered for all who mourned his passing in chapel services the following Sunday.

The news took nearly three weeks to reach North Dakota.

*****

WESTERN UNION

```
FJ-A
32 Govt Washington DC 1010pm Jan 12

        Mrs Mabel Emerson Pembina N Dak
     The Secretary of War desires me to
express his deepest regrets that your son
Captain Donald Emerson was killed in
action on twenty five December in European
area confirming letter follows

     Dunlop Acting the Adjutant General
            * * * * *
```

The messenger delivered the telegram to the Emerson farm on January 13th. In shock and abject bereavement, brother John drove the six miles to Pembina to make the necessary calls; he couldn't trust the crackling line of the recently installed telephone with the transmission of his heart-wounding message. As he walked toward the Central Telephone Office, the townspeople who saw him on the street that day could read the front-page news on his ravaged, tear-stained face before the *New Era* printed it.

After first calling his sister, he contacted his parents in Seattle and the Roswells at Halma. And although he didn't remember doing it, he was also the one who told Elinor Lindemann in New York. Her anniversary roses from Donald were still in the vase.

As more details were received and he heard from his parents again, he wrote a note to his sister saying, "Daddy sounded strong and brave but not Mom, but don't blame her. I sure felt bad today."

Donald's parents came home to North Dakota on the 24th of January, Mabel's 53rd birthday. Memorial services were then planned in both states that claimed him. In February, Reverend Sumner Williams conducted a special service at the Joliette Methodist Church, and in March, a double tribute was held in Karlstad at the First Lutheran Church in remembrance of Donald and Stanley Hams, another young local man recently killed in the war. Donald's old friend Pastor E.B. Kluver officiated.

Friends would remember Donald as a joy to be around and for his ever-present smile. The men who flew with him would recall his calm and cordial demeanor, his strong, determined spirit ... and remember him as being very quiet and serious — not the boisterous type, like so many of them were ... and they said he wasn't just another "yard bird," but one of only a few to routinely refuse time off, and to volunteer for a second tour. They admired him as one of the best fighter pilots in the 4th Fighter Group — an expert flyer who was methodical ... meticulous ... dependable ... super ... exceptional ... and one who had that something extra. "The little guy with a big heart" had earned their tremendous respect as an air combat leader, and as a first-rate officer and friend.

This "lazy" farm boy was cited by the War Department for extraordinary achievement and heroism in aerial combat over enemy-occupied Continental Europe, and for the skillful and zealous manner in which he sought out the enemy and destroyed him; he was recognized as an inspiration to his fellow flyers, for devotion shown to duty, and his courage under all conditions. He was awarded the Distinguished Flying Cross with two Oak-leaf Clusters, the Air Medal with one Silver and two Bronze Oak-leaf Clusters, and the Purple Heart.

Donald and his fallen comrades would be immortalized on memorials and monuments in England as well as the States, and the bomb-damaged apse of St. Paul's Cathedral — which he had viewed with Don Patchen on their London holiday — would be rebuilt as The American Memorial Chapel. When it was finished General Eisenhower officially presented and helped dedicate The Roll of Honour, inscribed with the names of the 28,000 Americans who lost their lives while based in the British Isles.

The Battle of the Bulge was to be the final Nazi offensive in the war. After Christmas Day the Germans were turned back by the all-out Allied counterattack directed by Eisenhower, and in another month it was over.

The same type of heavy cloud cover which had first hindered air operations over Germany now draped England, and the weather was almost as tough on the 4th FG pilots as the war. Richard Rinebolt was injured when he crashed trying to land, and though he'd keep a private pilot's license after the war, he never flew in combat again. (A month later his 20-year-old brother Harold was killed while serving with the 9th Infantry in Belgium; Dick wasn't properly notified, and first heard of his brother's death from a friend when he got back to the States.) Morton Savage flew into a radio tower in the fog, Alvin Wallace spun into the ground, and Frederick Hall crashed while trying to land — all three dying in England. Robert Stallings and William Bates were killed over the North Sea, and four more were struck down over Germany; Victor Rentschler lived to be taken prisoner, but Arthur Senecal, Paul Santos, and Henry Kaul died.

The Marines persevered with their invasion of the Philippines, and when MacArthur finally fulfilled his pledge to return to Manila it was well staged and documented. In Poland, the Russians had driven out the Germans and were now well into eastern Germany. A victorious end in sight, Roosevelt, Churchill and Stalin met in Yalta for strategy talks outlining the final stages of the European war and for the time of peace to come.

But with no sign of surrender forthcoming from Hitler, the pummeling of German cities and its dwindling targets by the Allied air forces was uninterrupted. The strategic bombing campaign — once a questionable experiment — now rolled on like some gigantic and unstoppable beastly robot, leaving a trail of unspeakable devastation.

Until the madness stopped the show went on, and the Mustang pilots of the 4th reprised their strafing performances after playing their roles in support of the featured bombers of "The Mighty Eighth."

By the end of March, another 16 of the 4th's pilots had been downed — most of them while strafing. Flak hit Art Bowers' canopy; though wounded in the neck, he flew on home. Two others bailed out and successfully evaded the enemy. John McFarland landed in Denmark and made it to Sweden; Pierce

McKennon evaded the Germans for the second time — this time his wingman, George Green, followed him down, picked him up and flew him back to Debden, riding double. Eleven men were captured by the Germans: John Fitch, August Rabe, Andrew Lacy, Alvin Hand, Kendall Carlson, Harold Crawford, Robert Voyles, Kenneth Green, George Davis, Robert Cammer and Kenneth Foster. Albert Davis and Earl Hustwit were both killed attempting to bail out of their faltering P-51s, and on March 26th, a possible mid-air clash involving Donald's old "Donald Duck" Mustang brought it crashing down in flames, killing its pilot, Harry Davis.

The battle in the Pacific Theater for Iwo Jima had ended and the American forces had moved on to Okinawa when President Roosevelt died on April 12th. The announcement was received with an airy hope by Hitler in his Berlin bunker, who foolishly thought that the death of a democracy's leader could unsettle things long enough for him to reverse the inevitable outcome of the war. He held fast to his delusions even as the Russians raced toward him from the east and the Americans moved in from the west, converging in the capture of Germany's capital city.

In this last month of struggle, fifteen more 4th Fighter Group pilots would be lost. Edward Wozniak and Robert Miller were wounded in action — Wozniak crashed due to engine failure, and Miller was hit by gunfire. Homer Smith was killed in a flying accident, and Herman Rasmussen, Robert Bucholz, and Robert Davis were all killed by flak. Eight pilots were shot down in a twenty-minute span while strafing a heavily defended Czecho-slovakian airdrome; William Ayer, Benjamin Griffin, Maurice Miller, Edward Gimbel, Edward McLoughlin and Sidney Woods were taken prisoner; Leroy Carpenter and Carl Alfred were both killed. The last to go down during combat was William Hoelscher. On April 25, 1945, he bailed out over Czecho-slovakia when his plane was torn up by flak; he landed unhurt and eluded capture.

Nazi resistance in all sectors was falling apart. In Northern Italy, where Mussolini was still being harbored by his Nazi cohorts, partisans chased him down and caught him as he tried to run for his life. After a speedy trial he was shot and hung up by his heels from a street light, and the total surrender of German forces still in Italy soon followed.

The misery endured by the thousands of Allied POWs held by the Germans had been compounded when the Russians began getting uncomfortably close. Ill-clothed for the bitterest of winter weather, they had been shunted hundreds of miles from Sagan to Nuremburg, either traveling on foot, or jammed aboard over-crowded trains. When spring came the prisoners were again put on the march — this time to Moosburg, because the Americans were closing in. It was here that Patton's tanks rolled in to free them on April 29th, with the general himself standing on the lead tank.

As the Allied armies made their liberating sweep across the once-proud Reich, its concentration camps, gas chambers and crematoriums became known, and the full scope of Nazi atrocities was revealed to the rest of the world.

Hitler finally ran out of even irrational solutions as the avenging forces zeroed in to flush him from his hideout, and seeing only one route of escape, the cowardly Führer killed himself before he could be charged by an earthly court for the despicable deeds spawned by his most arrogant inhumanity.

What was left of Germany unconditionally surrendered within days, and the 8th of May was declared "VE Day" for victory in Europe.

In the pastoral villages and small towns there may have been a few clanging cow bells and pots and pans to mark the event, but VE Day was more often observed with prayer services of thanksgiving and chiming church bells. Big cities, however, leaned more toward excess in demonstrating the exhilaration of triumph, and New York City was the paradigm. The parades and celebrations topped any pandemonium ever witnessed on any New Year's Eve, and this was but a dress rehearsal for the blowout to come in August.

Forty-five years after Uncle John telephoned Elinor in New York, my mother called her. Long distance phone calls were no longer the luxury they had once been, and by this time not even my mother wrote letters very often.

Our many months of remembering Donald had caused her to think so much about Elinor that she had been impelled to track her down. Among Grandma's old letters was one Elinor had written in 1965; directory assistance supplied a phone number at the same New Jersey address, and less than ten minutes later the "two Eleanors" were talking with each other for the first time.

They had talked for nearly an hour; there was so much to catch up on. After repeating nearly their entire conversation to me, my mother said, "I told Elinor that I knew if I ever went to see Donald's grave I would cry."

I was completely surprised to hear her say this — I never knew she had ever dreamed of going to Holland.

"I was thinking," she continued " — wouldn't it be nice if we could go there sometime? You and me?"

After my audible gasp, I was even more surprised to hear myself say, "We SHOULD go there! If I'd known you wanted to go, we could have gone a long time ago."

As usual, my impetuous tongue had slipped free from the restraints of common sense. What had I promised? I'd never given any thought to foreign travel — I didn't even like to get on a bus! And what qualified me to judge Nannie for her lack of adventure anyway? Up until that very instant I'd planned every part of my own life and my work to minimize risk, always doing the safest, easiest thing — I'd even done my driving according to the accessibility of parking and around rush hours ... avoiding left turns.

But if my mother wanted to go to Holland, I had to find a way of getting her there. I would have to stop being so timid; if Donald could learn to fly a shooting, bombing warplane, I should at least be able to figure out how to book a couple of airline reservations to Europe. I could hardly wait to tell Bonnie — when our whole family visited her in California a couple of years earlier, she hadn't been able to talk Ma into going on a two-hour ride to San Francisco in a Lincoln Town Car! I'd call a travel agent.

"If we do go there," my mother said, "we should make the trip in May. May is the month of Memorial Day, and Donald's birthday."

The end of the war in Europe was also the end of the war for the 4th Fighter Group. Although they had expected to be sent off to fly P-47s in the Pacific, the fighting in that area began to wind down before their transfer could take place. Yet in May, while flying in peaceful duty, three last Debden pilots died. Richard Tannehill, Barnaby Wilhoit and Harold Fredericks were all killed in accidents.

By the time summer arrived the Japanese had been overrun in Okinawa, compelling thousands of their soldiers and civilians to commit suicide. Curtis LeMay had taken over the Pacific bombing early in the year and had begun sending fighter escorts from the reclaimed airbases on Iwo Jima to protect the hordes of B-29 Superfortresses as they approached Japan on their long haul from Guam and Tinian. These oversized bombers dropped thousands of tons of incendiary bombs, practically annihilating Tokyo, Yokohama, Nagoya, Kobe and Osaka — Japan's five largest cities. With the invasion of their home islands and unquestionable defeat imminent, the Japanese still held on. And when warnings of being hit with a new, more powerful weapon failed to induce their immediate surrender, President Truman authorized the use of the atom bomb.

Choosing to spare the religious and cultural city of Kyoto, the Allies targeted instead the industrial city of Hiroshima, population 350,000. On August 6th, the B-29 Superfortress *Enola Gay* dropped the aerial bomb which exploded above the urban center. Within one second, half of the city disappeared and more than one quarter of its inhabitants were killed, leaving the rest to suffer the horrendous, long-term effects of radiation; then, when there still was no sign of capitulation from the Japanese, the U.S. dropped a second atomic bomb over the city of Nagasaki on August 9th, wreaking similar results.

The Japanese surrendered the following day. The terms of surrender were accepted on the 14th, and the 15th was declared VJ Day, for victory over Japan. When the end of the war was announced on the radio, the world went wild in jubilation.

This was the day that Elinor Lindemann had been waiting for, when she said she was "not going to do anything but celebrate." The whole city was a mad house, and despite her personal loss, she went down to Times Square. Not quite as eager to celebrate as she once was, she still wanted to go on record as having been there. Her father, her sister, and her sister's boyfriend went with her. She had never seen so many people in one place; the streets were blocked off so cars could not get through, and there were people everywhere — blowing horns and whistles, screaming and throwing confetti, and dancing and climbing up lamp posts. If it were not for Elinor's father who kept pulling her out from under the feet of the mob, this slip-of-a-girl felt sure she would have been trampled to death. They did not stay long, and after just a sampling of the frenzied revelry went back home, their spirits more subdued and thoughtful than uplifted, feeling mostly thankful that no more boys had to be killed.

On September 2, 1945, the official documents were signed aboard the battleship *Missouri,* and nearly six years to the day after Hitler's march into Poland another global war had ended. Before all the radioactive dust had settled, old enemies were becoming friends, and former allies were considered suspect. And the world was left to ponder the sobering potential of nuclear power as a long cold war began.

As our travel plans took shape, my mother told me she thought she had talked her brother John into going with us to Donald's grave; a consoling milestone — the first sign that Uncle John might finally be coming around.

But my pleasant thoughts of a happy family threesome flying across the ocean turned out to be short-lived. A few weeks later my mother called again — this time to tell me he'd changed his mind.

"Johnny said that digging up all these old memories of Donald is making him too sad," she said. "He doesn't want to go there. He said nobody understands how he feels."

My heart dropped to my kneecaps when I heard this. "I never should have started any of this!" I told her. "I wish I'd left Donald and Uncle John and this whole business alone."

"NO! DON'T STOP NOW!" she protested with alarm. "It's a good thing you're doing — I'm sure Johnny thinks so, too — he just can't stand thinking about it. I told him I LOVED to remember — even if it makes me sad. I don't mind crying!"

But now she was having second thoughts about making the

trip, too, and wondered aloud if it had been a harebrained idea in the first place. She didn't know if she wanted to go all that way when she wouldn't actually see Donald — it wasn't as if he were really there, she said. The thought of going was one thing, but doing it quite another. And what would we do in Holland for a whole week anyway?

"We could do some sight seeing, take a couple of tours — see those famous windmills and tulips," I suggested.

"I don't know," she said warily. "I've heard that the plane trip takes about ten hours and it's really uncomfortable — not enough room to stretch out. You know how my back is. It's awfully hard for me to sit still like that for a long time. Maybe if we could go on that Concorde..."

"The Concorde doesn't fly out of the Twin Cities, Ma — or land in Holland."

I told her not to give it up yet, to think about it for a while and I'd call again in two weeks.

Maybe my mother was right; maybe the trip would be too strenuous for her. I decided to research it some more. I picked up a Fodor's Guide To Holland. *In it I read:*

Long-distance flying today is no bed of roses. Lines and delays at ever-more-crowded airports, perfunctory in-flight service and shrinking leg-room on board a giant jet with some 400 other people, followed by interminable waits for your luggage when you arrive, are the clearest possible signals that the glamour of air travel — if it ever existed — is very much a thing of the past.

How far we'd come. Great. I could feel the trip slipping away. Two weeks and one day later I called for my mother's decision.

"Well, what's the word?" I asked.

"Not good," she replied listlessly.

I could hear the answer in her voice. She wasn't sick, she said, but she was in bed, badly bruised from a fall the day before. My first guess was that she had been climbing up on something rickety to do her ritual spring cleaning, but I was wrong; her current predicament was brought on by an action almost eerie.

She had been going down the stairs after a nap, carrying her little dog Buffy, when she noticed the picture of Jesus she had recently hung on the stairwall was slightly askew. As she reached out to straighten it, she lost her footing and crumpled in a heap on the landing.

"So this means the trip is off?" I moronically asked.

"I think it pretty much settles things for me," she asserted.

I was sorry I hadn't called her one day sooner — if she had decided she didn't want to go, all she would have had to do was say so; I could have saved her all this pain and trouble — I wouldn't have dragged her thousands of miles to a cemetery against her will.

At first it seemed odd that she could so abruptly let go of a dream she'd had for so long. Then it dawned on me that she hadn't really given it up — she had simply given it to me.

I told her I was going anyway. I'd had a hunch she'd back out and had an alternate plan — because I really wanted to go; I couldn't explain why. I only knew I needed to go to Donald's grave, and my daughter could go in my mother's place.

In September of 1945, Lt. Col. William Becker took over the helm of the 4th Fighter Group from Col. Everett Stewart. By then all of the Mustangs and personnel had been dispatched from Debden and the air base was returned to the British.

The Brits' early trepidation of losing their women to the Yanks had not been ill-founded. The Americans finally did go back to the States, but several months later they were followed by a large fleet of ships, full of English war brides. Though many pilots certainly had chances for romantic dalliances, their tours overseas were usually too brief for serious courting, and in the 4th only a few married while in England. Robert Nelson, Willard Millikan, Chesley Peterson and Aubrey Stanhope were four who did, but they'd all first been in the RAF, which extended their time in combat. The most earnest Romeos were the men on the ground; a good share of them had been there for three years or longer. George Anderson was the only one stationed at Debden to find a bride in the tiny village itself, but the rest didn't have to go too far afield to find theirs — Bob Beeson found his in a phone booth in Cambridge! And Bill Gier, Sy Koenig, George Russel, Joe Lawrence and George Kalberg are but a small representation of the many enlisted men who married their British girlfriends. Surely the entire multitude of women wooed and won by the 4th Fighter Group would have filled a good-sized yacht.

In November the 4th FG was inactivated. Its unemployment was of short duration, however, and with a few changes went on to serve in other wars. The Army Air Corps would separate from the U.S. Army and trade their "pinks and greens" for uniforms of Air Force blue, and eventually the 4th Fighter Group became the 4th Fighter Wing of the Ninth Air Force, its 334, 335 and 336 Squadrons still intact.

When the final scores were tallied, the 4th Fighter Group had narrowly edged out the 56th for the highest number of enemy aircraft destroyed during the war, but the performances by both groups were superlative, with each recording totals of more than 1,000 victories.

World War Two produced hundreds of fighter aces — pilots credited with the destruction of five enemy aircraft; there were at least eighty aces in the 4th Fighter Group alone. Group and individual scores would be disputed and adjusted for years to come as gun camera film was dissected and examined and combat reports were reviewed; aircraft claimed to have been destroyed were sometimes judged only damaged, and whole credits originally awarded might later be divided among other pilots. About all that can be said with certainty is that not all lists agree.   Donald's own published credits vary from 3.5 aerial victories, to as many as 10 when including ground kills. He believed he had whole or partial credit for the destruction of 11 different enemy planes. He came pretty close to reaching his goal of 100 combat missions; his mouse-nibbled log book has disappeared, but 89 mission reports bearing his name are on file in the National Archives. They offer proof that Donald never once turned back early from, or aborted any of his missions — attesting as much, perhaps, to the high quality of workmanship by the men on the flight line as it does to his own courage.

Of the 550-plus pilots who served with the 4th Fighter Group in the Second World War, easily forty-five percent of them became casualties. About half of that number died, and many were wounded. With the exception of a couple dozen evaders, the rest of the downed survivors became prisoners of war.

A few of the top aces, whose lives had seemed invincible in combat, survived the war only to perish while still in their prime. Duane Beeson's early death was caused by a brain tumor, and

Johnny Godfrey died of Lou Gehrig's disease. Don Gentile, Pierce McKennon and Fred Glover were all killed in plane crashes; and Gerald "Monty" Montgomery was lost in the Korean War.

Of the war veterans lucky enough to be around long after, famous or not, there was no dispute found within their ranks; they avowed that as young men joined together in this noble cause they'd climbed life's highest peak, and nothing that had happened since — no matter how wonderful or horrible — had been able to eclipse or equal the intensity of that experience. But sometimes, when they got together again, or saw an old warplane overhead, they came very close to reliving it.

Though their magnificent P-51 Mustangs were flown for several more years by the United States as well as other countries, most of them were subsequently sold off as surplus or salvage. But as the jet age and computerized warfare hastened its descent into obsolescence, this fighter plane found a permanent place in the affections of aviation enthusiasts and vintage airplane collectors. And nearly fifty years after Mustangs reigned trium-phant over European skies, one of these authentic war birds would rise like the mythical phoenix, reincarnated as Captain Emerson's personal craft, and "Donald Duck" would fly again.

That first winter after the war held no travel plans for the Emersons. Another harvest season had come and gone, and when they'd battened down for North Dakota's hibernal limbo, Donald's father attempted the impossible — to compose a poem worthy of his martyred son. His wish was to complete it in time to commemorate the first anniversary of Donald's death. This was the most difficult thing he'd ever tried to write, and as Christmas drew near, he sent what he had written in a letter to his daughter.

Pembina, N. Dak.
Dec. 22, 1945

Dear Eleanor and all:

Just a few lines this morning ... as you know Sunday is
tomorrow and that interferes with the mail. I have been trying
to write a few lines in memory of Donald but my thoughts do
not seem to rhyme very well.

Christmas cheer adorns the year
With notes of rising peace;
The price of our beloved sons
Who gave their lives at least.

That blood since spilt on battle fronts
Should not be spent in vain
But triumphs of a simple trust
Should calm this world again.

Freedom is no idle dream
To charm the fretted brow,
But rises only in omen
To actions we endow.

With Christmas cheer that comes each year
First voiced in Bethlehem,
Where God first gave His own dear son
That all in turn may mend.

C.F. Emerson

I do not think this hits the bulls-eye though. You try a line
and we could possibly make something out of our combined
efforts.

Merry Xmas, Love to all.
Dad.

The letter from her father arrived on Monday. Eleanor read over his poem a few times — tried substituting a word or a line here or there, but soon gave up on it; a houseful of exuberant children on Christmas Eve was not a favorable atmosphere in which to fashion serious poetry.

Elinor Lindemann was nervously waiting at New York's Penn Station. She hadn't seen her college boyfriend, Bob Houston, for three and a half years, and now he was on his way from his Arkansas army camp to spend Christmas with her. Though their romance had ended, they had remained close friends and confidants, and Bob had always known everything about Donald. Unsure of how Donald's interception might impact their lives, Bob had fostered "a natural resentment" toward Donald, "... compounded, of course, by the inherent animosity of the dog-face toward the fly-boy...until the weather lifted over Bastogne!" he admitted, alluding to the Battle of the Bulge. Bob hoped to find out during the holidays if he and Elinor could pick up where they left off.

Two years after they were reunited Elinor and Bob were married, but none of the Lindemanns could ever forget Donald; Elinor's younger sister thought so highly of him that she named one of her sons Donald, and he grew up to become a captain in the Air Force, flying jet fighters.

Betty Cummins, another brown-eyed and brown-haired young charmer, went to work for the Emersons in 1947, continuing the time-honored tradition of mother-encouraged love match between son and hired girl. She married Donald's brother John in 1948, and the first of their three left-handed sons, Donald Arthur, was born the following March. His cousin Susan, Eleanor and Hot's final daughter was born three months later.

In 1950, Max Short built a second house on the farm for Frank and Mabel, making room in the old house for John and Betty's growing family; Darryl was due to arrive the next spring, and David, six years after that. Donnie would one day leave the farm he loved to serve in Vietnam, and both Darryl and David would learn to pilot airplanes.

C.F. Emerson never did finish the poem for Donald to his satisfaction, and he finally put it aside, unpublished. But Donald lived on in the hearts of his family, and for the next forty-six years, at some point each Christmas Day, a woman's voice would remind those assembled, just how many years it had been, since Donald.

Before we left for Holland in May of 1990, my mother called to say she was sending me some money; she had talked it over with Uncle John and they wanted me to buy flowers to put on Donald's grave. Of course, I'd do that, I told her — I would have done it anyway.

"Be sure to get a couple of those ribbons that say 'Brother,' " she added.

Then I asked if she wanted me to do anything else when I got there, expecting she would like me to do or say something at least marginally religious, but she said, "Just tell him that I miss him."

After the overnight transatlantic flight from the U.S. we expected to drive the last lap in about three hours, but it took us twice as long to reach our destination in the southern tip of Holland. Our fatigue and unfamiliarity with foreign directional signs had compounded our confusion, and we had zig-zagged, backtracked, and spent an inordinate amount of time just plain off the track. We had likely circled, many times, the area in which Donald's plane was shot down. We were exhausted and my daughter was angry and no longer speaking to me. I had been in charge of the map and of asking directions, so it was all my fault. I had squandered the day begging for assistance from many helpful inhabitants along the way. Among the first was a very surprised man I threw myself on as he sat sipping beer on a Belgian bar stool. When we discovered we were in Antwerp I had run into the first open establishment. Could I speak Spanish? — he had asked in a sincere attempt at finding a common language. Sorry. No. Some time later I tried a pizza parlor — what could be more American than that? The manager wore a turban and threw up his hands in utter dismay. My final plea was lobbed at two truckers in an isolated, wooded rest area in West Germany. By that time I was no longer afraid of anything. They very patiently tried to explain the highway system, and then drew us a map — ending our search for the Hotel-Cafe Wippelsdaal.

Susanne and Jan, the proprietors, were expecting us; Stacey charged up to our room and plunged, livid and still speechless, into bed.

I was too keyed up to sleep and decided to explore the area. Susanne told me the cemetery was only about a mile away, and on a clear day they could see its tower. There was a footpath that cut across the pastures; I could easily walk there in 20 or 30 minutes. I was tempted, but as it had been raining periodically throughout the day and the skies were still overcast, I was afraid I'd get caught in the rain. And I didn't dare to attempt driving the Opel we rented at Schiphol Airport; I hadn't driven a car with a stick shift in nearly 30 years. In any case, the cemetery gates would be locked in a couple of hours. I'd have to wait until the next day.

Because of jet lag, the time change or excitement — I'm not sure which — I popped wide awake in the middle of the night. I could hear the occasional murmuring sounds of the cows in the attached stable. I got out of bed and went to the window. The sky was so clear and bright with stars that I was momentarily

*startled to see the Big and Little Dippers, just the way they used
to look when I was a kid up north. It felt more like home to me
there than it did in many places in the States. A rooster started
crowing; it was almost morning, and soon we would visit Donald.*

Susanne had given us a map with directions to the village of
Margraten and where we could go to buy flowers for the grave.
I carried in my hands the big white bow I bought at the florist's
in St. Paul before I left home; it had three white streamers: two
with "Brother" written in gold lettering, and one with "Uncle."

     It was just a short distance and we soon found the small shop
with the familiar FTD sign in the window. The cheerful young
clerk understood exactly what we wanted; cemetery visitors
accounted for a lot of their business. He quickly put together a
large, mixed bouquet of yellow and white flowers, the stem ends
in a plastic bag filled with water, covered by a pleated white
paper ruff.

     While we drove the last half-mile, I attached the ribbon to the
bouquet and tried hard to imagine the belligerent armies of
Hitler and Napoleon ever marching down that peaceful, narrow
highway.   Then turning off the road we drove through the
entrance gate and parked the car. As we walked up the stone
steps to the visitors' center we were welcomed by a smiling young
Dutchman; he couldn't have looked happier if he had personally
been waiting for us for the past 45 years. He asked if we had
come to visit any particular grave, and when we explained our
pilgrimage his delight was even further heightened. He darted
into his office to search through the files and came back with a
diagram of the burial area with the location of Donald's grave
marked by an X. Plot B, row 15, grave 21. He suddenly thought
to ask if we had ever received our "next-of-kin package." I said
I didn't think so and he said I could have as many as I wanted for
family back home. I took three: one for me, one for Ma, and one
for Johnny's boys. He asked me to write my name, address, and
relationship to the deceased in a couple of registers, and then he
asked if I knew that during and right after the war the graves had
been adopted — cared for — by Dutch families. I had heard
many were, I answered, but I hadn't known they all had been.
Oh, yes, he said; there even were waiting lists of people eager to*

do something to show their gratitude to the Allied heroes for liberating Holland, and he promised if he could find out the names of the people who adopted Donald's grave he would send the information to me. He offered to accompany us to the grave site, but we thanked him and said we thought we'd be able to find it without any problem.

We walked beside a long reflecting pool toward the towering chapel at the other end of the courtyard; the walls engraved with the names of the missing sheltered us on either side. At the end of the pool stood a large bronze statue of a mourning woman; bronze doves hovered around her shoulder. We went up a few more steps on the left side of the chapel and saw the brilliant spread of emerald green grass studded by thousands of stark pearly-white marble markers; plot B was directly in front of us. The sight was breathtaking.

I needed to stop and collect myself — I wasn't ready. But my impatient, sprightly companion raced ahead, fairly dancing between the graves, rapidly counting off the 15 rows, and seconds later yelled, "HERE HE IS!" as she stopped at grave 21.

I kept walking and caught up despite my reluctance. So this was it, his shady spot, shared by exactly eighty-three hundred other forever-young arrows. Right there at my feet. I leaned the flowers up against his cross and touched the cool white marble; the fine-grained surface felt exactly like a block of salt. Then I ran my hands over the sharply chiseled inscription:

DONALD R. EMERSON
CAPT 336 FTR SQ 4 FTR GP
NORTH DAKOTA DEC 25 1944

It wasn't turning out at all the way I'd planned. I told her to stop taking pictures of me — where were my sunglasses, anyway? I looked and felt positively dreadful. I had mentally pictured that moment: Me, standing triumphantly at the end of my journey beside my uncle's grave — one of those magazine-cover moments, like Neil Armstrong stepping on the moon. I couldn't help it, I told her; it was the saddest place I'd ever been. And he'd been there since he was just her age.

*****

I slumped heavily in the passenger seat as we left the cemetery behind, my daughter in complete control. She navigated the highways like a native and kept cheerily reminding me of all the fun we were going to have in "Aahm-stah-daahm," as she pronounced it, in perfect mimicry of the Netherlands' speech.

I knew we would have a good time in Amsterdam; there was a whole list of things we wanted to do. I wanted to look at the buildings, see the museums, Anne Frank's house and the canals. She wanted to find the retail district, the antique stores and the flea markets. I wanted to see it; she wanted to shop it. My daughter was born with an eye for the finer things.

Upon our return home, I immediately called my mother.

"We're back, Ma — we made it!" I said — without first even saying hello.

"What day were you at the cemetery?" she asked, also skipping any preliminaries.

"Thursday —"

"His birthday!"

"Yes, I know."

"He would have been 67," she reminded me, rather pensively.

"I thought we would have been there by Wednesday," I hurried on breezily, "but it took a lot longer to find the place than I expected."

"I was thinking of you that day — wondering if you had been there yet," she said.

"We were there about 10 o'clock in the morning — 3 AM back home; Holland is seven hours ahead of us," I informed her in the most controlled tone I could muster.

"He was born about 3 o'clock in the afternoon."

I knew where she was going.

Trying to head her off, I started telling her everything I could remember about the cemetery — the friendly young Dutchman, the trees and the flowers, the perfect green grass — stupidly thinking that if I could keep talking I wouldn't cry.

"That's good to hear," she said. "So many graveyards are awfully neglected and seedy looking."

But even though I babbled away like a demented tour guide, she was only half-listening. She was already taking a trip of her own, flying back in time to 1944, and still traveling.

"It was best, then, that we left him there, you think? We could have had him brought home after the war, you know, but we all agreed to leave him there. I always had a feeling that if we could have asked Donald, he would have said he wanted to stay with his buddies."

"Yes, I think so, too," I agreed, before feebly attempting to go on with my travelogue. "I just can't get over how nice it was there — so much like home. And there were cows everywhere — big black and white ones. Holsteins, aren't they? Cow pastures border three sides of the cemetery!"

"You'll have to be sure to tell all this to Johnny. I hope you took a lot of pictures."

"Stacey took a bunch, but I don't know how they'll turn out," I said, remembering my tear-streaked face and red, swollen eyelids. "I hope they're good enough so you can get some idea of what the place looks like. It just couldn't have been a more perfect day — it had been raining the day before. It was about 70 degrees, only fluffy white clouds in the sky. The sun was so bright everything just glowed — "

"It was exactly that kind of day when Donald was born, too," she began. "A beautiful spring day. When we came walking home from school that afternoon and saw the doctor's car in the yard we started running as fast as we could. Donald had just been born..."

Eleanor & Donald

Sandra at Donald's grave

Bob & Elinor Houston

Capt. Donald Wolff, Elinor's nephew

Betty & John Emerson

Darryl, David & Donnie Emerson

*Eleanor & girls in front of
peonies & lilacs*

*Emerson
farm*

*Beverly, Donnie, Bonnie, Sandy, Susie & Darryl on
steps of new farm house*

Baby Susan with sisters

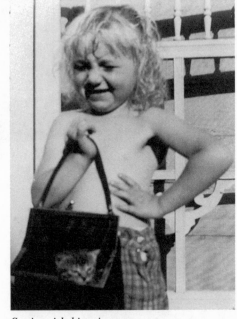

Susie with kitty in purse

Baby David Emerson

Darryl, Donnie & piglets

Frank & Mabel Emerson, Christmas, 1961

Nannie Roswell & her dog Patty

Harold & Eleanor Torkelson with granddaughter Kim, daughters Sue, Sandy, Bev, Bonnie, and dog Buffy

John & Betty Emerson

Emerson men, 1968

Postscript

My mother encouraged me to write Donald's story right up to the end of her life; she tried so hard to think of anything and anybody that could help me.

"Write to that Charles Foch," she had said at the start. "He'd be able to tell you something — and he might know others who'd remember Donald."

But my search for Donald's friends soon brought back questions of her own that had gone unanswered: Was Donald buried in a coffin? Where were his wounds? Was he conscious at all before he died? Had he known he was dying? Did he have time to pray?

Charles Foch, the air force mechanic who had phoned the Emersons on the 40th anniversary of the Battle of the Bulge, was no longer where he'd once lived in Tennessee, and I couldn't find him; I was unable to find answers to some of my mother's old questions as well.

Regardless of some early failures, as soon as I was committed to doing the job I almost felt myself being led around, as if by an unseen hand. Before I knew what was happening, Donald's friends began forming up to help me with their memories and to support and guide me as I made my bumbling way.

Memories can be some pretty slippery things — even those held closely for fifty years, and squaring old lopsided accounts was sometimes a chore of diplomacy; I aimed high and toward the middle, and gave it my best shot. Most mere details are often unimportant anyway. Even my mother misremembered some things, and it should be noted here that it was Ralph Hay Emerson, not Ralph Waldo, who was the cousin lost in an RCAF bomber the day after Donald died.

My mother was so very pleased and elated to read the accolade-filled letters I got from Donald's friends, and because she knew her own opinions were naturally biased she was gratified to have them confirmed by others.

"I just know Donald's getting a big kick out of all this," she'd say. "I know he's watching you."

Of course I couldn't resist telling her that more than once, when someone was asked if he remembered Donald Emerson, the very first response had been, "Yeah... little short guy."

She bristled at that, and in righteous indignation snapped, "Well! He would have been taller if Grandpa Roswell hadn't been so short!"

Before I had a chance to meet any of Donald's friends in person, from out of the blue — literally — came word of an utterly dazzling development: Bob Tullius, a sports car racing figure from Winchester, Virginia, had bought an original WWII P-51D Mustang with the intention of duplicating one flown in combat, and the model he had chosen was Donald's "Donald Duck" plane! He had also indicated that someday he would have an official dedication of the airplane, and he welcomed the participation of the Emerson family.

When I told my mother about this incredible honor, she was as thrilled as I was, but the best part was that when she passed along the news to uncle John, they talked together about Donald for the first time since his death. A month later would have been too late; her health was already taking a dramatic dive.

A couple of weeks later my sisters and I were back home in Karlstad for our annual summer visit with our parents. We didn't know that our coming together that July as a whole family would be the last while our mother still lived. As we sat talking idly around the kitchen table one day, our mother listened from upstairs in her sickbed. When our usual food-centered conversation shifted to a famous, much-maligned Minnesota product, she could no longer remain silent.

"SPAM!" She hollered. "DONALD FIRST TASTED SPAM WHEN HE WENT TO RUSSIA!"

Laughing at the weird connection, I dashed up to her room. "You just can't stop, can you?" I said.

"I still remember lots of things, don't I?" she asked, looking thoroughly pleased with herself.

"You sure do, Ma," I sighed.

Then she asked if I remembered her telling me about the dream she'd had, shortly before Donald died.

I told her I did — I'd heard it so many times it was almost as if I had dreamed it myself. In it, Donald, dressed in uniform, is *walking alone down a long road. He walks slowly and steadily, looking unhurt and unafraid.*

She'd had that same dream again, she said, but this time she was the one walking down the road.

I listened without comment, and she said nothing more. Two weeks later, August 4, 1991, she suffered a severe stroke, and she was never able to speak again.

On the bedside table in her hospital room sat a stack of photographs of Bob Tullius's P-51. Bob had flown the newly restored plane home to his hangar just hours before my mother's seizure; he was so eager for Donald's family to see the finished results that he immediately shot and developed a roll of film and sent the prints to us by next-day mail.

The airplane looked beautiful, and except for some minor modifications it was a meticulous replica of Donald's favorite Mustang. It was complete down to the invasion stripes, Donald's name, ID markings, seven victory crosses, and the fighting-mad Donald Duck painted on its side — Don Allen had even been found and commissioned to direct the duplication of his original WWII noseart! The P-51 was exactly as Donald's had looked in August, 1944.

My mother held one of the pictures in her hand and stared mutely at it. I told her that at that very moment people were swarming around the plane at its first air show in Geneseo, New York, and they'd all be able to read the name printed on the side of the cockpit: Capt. Donald R. Emerson.

Pop picked up one of the photos, studied it for a minute and said, "Sure is funny that out of all those pilots he would pick Donald."

My mother was bursting with the answer, but all she could do was roll her head from side to side on the pillow. Her wide-open eyes swept the room until they found mine; the command in them was explicit.

"It was because of Donald Duck," I said, taking my cue.

My mother nodded slightly as I began explaining it for her.

"He wanted to honor a 4th Fighter Group pilot — an ace who'd taken part in D-Day. But he also wanted a plane with interesting noseart... so what really decided it for him was

Donald Duck — he's always been a big Donald Duck fan."

Any hope I'd had of writing Donald's story in my mother's lifetime was fading as fast as she was, but seeing the tension leave her face as I talked about the airplane, I felt the weight of that obligation lighten. It didn't really matter anymore if I wrote a memoir about Donald. Because of Donald Duck, and the magnanimous act of a stranger, Donald was going to be remembered by thousands of people who had never even heard of him before.

On August 20, 1991, my mother died, her mission to remember Donald ending just as mine was about to take off.

The following year, on August 29, 1992, fifty summers after Donald joined the army, the dedication of the P-51 took place. Bob Tullius and his good friend, Brian Fuerstenau, flew it all the way to Pembina, North Dakota, for the ceremony. In another bit of magic, the Pembina airport's airstrip had been extended just the fall before, making it long enough to accommodate a Mustang.

The heavens were an inviting shade of blue the day before the festivities — perfect flying conditions — and I had the distinct privilege of going up in "Donald's" plane. I barely re-membered to count off the five seconds to take-off, as Bob "Buffalo Grass" Nelson said I should if I ever got to ride in the Mustang, and then we were airborne and went soaring high above Pembina and on to Karlstad. I could pick out below the geometric-shaped game-board pieces of my life: the buildings on the Emerson farm... Karlstad High School... my old pink stucco home. I was far too excited to be afraid, but it was abundantly clear, even before Tullius buzzed the railroad tracks like a malevolent strafer, that I had not inherited Uncle Donald's intestinal fortitude.

Dedication Day thundered in with weather more typical of England. But despite strong winds, pouring rain and an ominous forecast, hundreds of American and Canadian veterans and airplane aficionados came to the airport to see the Mustang and to join Donald's family and friends for the tribute.

The planned outdoor program was definitely at risk, but then, just in time, "like somebody punched a hole in the clouds," as someone was heard to remark, a small patch of sky cleared over the airport, and the dedication of the flying monument to freedom went ahead on schedule.

If Donald could have seen us that day, I know he would have been humbled at the turnout — and heartened to see so many familiar faces in the crowd. Phil Kiner, Lela Pederson Spilde, Bertha Turnwall, and eight of the twenty-five members of his high school class were there. And Dr. Charles Short from California, and two of Donald's fighter pilot buddies — Don Patchen from New York, and Bob Planck from Ohio — all made the special trip and took part in the program.

I still had thousands of miles to go before I was through, but when the dedication was over I shifted into a higher gear.

A month after the dedication I flew with the Association of the 4th Fighter Group to England to celebrate the 50th anniversary of the formation of the 4th. We toured London and the old Debden air base, which was then occupied by the Queen's Royal Lancers. Lee, my son and faithful WWII reunion escort, accompanied me.

Many of Donald's dear friends became good friends of mine, and in late May, 1994, when I embarked on a transatlantic cruise on the QE2, heading for England and France to commemorate D-Day plus 50 years, my traveling companion was Elinor Houston, Donald's wartime love, just widowed the year before.

By the time I finished writing Donald's story, the Second World War had been over for 50 years; it had taken me exactly as long as it took the Allies to defeat the Nazis. I had climbed on a lot of tour buses, met all kinds of people, and I'd made some major left turns. I certainly had the "great adventure" that Otey Glass had predicted for me, and my life would be forever changed. I can only echo Donald's words to describe the whole experience: "Oh well we live and learn and boy I sure have learned a lot on this trip! I wouldn't have missed it for any-thing... I've seen so many things that have bulged my eyes out it would take a book to tell about them all...so whenever time hangs heavy on my hands, I'll tell everything."

Chuck Konsler & Bob Tullius

Frank Frison & Ed Kueppers of the 8AFHS

Lee Troska & Otey Glass

Sandra Merrill & Don Patchen

Sandra with Bill Dunn, 1st U.S. Ace in WWII

Marcella Carlson Turnbull

Leonard Pierce's sisters, Chris Dailey & Helen Gerlock, by his memorial marker on their parents' tombstone in New York

Sandra (wearing 336 SQD photo button) & Elinor Houston at D-Day commemorative ball on the QE2

Bob Tullius & Brian Fuerstenau

Tom Nord, Pembina Airport Manager

Sandra & Cousin Charlie Short

Flying high over Karlstad home in P-51
(speck at upper right)

Betty & Don Patchen, Bob & Vivian Planck

Sandra, struggling to recover after ride

DEDICATION DAY

Brian Fuerstenau,
Harold Torkelson,
Bob Tullius &
Don Patchen

Cope Kern (Cmdr. Pembina American
Legion Post) & Donald A. Emerson

Rev. Grafenstein,
Hetty Walker
(Pembina Mayor),
Sandra, Bob Tullius

George
Wikstrom, Jr.,
Karlstad Mayor

Legionnaires

Bob Tullius with
Sandra, christening
"the duck" with
Cold Duck (IN
CELEBRATION
OF FREEDOM,
CHEERS TO THE
DUCK!)

Bertha Turnwall,
Legion Auxiliary

WWII ORIGINALS WITH BOB'S MEMORIAL COPY

Elinor Houston

Don Patchen

Tullius & Patchen

Don Blakeslee & Bob Tullius

Bob inviting Don Allen for a ride

Don Patchen, Marvin Arthur, Frank Speer, Joe Higgins & Jim Goodson (all 4th FG pilots)

FOREIGN SCENES

Stacey Troska in Amsterdam

Sandra across from Anne Frank's house

At Duxford, England, with Helmut Peter Rix, Luftwaffe pilot & POW

Elinor Houston, Mitchell Wright & Sandra in "Parade of Ships" in English Channel, 6-5-94

Judge Dick Rinebolt at Anglo-American Memorial in Saffron Walden, England

Joe Fodor & Joe Sills placing wreath at American Military Cemetery in Cambridge, England

American Cemetery in Margraten, Netherlands Flowers on Donald's grave